D0891468

A SOURCEBOOK FOR HISPANIC LITERATURE AND LANGUAGE

A Selected, Annotated Guide to Spanish, Spanish-American, and Chicano Bibliography, Literature, Linguistics, Journals, and Other Source Materials

SECOND EDITION

by

DONALD W. BLEZNICK

The Scarecrow Press, Inc.
Metuchen, N.J., & London
1983

First edition published in 1974 by Temple University Press, Philadelphia.

Library of Congress Cataloging in Publication Data

Bleznick, Donald William, 1924–
    A sourcebook for Hispanic literature and language.

    Includes indexes.
    1. Reference books--Spanish philology.   2. Spanish
philology--Bibliography.   I. Title.
Z2695.A2B55   1983   [PC4071]   016.86   83-3060
ISBN 0-8108-1616-4

RoJoSu,
sweet joy of life.
Though first, second, and third in order of appearance,
equally compete in this existence.

CONTENTS

v

PREFACE

This revised, enlarged edition of the Sourcebook now has
1,412 entries, a considerable increase from the 1,075 in the
first edition published by Temple University Press in 1974.
This represents a real gain of 384 new items since 47 out-
moded citations were deleted. Moreover, a systematic effort
was made to revise bibliographic data and annotations for the
entries retained from the original edition in order to reflect
the appearance of new editions during the last decade. In
sum, about 36 percent of this book consists of new entries
and over 60 percent of the other items have been changed,
with some of these revised to a large extent.

A new chapter on Chicano Bibliography and Literature
has been added. The Table of Contents has been modified to
accommodate this new chapter, and it also reflects the following revisions: the switching of the order of Chapters 2 and
3; the combining of the former chapters 6, 7, and 8 into one
under the rubric "Histories of Hispanic Literatures"; and the
melding of the former Chapters 17 and 18 into one revised
grouping under the title "Selected Publishers and Book Dealers." This second edition of Sourcebook now includes two
indexes: one of authors and corporate entities and another
of titles.

Below are repeated (in slightly emended form) several
paragraphs from the Preface of the first edition since they
have validity in expressing the reasons for my preparation
of this work and the method followed.

*   *   *

When the idea for this book came to mind a long time ago,
I planned to prepare a practical guide to bibliography and
other basic materials which would serve budding and even

mature Hispanists in literary and linguistic research. Mindful of the vast array of bibliographic lists and studies that has proliferated in the past several years, I never doubted the need to be selective in compiling a manageable vade mecum. The guiding principle that emerged was to identify essential books--occasionally articles when adequate books do not exist--and journals in those areas most central to research in Hispanic literature and language. A corollary aim has been to incorporate current works, many of which are in print and should be available in college and university libraries. Even the fledgling investigator soon learns that one work leads to another, and it is expected that this Sourcebook will provide ample resources for research projects ranging from the undergraduate term paper to the doctoral dissertation and beyond.

Motivated by a desire to provide a vehicle for meaningful and rapid reference, I felt it imperative to annotate the books selected. The traditional bibliographic listing, providing only author, title, and date of publication, often fails to offer sufficient clues about a work's contents, and, therefore, I supply succinct descriptions of the scopes of the books included and at times add critical assessments for entries with exceptional merit or some defects. The annotations are generally purposefully brief so that the reader can determine quickly whether items may be pertinent to his or her investigation. Very few items are not annotated; this is the case when the title of an entry adequately indicates its contents (and the work has no more than average value) and on the rare occasion when it was not obtainable but its inclusion was deemed necessary for the purpose of having more complete coverage in some areas, particularly the literatures of some Spanish American countries.

The Table of Contents has been carefully designed to set out in a clear and detailed manner all the areas encompassed by this book. One will find the usual items expected in a volume of this kind: works on aims and methods of research, style guides, general bibliographic guides and references, bibliographies of Spanish and Spanish American literature, and guides to libraries and dissertations. However, this is not merely a bibliography of bibliographies. My purpose is to provide information on various other types of books which students of Hispanic literature and language often need in their work. Accordingly, sections have been introduced to augment the usefulness and uniqueness of this Sourcebook: literary dictionaries and encyclopedias; general and specific histories and anthologies of Hispanic literature; a new Chicano chapter; books on metrics; bibliographies of literature in translation; a chapter on linguistics, which also devotes a good deal of attention to various types of dictionaries (historical, etymological, grammatical, American Spanish, bilingual, etc.); a guide to 124 journals in the Hispanic field (an increase of 36 since 12 from the first edition have been deleted); such helpful references as biographical dictionaries, encyclopedias, handbooks, and works on Hispanic history and philosophy; and current lists of publishers and dealers in Hispanic countries, North America, and Europe.

The date assigned to each book usually indicates the edition examined, and a date in parentheses denotes the first edition. In many cases, books that are merely reprinted are so marked. It was felt that it would help the reader if the pagination of one-volume works were given, since one would normally expect a vast difference in coverage between a manual of literature that purports to cover a country's literature in 100 pages and one that does so in 500 pages. Standard abbreviations have been used throughout. The numbers found in the Index refer to the entry numbers in the text.

The books chosen in the sections on Spanish and Spanish American literature and anthologies as well as those in linguistics are what I consider basic. It is understandable that some may fault me for "glaring" omissions or for including works of little value, but in line with my intent to be selective rather than exhaustive, I have relied on my experience and the opinions of colleagues and students. In general, my cutoff date has been the summer of 1982. Despite my attempts to be current in all sections, it is obvious that I may be unaware of worthwhile publications that have come out lately. Consequently, I invite suggestions for improving the content and organization of this Sourcebook.

*   *   *

During the time spent on the revision of the Sourcebook, I am indebted to a number of people. Foremost among them is Hensley C. Woodbridge, one of the world's leading bibliographers in the Hispanic area, who has once again, as in the preparation of the first edition, selflessly devoted countless hours to suggesting and supplying useful material and to reading so carefully the first draft of the manuscript.

I am also grateful for the advice and help of Seymour

Menton, Richard V. Teschner, Frank H. Nuessel, Jr.,
David S. Zubatsky, Charles M. Tatum, Ernestina N. Eger,
and Máximo Torreblanca. Special thanks are proffered to
my wife, Rozlyn, who was very helpful in assembling the
manuscript, and to Delia V. Galván, whose assiduous assistance and research talent were vital to the completion of
this book.

                                                    D. W. B.

1. AIMS AND METHODS OF RESEARCH

1. Altick, Richard D. The Art of Literary Research. Rev.
   ed. New York: W. W. Norton & Co., 1975 (1963).
   xii, 304 pp.
   Deals with the spirit of scholarship, textual study,
   problems of authorship, searching for materials, libraries, note taking, and writing. Bibliography.

2. Barzun, Jacques, and Henry F. Graff. The Modern Re-
   searcher. 3d ed. New York: Harcourt, Brace &
   World, 1977 (1957). xix, 378 pp.
   Illustrates the theory and practice of research and
   report writing.

3. Corstius, Jan Brandt. Introduction to the Comparative
   Study of Literature. New York: Random House, 1968.
   viii, 212 pp.
   Offers a view of various approaches to the study of
   Western literature. Extensive bibliographies.

4. Downs, Robert B., and Clara D. Keller. How to Do Library Research. 2d ed. Urbana: University of Illinois Press, 1975 (1966). 298 pp.
   Guide to a library and its resources.

5. Foerster, Norman, et al. Literary Scholarship: Its
   Aims and Methods. Chapel Hill: University of North
   Carolina Press, 1941. iv, 269 pp.
   Series of articles by several authors on study of
   letters, language, literary history, literary criticism,
   and imaginative writing.

6. Gibaldi, Joseph, ed. Introduction to Scholarship in
   Modern Languages and Literatures. New York: The
   Modern Language Association of America, 1981. xi,
   143 pp.

Contains a Preface by the editor, an Introduction
by Joel Conarroe, and six essays: "Linguistics,"
Winifred P. Lehman; "Textual Scholarship," G.
Thomas Tanselle; "Historical Scholarship," Barbara K.
Lewalski; "Literary Criticism," Laurence Lipking; "Literary
Theory," Paul Hernadi; and "The Scholar in Society,"
Wayne C. Booth.   Selected bibliographies accompany
each essay.   A basic book on the aims and methods
of scholarship.

7.   Guerin, Wilfred L., et al.   A Handbook of Critical Approaches to Literature.   2d ed.   New York: Harper
and Row, 1979 (1966).   350 pp.
Excellent introduction to the major approaches of
literary criticism, with practical application.   Treats
the following approaches: traditional, formalistic, psychological, mythological.   Also includes structuralism,
stylistics, the phenomenological approach, feminist
criticism, etc.   Useful glossary of literary terms,
bibliography, and index.

8.   Kayser, Wolfgang.   Interpretación y análisis de la obra
literaria.   4th ed.   5th printing.   Madrid: Gredos,
1981 (1954).   594 pp.
Extensive treatment that deals with textual study,
analysis of a literary work, poetry, rhetorical devices,
structure of a literary work, techniques and structures
of the different genres, and style.   Ample bibliography.

9.   Simón Díaz, José.   La bibliografía: Conceptos y aplicaciones.   Barcelona: Planeta, 1971.   331 pp.
Of special interest should be the section entitled,
"La investigación bibliográfica sobre temas españoles."

10.   Thorpe, James, ed.   The Aims and Methods of Scholarship in Modern Languages and Literatures.   New York:
Modern Language Association, 1963.   69 pp.
Four essays on linguistics, textual criticism, literary history, and literary criticism.

11.   _____.   The Relations of Literary Study: Essays on
Interdisciplinary Contributions.   New York: Modern
Language Association, 1967.   xiv, 151 pp.
Seven essays on the relations of literature to history,
myth, biography, psychology, sociology, religion, and
music.

12. Van Tieghem, Paul. <u>La littérature comparée</u>. Rev. ed. Paris: Armand Colin, 1951 (1931). 224 pp. Presents the theory and method of comparative literature and its history.

13. Wellek, René, and Austin Warren. <u>Teoría literaria</u>. 4th Spanish ed. Madrid: Gredos, 1974 (1953). 430 pp. Original English version, <u>Theory of Literature</u> (New York: Harcourt, Brace, 1942). Analyzes the natures and functions of literature, literary history, general and comparative literature, the extrinsic approach to literature (biography, psychology, society, and ideas), and the intrinsic approach (literary art, rhythm and meter, style and stylistics, imagery, metaphor, symbol and myth, literary genres, etc.). Many notes and extensive bibliography. Prologue by Dámaso Alonso.

2. STYLE GUIDES

14. The Chicago Manual of Style. 13th ed. Chicago: The University of Chicago Press, 1982 (1906). 752 pp.
    A fundamental reference for authors, editors, copywriters, and proofreaders. Contains new material on preparing the manuscript for the typesetter, index making, composition, printing and binding, a new table of diacritics and a chapter on rights and permissions under the new copyright law.

15. MLA Handbook for Writers of Research Papers, Theses, and Dissertations. New York: MLA Publications Center, 1977. 176 pp. Supersedes William R. Parker's The MLA Style Sheet (1951, 1970).
    Widely adopted by language and literature departments in the United States and Canada. Includes information, with many examples, on writing research papers, the mechanics of writing, and the preparation of a manuscript, along with sample pages of a research paper and a detailed subject index.

16. Turabian, Kate L. A Manual for Writers of Term Papers, Theses and Dissertations. 4th ed. Chicago: University of Chicago Press, 1973 (1955). viii, 216 pp.
    Explains and illustrates all phases of writing and typing a formal paper. Follows the University of Chicago Press's Manual of Style, now entitled The Chicago Manual of Style (see no. 14 above).

3. GENERAL BIBLIOGRAPHIC GUIDES AND REFERENCES

17. Arnaud, Emile, and Vicente Tusón. Guide de biblio-
    graphie hispanique. Toulouse: Privat-Didier, 1967.
    353 pp.
    Covers wide area including general bibliographies,
    periodicals, homage volumes, geography, history, fine
    arts, music, dictionaries, and language. Greatest em-
    phasis given to literature.

18. Baldensperger, Ferdinand, and Werner P. Friedrich.
    Bibliography of Comparative Literature. Chapel Hill:
    University of North Carolina Press, 1950. xxiv, 701
    pp. Reprint, New York: Russell & Russell, 1960.
    Contains sections on Spanish contributions, including
    plays and novels, and their influence on writers of
    other countries. The Yearbook of General and Com-
    parative Literature (vols. 1-19) contains an annual sup-
    plement to this bibliography.

19. Besterman, Theodore. A World Bibliography of Bibli-
    ographies. 4th rev. ed. Lausanne: Societas Biblio-
    graficas-Lausanne, 1965-66 (1939). 5 vols.
    Contains bibliographies through the centuries. Vol-
    ume 5 has indexes by subject, title, and author.

20. Bibliographic Index: A Cumulative Bibliography of Bibli-
    ographies. New York: H. W. Wilson & Co., 1938- .
    Annual supplements.
    Entries listed by subject.

21. Bibliographische Berichte. Frankfurt-am-Main: Vittorio
    Klostermann, 1958- .
    Current bibliography of bibliographies with sections
    on national bibliographies as well as on literature.

5

22.   Bibliothèque Nationale.   Catalogue générale des livres
      imprimés de la Bibliothèque Nationale.   Paris: Im-
      primerie Nationale, 1897-1980.   230 vols.   Supple-
      ments published at five-year intervals.
      Mainly a short-title bibliography alphabetized by
      author.

23.   British Museum.   General Catalogue of Printed Books.
      London: British Museum, 1959-66.   263 vols.   1956-
      65 Supplement, 50 vols.   (1968).   1966-70 Supplement,
      26 vols. (1971-72).
      A listing of the holdings of one of the most impor-
      tant libraries in the world.

24.   British Union-Catalog of Periodicals....   Ed. by James
      D. Stewart, Muriel E. Hammond, and Erwin Saenger.
      New York: Academic Press, 1955-1958, 4 vols.   Sup-
      plement to 1960 (New York: Academic Press, 1962.
      991 pp.); New Periodical Titles, 1960-1968, 1969-1973
      (London: Butterworths, 1970-1976, 2 vols.); New Pe-
      riodical Titles, 1974-   (London: Butterworths,
      1974-).
      British equivalent to Union List of Serials.

25.   Collison, Robert L.   Bibliographies, Subject and National:
      A Guide to Their Contents.   3d ed.   New York: Haf-
      ner Publishing Co., 1968.   xviii, 203 pp.
      Chapter on language and literature contains material
      of interest to Hispanists.

26.   Columbia Dictionary of Modern European Literature.   Ed.
      by Jean-Albert Bédé and William Edgerton.   2d ed.
      New York: Columbia University Press, 1980.   872 pp.
      More than 1,800 biographies of writers and critics,
      with bibliography and notices of English translations
      representing 33 languages of Continental Europe.

27.   Conover, Helen F.   Current National Bibliographies.
      Washington, D.C.:   Library of Congress, 1955.   vi,
      132 pp.   Rpt., New York: Greenwood Press, 1968.
      Annotated index of periodical articles, government
      documents, and directories of periodicals and news-
      papers.   Revision and expansion of Current National
      Bibliographies: A List of Sources of Information Con-
      cerning Current Books of All Countries, by L. Heyl,
      first published in 1933.

28. Downs, Robert B. American Library Resources: A
     Bibliographical Guide. Chicago: American Library
     Association, 1951. 1950-61 Supplement (1962), 1961-
     70 Supplement (1972), 1971-80 Supplement (1981).
     Broad coverage. Includes printed library catalogs,
     union lists of books and serials, special collections,
     library holdings, and special library reports. Besides
     linguistics and literature, such areas as philosophy,
     psychology, religion, and science are covered.

29. Gesamtverzeichnis ausländischer Zeitschriften und Serien:
     Hauptband 1939-1958. Wiesbaden: Otto Harrassowitz,
     1978. 2 vols.; supplements for years 1959-67, 5 vols.
     Journals, international congresses, and reports of
     conferences. Includes Spain and Latin America.

30. Irregular Serials and Annuals: An International Direc-
     tory. 7th ed. New York and London: R. R. Bowker
     Co., 1982. 1,542 pp.
     Provides data on some 35,000 serials, annuals,
     continuations, etc. Entries are arranged alphabeti-
     cally by title under 270 subject headings.

31. Lasso de la Vega, Javier. Catálogo abreviado de una
     selección de libros de consulta, referencia, estudio y
     enseñanza.... Madrid: Junta de Intercambio y Ad-
     quisición de Libros para Bibliotecas Públicas, 1953.
     xxiii, 925 pp.
     More than 11,000 items. All subjects covered,
     with an excellent representation of Hispanic titles.
     Bibliographies, criticism, and works are all listed.

32. Malclès, Louise-Noëlle. Les sources du travail biblio-
     graphique. Geneva: E. Droz, 1950-58. 3 vols. in
     4. Rpt. (1966).
     General and specialized bibliographies including bib-
     liographical information on languages, grammars, dic-
     tionaries, and literature. Hispanic studies included
     (vol. 2, pp. 324-38).

33. Modern Language Association International Bibliography
     of Books and Articles on the Modern Languages and
     Literatures. New York: Modern Language Associa-
     tion, 1921- . Published annually.
     Fundamental bibliography of journal articles and
     books. Broadest coverage of annual bibliographies in

the field since 1956 when it attempted international coverage. In 1969 it began to appear in a four-volume format which includes such major sections as English, American, and other literatures, linguistics, and pedagogy. Volume 2 covers Romance and Germanic literatures, and volume 3 covers linguistics. The bibliography for 1981 has been reorganized into the following volumes: National literatures (1 and 2), Linguistics (3), General Literature and Related Topics (4), and Folklore (5). Spanish and Spanish American literature are in volume 2.

34. New Serial Titles. Washington, D. C.: Library of Congress, 1961- . 1950-60, 2 vols. (1961); 1961-65, 3 vols. (1966); 1966-69, 2 vols. (1970). Monthly, then annual, cumulations. Latest: 1976-80 (1981).
Entries arranged alphabetically by title.

35. Palfrey, Thomas; Joseph Fucilla; and William Holbrook. A Bibliographical Guide to Romance Languages and Literatures. 7th ed. Evanston, Ill.: Chandler's, 1969 (1939). 122 pp.
Books listed chronologically according to subject. Occasionally annotated.

36. Romanische Bibliographie/Bibliographie romane/Romance Bibliography, 1961/62- . Tübingen: M. Niemeyer, 1967- . Supersedes the bibliographic supplements of the Zeitschrift für romanische Philologie (see no. 55 below). The bibliography for 1961-62 was published in four volumes (1965-68); for 1963-64, in three volumes (1968-69).
Issued biennially in several volumes.

37. The Romantic Movement Bibliography, 1936-70. Edited by A. C. Elkins, Jr. and L. J. Forstner. New York: Pierian Press and R. R. Bowker Co., 1973. 7 vols.
Largely descriptive, with occasional annotations of books and articles on English and Continental romanticism. Items previously published in ELH (1936-49), Philological Quarterly (1950-64), and English Language Notes (1965-78).

38. The Romantic Movement: A Selective and Critical Bibliography for 1979- . New York: Garland, 1980- . Compiled by David V. Erdman with the assistance of Brian J. Dendle, et al.

Earlier bibliographies included the movement in Spain and Spanish America while recent ones are limited to Spanish literature.

39. Sabor, Josefa. Manual de fuentes de información; obras de referencia; enciclopedias, diccionarios, bibliografías, ... 2d ed. Buenos Aires: Kapelusz, 1967 (1957). xv, 342 pp.
    Annotated listing of general reference works which includes works covering Spain and Latin America, especially Argentina.

40. Sheehy, Eugene P. Guide to Reference Books. 9th ed. Chicago: American Library Association, 1976. 1,015 pp. Supplement for years 1974-78 published in 1980. 305 pp.
    Supersedes Constance Winchell's Guide to Reference Books (see no. 51 below). A comprehensive guide to reference sources in all fields. Useful in suggesting places to search when subject bibliographies do not solve a research problem. Use the American Reference Book Annual to cover reference books published after Sheehy.

41. Titus, Edna Brown. Union List of Serials in the Libraries of the United States and Canada. 3d ed. New York: H. W. Wilson & Co., (1965). 5 vols. Rpt. 1968.
    Each entry includes bibliographic data. Holdings of more than 600 libraries are included.

42. Ulrich's International Periodicals Directory: A Classified Guide to a Selected List of Current Periodicals, Foreign and Domestic. 20th ed. New York: R. R. Bowker Co., 1980 (1932). 2,212 pp.
    Provides basic information about a wide variety of periodicals, including many foreign ones.

43. UNESCO. Bibliographie générale de littérature comparée. Paris: Librairie M. Didier, 1949-58. 5 vols.
    Treats such topics as bibliographies, theory, style, literary influences, current movements, and genres.

44. Union List of Serials in Libraries of the United States and Canada. 3d ed. New York: H. W. Wilson & Co., 1965. 5 vols.

Information on periodical holdings of more than 600 libraries.

45. U. S. Library of Congress. A Catalog of Books Represented by Library of Congress Printed Cards Issued to July 31, 1942. Ann Arbor, Mich.: J. W. Edwards, 1942-46. 167 vols. Supplements: 1942-47, 42 vols. (1948); 1948-52, 24 vols. (1953).

46. _____ . Library of Congress and National Union Catalog Author Lists, 1942-1962. Detroit: Gale Research, 1969- .

47. _____ . Library of Congress Catalog--Books: Subjects, a Cumulative List of Works Represented by Library of Congress Printed Cards. Washington, D. C., 1950- . Cumulative supplements every 5 years. Quarterly and annual.

48. _____ . The National Union Catalog, 1952-55 Imprints: An Author List Representing Library of Congress Printed Cards and Titles Reported by Other American Libraries. Ann Arbor, Mich.: J. W. Edwards, 1961- . 30 vols. Supplements: 1953-57 (1958); 1958-62 (1963); 1963 (1964); 1963-67 (1969).

49. _____ . The National Union Catalog, Pre-1956 Imprints. London: Mansell, 1968-80. 685 vols. Supplements: vols. 686-754 (1980-81). Continuing.
A cumulative author list representing Library of Congress printed cards and titles reported by other American libraries. This represents an attempt to make one union list of Library of Congress entries and those of other collections published before 1956.

50. Walford, Albert John. Guide to Reference Materials. 3d ed. London: Library Association, 1975-77 (1959). 3 vols.
Lists recent reference books by country and subject. Contains many items for Spain and Spanish America in sections on bibliography, language, and literature. Emphasis is on items published in Britain.

51. Winchell, Constance M. Guide to Reference Books. 8th ed. Chicago: American Library Association, 1967 (1902). xx, 741 pp. Supplements compiled by Eugene P. Sheehy: 1965-66 (1968); 1967-68 (1970); 1969-70 (1972).

Very useful, well-organized reference. (See Sheehy, no. 40 above.)

52. Wortman, William A. A Guide to Serial Bibliographies for Modern Literatures. New York: MLA, 1982. xvi, 124 pp.
A guide to current bibliographies in all modern literatures as well as in nonliterary fields important to literary scholars. Includes all current serial bibliographies for national literatures, literary periods, genres, themes, subjects, and authors. Contains a bibliography and subject and title index.

53. The Year's Work in Modern Language Studies. Cambridge: Modern Humanities Research Association, 1931-40; 1950- .
Annual critical survey of work done in modern languages and literatures. Indexes of subjects and names.

54. Zamarriego, Tomás. Enciclopedia de orientación bibliográfica. Barcelona: Juan Flors, 1964-65. 4 vols.
International in scope but with heavy concentration on Spanish, especially humanities and religion. Fifth part of volume 3 deals with literature. Each entry is well annotated.

55. Zeitschrift für romanische Philologie. Supplement: Bibliographie, 1875-1960. Tübingen: M. Niemeyer, 1878-1964. Superseded by Romanische Bibliographie (see no. 36 above). It was published as an annual or biennial bibliographic supplement to ZRP until 1939. Supplements for 1940-50 (vols. 60-66) published in 1957; for 1951-55 (vols. 67-71) published in 1960; for 1956-60 (vols. 72-76) published in 1964.
Very comprehensive bibliography for the Romance literatures and languages.

4. BIBLIOGRAPHIES OF HISPANIC LITERATURE

For bibliographies besides those listed below, consult section 12 for ones included in major journals in the Hispanic field. Especially useful are the bibliographies in the Nueva revista de filología hispánica (México, 1947-) for literature and linguistics of Spain; the Revista de filología hispánica (Buenos Aires and New York, 1939-46), superseded by NRFH, for Hispanic literature and linguistics; the Revista hispánica moderna (New York, 1935-68) for Spanish American literature and linguistics; the Revista de filología española (Madrid, 1914-) for Spanish linguistics and literature; the Revista de literatura (Madrid, 1952-) for Spanish literature; and La torre (San Juan, 1953-) on Hispanic literature.

SPAIN AND SPANISH AMERICA

56. Alarcón, Norma, and Sylvia Kossnar. Bibliography of Hispanic Women Writers (From the MLA 1922-1978). (Chicano-Riqueño Studies Bibliography Series, I.) Bloomington, Ind.: Chicano-Riqueño Studies, 1980. 86 pp.
   Useful for its time-saving qualities. Contains data on almost 150 women writers concerning whom material is listed in the MLA bibliographies.

57. Anderson, David L., et al. Symbolism: A Bibliography of Symbolism As an International and Multi-Disciplinary Movement. New York: New York University Press, 1975. xxi, 160 pp.
   Includes about 300 Spanish, Spanish American, and Portuguese items in Section II, National and Interna-

tional Movements. A good starting point for those interested in symbolist criticism.

58. Bibliografía histórica de España e Hispanoamérica. Barcelona: Teide, 1953-1957. Three numbers published
annually.
Annotated listing of books and articles. Though this
is a general bibliography, entries pertaining to literature are numerous.

59. Catálogo general de la librería española e hispanoamericana, 1901-1930. Madrid: Instituto Nacional del Libro
Español, 1932-51. 5 vols.
Bibliographical data on 92,670 items (separately published books and pamphlets) published between the years
indicated. Includes Spanish American publications.

60. Catálogo general de la librería, 1932-1950. Madrid: Instituto Nacional del Libro Español, 1957-65. 4 vols.
Publishers and variant editions, prices, and numbers of pages of 69,575 entries. Books deal with
Spanish America, France, Italy, and Spain.

61. Foster, David W., and Virginia Ramos Foster. Manual
of Hispanic Bibliography. 2d ed. New York and London: Garland, 1977 (1970). xiii, 329 pp.
Comprehensive bibliographic guide to general bibliographies of Spanish and Spanish American literatures.
Also includes guides to libraries and collections, periodical literature, and theses. For Spanish America,
entries are listed according to country and by periods.
Index included. Covers 1,050 items versus 796 in
first edition.

62. Golden, Herbert H., and Seymour O. Simches. Modern
Iberian Language and Literature: A Bibliography of
Homage Studies. Cambridge, Mass.: Harvard University Press, 1958. x, 184 pp. Rpt., Millwood,
N.Y.: Kraus Reprints, 1971.
Lists studies in homage works up to 1956. Concerned primarily with the Catalonian, Portuguese, and
Spanish languages and literatures, with some articles
relating to Spanish America and Brazil. Linguistic
section updated by Zubatsky (see chapter on Linguistics).

63. González Ollé, F. Manual bibliográfico de estudios es-

pañoles. Pamplona: Ediciones Universidad de Nava-
rra, 1976. xiv, 1,375 pp.
More than 35,000 items with a cut-off point of 1973.
Spanish American items are included. Covers literature, language, and culture. Contains useful author,
alphabetical subject, classified subject, and general indexes.

64. Grismer, Raymond L. A Bibliography of Articles and
Essays on the Literature of Spain and Spanish America.
Minneapolis, Minn.: Perine Book Co., 1935. 423 pp.
The scope of this work is from the Middle Ages to
the 20th century. Sections on dialects, individual
American countries, and interrelationships of differ-
ent languages.

65. _____. Bibliography of the Drama of Spain and Spanish America. Minneapolis, Minn.: Burgess-Beckwith,
1967-69. 2 vols.
Alphabetical listing by critic. Contains a dramatist-
critic index.

66. _____. A New Bibliography of the Literatures of
Spain and Spanish America. Minneapolis, Minn.:
Perine Book Co., 1941-46. 7 vols.
Listing is by author, but covers only from "a" to
"cez." Books and magazines in subjects other than
literature are included.

67. Hatzfeld, Helmut A. A Critical Bibliography of the New
Stylistics Applied to the Romance Literatures, 1953-
1965. Chapel Hill: University of North Carolina
Press, 1966. 183 pp. Rpt., New York: Johnson
Reprint Co., 1972. Spanish version, Bibliografía
crítica de la nueva estilística aplicada a las literaturas románicas (Madrid: Gredos, 1955).
Contains almost 1,900 concisely annotated entries.
This meticulously organized work covers such categories as theory of style and stylistics, explication
de texte, translations, stylistic parallels and variants,
style and structure of literary works, aspects of style,
and motifs. It also has two useful indexes: one of
style investigators and the other of authors, titles,
and terms.

68. Libros en venta en Hispanoamérica y España. New York:
R. R. Bowker, 1964-73. 2d ed. Buenos Aires: Bow-

ker, 1974. 2 vols. 2,185 pp. Supplements: Buenos
Aires, 1967, 1969, 1974, 1977. 1st supplement of 2d
ed.: Buenos Aires: Turner, 1979 (for years 1973-
78). Supplements for 1979-80 (1981) and 1981 (1982)
published in San Juan by Melcher.
Equivalent to Books in Print and supplements. Imprint varies. Arranged by author, title, and subject.

69. Palau y Dulcet, Antonio. Manual del librero hispanoamericano. Inventario bibliográfico de la producción
científica y literaria de España y de la América Latina.
2d ed. Barcelona: Librería Palau, 1948-1977. 28
vols. Index by Agustín Palau Claveras. Vol. 1 (A-
Carvino), Barcelona/Oxford: Palacete Palau Dulcet/
Dolphin Book Co., 1981. vi, 507 pp. Vol. 2 (Cas-
Espanya), Barcelona/Oxford: Palau/Dolphin, 1982.
457 pp. 5 or 6 volumes projected.
   Most complete bibliography of Spanish publications
up to the 20th century. Some noteworthy editions of
this century are listed. Alphabetical index of titles-
subjects.

70. Sainz Rodríguez, Pedro. Biblioteca bibliográfica hispánica. Madrid: Fundación Universitaria, 1975-80. 5
vols.
   Useful despite some errors and omissions. Entries
are usually well annotated. More attention devoted to
Spain. Includes bibliographies of biographical and biobibliographical dictionaries, bibliography of Spanish
national bibliographies, index of periodical publications,
and bibliography on the history of printing in Spain.
Many indexes.

71. Schanzer, George O. Russian Literature in the Hispanic
World: A Bibliography. Toronto: University of Toronto Press, 1972. xlvi, 312 pp.
   Listing of Spanish collections and anthologies of Russian literature, individual translations, criticisms both
general and specific, and sections of semiliterary writings from 1838 to 1965. Some annotations.

72. Simón Díaz, José. Bibliografía de la literatura hispánica. Madrid: Consejo Superior de Investigaciones Científicas, 1950- . 12 vols.
   Volume 1: literary history, collections of texts,
anthologies, monographs, comparative literature; Catalan, Galician, and Basque literatures with many of the

same major divisions. Volume 2: bibliography of bibliographies, biography and biobibliography, general bibliography, catalogs of libraries, catalogs of periodicals,
catalogs of archives, indexes to periodical publications,
general and partial literature bibliographies, bibliographies of other subjects. Same for Catalan and Basque.
Volume 3, in two parts: medieval literature. Volumes 4-12: Renaissance and Golden Age Spanish literature.

73. Thompson, Lawrence S. A Bibliography of Spanish Plays
    on Microcards. Hamden, Conn.: Shoe String Press,
    1968. viii, 490 pp.
       Six thousand Spanish, Catalonian, and Spanish Amer-
    ican plays from the 16th century to the present, based
    on holdings in the University of Kentucky Library.

74. Vindel, Francisco. Manual gráfico-descriptivo del bibliô-
    filo hispanoamericano, 1475-1850. Madrid: Imprenta
    Góngora, 1930-34. 12 vols.
       Reproductions of covers and fragments of several
    thousand books. Brief descriptions.

75. Wilgus, A. Curtis. Latin America, Spain and Portugal:
    A Selected and Annotated Bibliographical Guide to Books
    Published in the United States, 1954-1974. Metuchen,
    N.J.: Scarecrow Press, 1977. xv, 926 pp.
       Useful despite some omissions and errors. De-
    scriptive annotations. Cutoff year is 1973.

76. Woodbridge, Hensley C. Spanish and Spanish American
    Literature: An Annotated Guide to Selective Bibliogra-
    phies. New York: MLA, 1983.
       This compilation of over 350 items is selective and
    lists mostly works published since 1950. The Spanish
    literature section is arranged chronologically by peri-
    ods and the Spanish American sections are arranged by
    country. Annotations are very helpful in determining
    the contents of the works included and a number of
    items are evaluated critically. This bibliography is
    very current and extremely valuable for students and
    scholars.

SPAIN

General

77. Aguilar Piñal, Francisco. Bibliografía de autores españoles del siglo XVIII. Madrid: C. S. I. C., 1981- , 1- . 10 vols. projected.
    Tome I, A-B, has 5,377 entries and five indexes. Bibliography for each author generally covers manuscripts, published works, and studies. This complements José Simón Díaz's Bibliografía de la literatura hispánica (no. 72).

78. _____. Bibliografía fundamental de la literatura española. Siglo XVIII. Madrid: Sociedad General Española de Librería, 1976. 304 pp.
    First bibliographic guide to 18th-century Spanish literature. Important studies on individual authors and desiderata for critical editions and studies.

79. El año literario español 1974-81. Madrid: Castalia, 1975-82. English version: The Spanish Literary Year 1974, 1975, 1976, 1977, 1978. Madrid: Castalia, 1979. 759 pp.
    Annual critical survey of the various genres. Includes regional literary production.

80. Antonio, Nicolás. Bibliotheca hispana nova. 2d ed. Madrid: Viuda de Ibarra, 1783-88 (1672). 2 vols. Facsimile ed., Turin: Bottega d'Erasmo, 1963. 2 vols.
    Written in Latin. Writers covered from 1500 to 1684. This first bibliography of Spanish literature is a basic tool for the study of Peninsular literature.

81. _____. Bibliotheca hispana vetus. 2d ed. Madrid: Viuda de Ibarra, 1788 (1696). 2 vols. Facsimile ed., Turin: Bottega d'Erasmo, 1963. 467 pp.
    Written in Latin. From Augustine Empire to 1500. This second bibliography of Spanish literature is a basic tool for the study of early Peninsular literature.

82. Armistead, Samuel G. "Critical Bibliography of the Hispanic Ballad in Oral Tradition (1971-1979)." In El romancero: Historia, comparatismo, bibliografía crítica.

Ed. by Samuel G. Armistead, Diego Catalán, Antonio
Sánchez Romeralo. Madrid: Gredos Cátedra Seminario
Menendez Pidal, 1977, pp. 3, 199-310.
Brief commentary on every publication on the Hispanic ballad that has come to Armistead's attention for
the years 1971 to 1978. Books and articles published
prior to this period, but reviewed after 1971, have also
been listed, but without critical commentary. Excellent
critical, annotated bibliography by a leading expert on
the subject.

83. Avila, Pablo Luis. Contributo a un repertorio bibliográfico degli scritti pubblicati in Italia sulla cultura
spagnola (1940-1969). Pisa: Università di Pisa, 1971.
111 pp.
Contains articles and books. An unannotated alphabetical listing. Author and subject indexes.

84. Bainton, A. J. C. Comedias sueltas in Cambridge University Library: A Descriptive Catalogue. Cambridge:
The University Library, 1977. 281 pp.
Includes 919 entries, many of which have never been
catalogued before.

85. Barrera y Leirado, Cayetano Alberto de la. Catálogo
bibliográfico y biográfico del teatro antiguo español,
desde sus orígenes hasta mediados del siglo XVIII.
Madrid: M. Rivadeneyra, 1860. 2 vols. Facsimile
eds., Madrid: Támesis, 1968; Madrid: Gredos, 1969.
A short biographical sketch of each author with a
chronological list of his works. Various appendixes
are included. Valuable source of information for study
of early theater.

86. Beardsley, Theodore S. "Spanish Literature." In The
Present State of Scholarship in Sixteenth-Century Literature. Ed. by William M. Jones. Columbia: University of Missouri Press, 1978, pp. 71-100.
Valuable survey that updates Green's article (no. 96)
through 1974. The bibliography comprises bibliographies, surveys of scholarship, catalogs and surveys of
Renaissance texts, general and comprehensive studies,
specialized studies, and linguistics.

87. Bergman, Hannah E., and Szilvia E. Szmuk. A Catalogue of "Comedias Sueltas" in the New York Public
Library. (Research Bibliographies and Checklists,

32.) Vol. I.   London: Grant and Cutler, 1981. 154
pp.
A checklist of 612 comedias sueltas. Volume I covers A-H. The projected volume II will complete coverage and include indexes and checklists for both volumes. Identifies editions primarily printed before the
end of the 18th century, but the cutoff year is 1833.

88. Brown, Reginald F. La novela española, 1700-1850.
Madrid: Servicio de Publicaciones del Ministerio de
Educación Nacional, 1953. 221 pp.
The main section is an annotated chronological list-
ing of novels.

89. Cárdenas, Anthony; Jean Gulkinson; John Nitti; and Ellen
Anderson. Bibliography of Old Spanish Texts: Literary
Texts. 2d ed. Madison, Wisc.: Hispanic Seminary
of Medieval Studies, 1977 (1975). 128 pp.
Computer-produced compilation of 1,869 manuscripts
of literary works and of works printed before 1501.
Contains nine indexes.

90. Catálogo colectivo de obras impresas en los siglos XVI
al XVII existentes en las bibliotecas españolas. Madrid: Biblioteca Nacional. Edición provisional, 1972- .
Provides photographic reproduction of library catalog cards with an indication of which libraries hold the
books. It has been published through the letter "S"
(1979). Coverage of the 17th century has yet to appear.

91. Childers, James Wesley. Tales from Spanish Picaresque
Novels: A Motif-Index. Albany: State University of
New York Press, 1977. 262 pp.
A motif index of tales from 30 Spanish picaresque
novels with an introductory discussion of the picaresque
genre and its influence on Spanish and other literatures.
Useful to the scholar working in Hispanic folklore.

92. Cioranescu, Alejandro. Bibliografía franco-española
(1600-1715). Anejo XXXVI of Boletín de la Real Academia Española. Madrid: 1977. 705 pp.
Contains 4,769 entries. Includes grammars and dictionaries of the Spanish language published in French
or in France, travel accounts, and French works influenced by Spanish authors. Includes an author index
and one of cryptograms and pseudonyms.

93. Eisenberg, Daniel. Castilian Romances of Chivalry in
     the 16th Century. (Research Bibliographies and Check-
     lists, 23.) London: Grant and Cutler, 1980. 112 pp.
     Bibliography of major sources, general sources, the
     Romances themselves, texts and studies on chivalry,
     chivalric elements in early and Golden Age drama, and
     an Index of Names. Covers manuscripts from 1508 to
     1602.

94. Foulché-Delbosc, Raymond. Bibliographie hispanique.
     New York: Hispanic Society of America, 1905-17. 13
     vols.
     Listing of books, pamphlets, and articles on lan-
     guages, literatures, and histories of Spanish, Catalan,
     and Portuguese. Volumes for 1912-14 contain Biblio-
     graphie hispano-française of Foulché-Delbosc; volumes
     for 1915-17 have Bibliographie hispano-grecque, in col-
     laboration with Emile Legrand.

95. _____, and L. Barrau-Dihigo. Manuel de l'His-
     panisant. New York: G. P. Putnam's Sons, 1920-25.
     2 vols. Facsimile ed., Millwood, N.Y.: Kraus Re-
     prints, 1959.
     Essential bibliographical guide.

96. Green, Otis H. "A Critical Survey of Scholarship in the
     Field of Spanish Renaissance Literature, 1914-1944."
     Studies in Philology, 44 (1944), 228-62.
     Principally concerned with the history of ideas rath-
     er than with periods, genres, or authors. Covers the
     period 1473-1600.

97. Greene, Vinson Fleming. "A Critical Bibliography of
     the Spanish Pastoral Novel (1559-1633)." Diss. Uni-
     versity of North Carolina, 1969. 120 pp.
     Critically annotated bibliography of 403 items re-
     lating to 20 pastoral novels.

98. Haebler, Konrad. Bibliografía ibérica del siglo XV:
     Enumeración de todos los libros impresos en España
     y Portugal hasta el año 1500 con notas críticas por
     Conrado Haebler. New York: Burt Franklin Reprints,
     1960 (1903-17). 2 vols.
     Lengthy annotations of more than 700 works.

99. Hitchcock, Richard. The Kharjas: A Critical Bibliog-
     raphy. (Research Bibliographies and Checklists, 20.)
     London: Grant and Cutler, 1977. 68 pp.

A list which includes all items concerned directly
with the interpretation and significance of the jarchas,
together with a representative selection of items dealing with their context, the problems they raise, and
less central issues.
Supplement with a critical evaluation of 24 items
by Samuel G. Armistead in "Some Recent Developments in Kharja Scholarship," La Corónica, 8:2
(1980), 197-203.

100. Instituto Nacional del Libro Español. Indices de la
producción editorial española (1968-1972). Madrid:
INLE, 1973. 636 pp.
Contains bibliographic data published in Libros
nuevos (until 1970) and Novedades editoriales españolas (no. 129).

101. Jauralde Pou, Pablo. Manual de investigación literaria: Guía bibliográfica para el estudio de la literatura española. (Biblioteca Románica Hispánica.
Manuales 48.) Madrid: Gredos, 1981. 416 pp.
Includes 1,996 items, many annotated, in 22 areas
such as general bibliography, encyclopedias and dictionaries, libraries, bibliography of Spanish literature, histories, manuals and anthologies of Spanish
literature, literature by centuries, metrics, and pro-
fessional journals. Coverage is uneven in the various areas. Contains an eight-page table of contents.

102. Kayserling, M. Biblioteca española-portugueza-judaica:
Dictionaire bibliographique des auteurs juifs, de leurs
ouvrages espagnoles et des oeuvres sur et contre les
juifs et le judaisme avec un aperçu sur la littérature
des juifs espagnols et une collection des proverbes
espagnoles. Reprint. New York: Ktav Publishing
House, 1971 (1890). 272 pp.
Dictionary of Jewish Iberian authors from early
times to the nineteenth century.

103. Laurenti, Joseph L., and Alberto Porqueras-Mayo.
The Spanish Golden Age (1472-1700): A Catalog of
Rare Books Held in the Library of the University of
Illinois and in Selected North American Libraries.
Foreword by N. Frederick Nash. (Reference Publi-
cations in Latin American Studies.) Boston: G. K.
Hall, 1979. 593 pp.
Items are arranged alphabetically by author with

each being described in detail. Includes an index of printers.

104. Library of Congress Hispanic Division. The Spanish Plays Collection (microfilm edition), 1981. 161 reels. Includes 8,179 dramatic works published in Spain and written and performed between 1830 and 1920. Acquired in 1938 by the Library of Congress from the Hispanic Society of America. Author index.

105. McCready, Warren T. Bibliografía temática de estudios sobre el teatro español antiguo. Toronto: University of Toronto Press, 1966. xix, 445 pp. Studies published between 1850 and 1950, dealing with the Spanish theater from early times to the beginning of the 18th century.

106. McGaha, Michael O. The Theatre in Madrid During the Second Republic. (Research Bibliographies and Checklists, 29.) London: Grant and Cutler, 1979, 105 pp. Chronological arrangement from the period April 14, 1931-July 18, 1934. Index of titles and one of authors, translators, and adapters.

107. Madrigal, José A. Bibliografía sobre el pundonor: Teatro del Siglo de Oro. Miami: Ediciones Universal, 1977. 56 pp. Includes 569 unannotated items on general studies and on three dramatists: Lope de Vega, Calderón de la Barca, and Rojas Zorrilla.

108. Paci, Anna Maria. Manual de bibliografía española. Pisa: Università de Pisa, 1970. 829 pp. Systematic listing of all articles relating to Spanish (and Catalan) literature in all issues of over 100 periodicals up to 1968 (10,246 items).

109. Penney, Clara Louise. Printed Books, 1468-1700, in the Hispanic Society of America. 2d ed. New York: Hispanic Society of America, 1965 (1929, 1938). xlii, 614 pp. A short-title alphabetical listing.

110. Pérez Pastor, Cristóbal. Bibliografía madrileña o descripción de las obras impresas en Madrid (1566-1625). Madrid: Huérfanos, 1891-1907. 3 vols.

Rpt., New York: Burt Franklin, 1967; Amsterdam:
T. Van Heusden, 1970-71.
Arranged chronologically and alphabetically by author. Useful annotations. A basic bibliography for
the period covered.

111. Ricapito, Joseph V. Bibliografía razonada y anotada
de las obras maestras de la picaresca española. Madrid: Castalia, 1980. 613 pp.
Survey of the critical works that have been written
about the Spanish picaresque and three major works
of this genre: Lazarillo de Tormes, Guzmán de Al-
farache, and El Buscón. Very useful.

112. Sáez, Emilio, and Mercé Rossell. Repertorio de me-
dievalismo hispánico (1955-1975). Barcelona: "El
Abir," 1976- . 5 vols. projected.
Arranged by author. Lists materials published,
in press and in preparation.

113. Salstad, M. Louise. The Presentation of Women in
Spanish Golden Age Literature: An Annotated Bibliography. Boston: G. K. Hall, 1980. xix, 129 pp.
Includes 372 well-annotated studies on women in
16th- and 17th-century Castilian literature.

114. Sánchez Romeralo, Antonio; Samuel G. Armistead; and
Suzanne H. Petersen, with the collaboration of....
Bibliografía del romancero oral. Madrid: Cátedra
Seminario Menéndez Pidal, 1980. xxv, 277 pp.
Includes 1,624 bibliographical references to primary sources and studies of the Romancero in modern oral tradition from 1700 to the present. Covers
the Romancero in Spain, Portugal, and Latin America.
Includes seven indexes. The authors say that this
very useful compilation is relatively complete but not
exhaustive.

115. Serís, Homero. Manual de bibliografía de la literatura
española. Syracuse: Centro de Estudios Hispánicos,
1948-54. 1,086 pp. in 2 pts.
Covers general works, biobibliographical studies,
literary genres, culture, art, and folklore.

116. Simón Díaz, José. Manual de bibliografía de la literatura española. 3d ed. Madrid: Gredos, 1980 (1963).
1,156 pp.

Lists studies of all aspects of Spanish literature
and a few linguistic studies. Author and subject indexes are very useful. Probably the most useful one-
volume bibliography of Spanish literature. Contains
26,924 entries.

117. Siracusa, Joseph, and Joseph L. Laurenti. Relaciones
literarias entre España e Italia: Ensayo de una bibliografía de literatura comparada. Boston: G. K.
Hall, 1972. ix, 252 pp. Continued by their "Literary Relations Between Spain and Italy: A Bibliographic Survey of Comparative Literature. First
supplement (1882-1974)." Anali. Istituto universitario orientales. Sezione romance, 19:127-199 (1977),
and "A Bibliography of Literary Relations Between
Spain and Italy," Hispano Italo Studies, 1:83-96 (1976).
This is a compilation of 2,188 mostly unannotated
items arranged by critic with an index of Spanish and
Italian writers mentioned in these references.

118. Steunow, Jacqueline, and Lothar Kanpp. Bibliografía
de los cancioneros castellanos del siglo XV y repertorio de sus géneros poéticos. (Documents, études
et répertoires publiés par l'Institut de Recherche et
l'Histoire des Textes, 22.) Paris: Edition du CNRS,
1975-78. 2 vols.; a 3rd vol. is projected.
Covers manuscripts and old editions of cancioneros
from the first third of the 14th century to the first
half of the 16th.

119. Stubbings, H. U. Renaissance Spain in Its Literary
Relations with England and France: A Critical Bib-
liography. Nashville, Tenn.: Vanderbilt University
Press, 1969. 138 pp.
Annotated bibliography of 364 items covering books,
monographs, and articles. Extensive index.

120. Thomas, Henry. Short-Title Catalogue of Spanish,
Spanish-American, and Portuguese Books Printed
Before 1601 in the British Museum. Rpt., London:
British Museum, 1966 (1921). xv, 169 pp.
Arranged alphabetically in three sections: Spanish,
Spanish American, and Portuguese.

Serial

121. Bibliografía española. Madrid: Ministerio de Educa-

ción Nacional: Dirección General de Archivos y Bibliotecas, 1958-63.
Annual general bibliography based on copyright receipts in the Biblioteca Nacional. Index of authors, titles, and subjects, and lists of publishers, series, and periodicals. Continues Bibliografía hispánica (no. 122).

122. Bibliografía hispánica. Madrid: Instituto Nacional del Libro, 1942-57.
Monthly bibliography classified by subject and by author. Continued by Bibliografía hispánica (see entry above) and superseded by El libro español (no. 127).

123. "Bibliography of Post-Civil War Spanish Fiction, 1978- ,"
Anales de la narrativa española contemporánea, 4-5 (1979-80); Anales de la literatura española contemporánea, 6- (1981-).
Creative works, critical books and essays, reviews, documents, and interviews are included.

124. Bibliotheca hispana: Revista de información y orientación bibliográfica. Madrid: Consejo Superior de Investigaciones Científicas, 1943- .
Annual bibliography covering wide range of subject matter, including philology and literature.

125. Boletín del depósito legal de obras impresas. Madrid: Ministerio de Educación Nacional: Dirección General de Archivos y Bibliotecas, 1958- .
Lists all books printed in Spain.

126. Indice español de humanidades. Madrid: Instituto de Información y Documentación en Ciencias Sociales y Humanidades (ISOC) y Centro Nacional de Información y Documentación, OSIC, 1, no. 1 (January-June 1978-).
The first issue contains tables of contents of 171 journals published in 1976. Key word index.

127. El libro español. Madrid: Instituto Nacional del Libro Español, 1958- .
Classified monthly listing of current and forthcoming books. Also contains brief articles on the literary world. Spanish equivalent of Publishers Weekly.

128. Libros españoles: Catálogo ISBN. Madrid: Agencia

Española del International Standard Book Number,
1973- .
Equivalent to U. S. Books in Print. Contains three
major sections of titles, authors, and subjects.

129. Novedades editoriales españolas. Madrid: Comisión
Ejecutiva para el Comercio Exterior del Libro, 1953-
57.
Contained literary articles and bibliographic data
on current literature, art, history, philosophy, etc.
Superseded by El libro español (see 127).

SPANISH AMERICA

General

130. Acuña, René. El teatro popular en Hispanoamérica:
Una bibliografía anotada. México: UNAM, 1979.
114 pp.
Covers Spanish "popular" theater antecedents and
Spanish American theater from pre-Columbian times
to 1970, and some beyond this date. The author is
unclear in the meaning he ascribes to "popular."
Gaucho theater is surprisingly omitted.

131. Amérique Latine: Bulletin analytique de documentation.
1978- . Paris: Institut des Hautes Etudes de l'Amérique Latine.
Includes books and periodical articles on Latin
America.

132. Anderson, Robert Roland. Spanish American Modernism: A Selected Bibliography. Tucson: University
of Arizona Press, 1970. 167 pp.
Critical studies on 18 authors plus a section of
general studies on the movement as a whole.

133. Anuario hispanoamericano. Madrid: Mundus, 1953-
54.
Includes literature and culture among broad range
of subjects covered.

134. Becco, Horacio Jorge. Fuentes para el estudio de la
literatura hispanoamericana. Buenos Aires: Centro
Editor de América Latina, 1968. 52 pp.

Covers bibliographies, literary histories, essays, anthologies, national bibliographies, and literary journals. Brief annotations.

135. _____, and David William Foster. La nueva narrativa hispanoamericana: Bibliografía. Buenos Aires: Casa Pardo, 1976. 226 pp.
An unannotated list of 2,257 items on the "new" novel and short story. It contains data on 15 authors.

136. Behar, D., and R. Behar. Libros antiguos y modernos referentes a América y España. Buenos Aires: Librería Panamericana, 1947. 371 pp.
Covers history, periodicals, bibliographies, and indigenous languages. Some annotations.

137. Berliner, J. J., and staff. Bibliography of Latin America. New York: J. J. Berliner, 1935-40. 6 vols.
Each volume gives chronologically arranged bibliographic information on general cultural material.

138. Bryant, Shasta M. Selective Bibliography of Bibliographies of Hispanic American Literature. 2d ed., expanded and revised. Austin: University of Texas, Institute of Latin American Studies, 1976 (1966). x, 100 pp.
About two thirds of these 662 entries are author bibliographies. Almost all items are annotated. The index is one of compilers and of authors and genres as subjects.

139. Cordeiro, Daniel Raposo. A Bibliography of Latin American Bibliographies: Social Sciences and Humanities. Metuchen, N.J., and London: Scarecrow Press, 1979. 280 pp.
Covers the period 1966-74. Supplements and follows format of Arthur Gropp's A Bibliography of Latin American Bibliographies (1968) and its Supplement (1971). See Gropp (no. 148) and Piedracueva (no. 166) below.

140. Dorn, Georgette M., comp. Latin America, Spain, and Portugal: An Annotated Bibliography of Paperback Books. 2d rev. ed. Washington, D.C.: Library of Congress, 1976 (1971). 322 pp.
Listing of 2,000 inexpensive paperbacks, mainly from the U.S. Includes a section on grammars, dictionaries, and textbooks.

141. Fichero bibliográfico hispanoamericano. San Juan, P. R.:
      Melcher Ediciones, 1961- . Formerly published by
      R. R. Bowker Co. (New York). Frequency has var-
      ied; since Oct. 1964 it has appeared monthly except
      for a combined Jan.-Feb. issue.
           Classified list of current publications in Spanish
      regardless of place. Over the years some countries
      have been covered considerably better than others.

142. Finch, Mark Steven. "An Annotated Bibliography of
      Recent Sources on Latin American Theater: General
      Section, Argentina, Chile, México and Peru." Dis-
      sertation. Cincinnati, 1979. 372 pp.
           Includes 884 well-annotated items concerning the
      Latin American theater and in particular the four
      countries mentioned in the title.

143. Flores, Angel. Bibliografía de autores hispanoameri-
      canos: A Bibliography of Spanish-American Writers,
      1609-1974. New York: Gordian Press, 1975. 311
      pp.
           Selected bibliography, with around 10,000 entries
      on almost 200 authors. A number of important omis-
      sions.

144. Foster, David William. The Twentieth-Century Spanish
      American Novel: A Bibliographic Guide. Metuchen,
      N. J.: Scarecrow Press, 1975. 234 pp.
           This unannotated compilation covers criticism per-
      taining to the 56 Spanish American novelists most
      commonly studied in the U. S. Contains the section
      "Basic monographic studies on the Spanish American
      novel"; material on most of the authors is divided
      into Bibliographies, Critical books, and Critical es-
      says.

145. Fretes, Hilda Gladys, and Esther Bárbara. Biblio-
      grafía del modernismo. Mendoza, Argentina: Uni-
      versidad Nacional de Cuyo, Biblioteca Central, 1970.
      138 pp.
           Contains 245 items with many extensive annotations.

146. Geoghegan, Abel Rodolfo. Obras de referencia de Amé-
      rica latina: Repertorio selectivo y anotado de enciclo-
      pedias, diccionarios, bibliografías, repertorios bio-
      gráficos, catálogos, guías, anuarios, índices,....
      Buenos Aires: Crisol, 1965. xxiii, 280 pp.

Annotates 2,694 works of reference, including books as well as articles from more than 165 periodical publications.

147. Grismer, Raymond L. A Reference Index to 12,000 Spanish American Authors: A Guide to Bibliographies and Bio-bibliographies. New York: H. W. Wilson & Co., 1939. xvi, 150 pp. Rpt., Detroit: Blaine Ethridge Books, 1971.
Indexes more than 125 reference sets, encyclopedias, and the like, covering writers in all genres.

148. Gropp, Arthur E. A Bibliography of Latin American Bibliographies. Metuchen, N.J.: Scarecrow Press, 1968. ix, 515 pp.
Greatly enlarged and updated version of the work of the same title by C. K. Jones published in 1942. Gropp published a supplement with the same publisher (1971, xiii, 277 pp.), which mainly covers the period 1965-69. For both volumes the arrangement of items is by subject, subdivided by country. Detailed indexes in each volume. See Cordeiro (no. 139) and Piedracueva (no. 166) for further supplements to this work.

149. Gropp, Arthur E. A Bibliography of Latin American Bibliographies Published in Periodicals. Metuchen, N.J.: Scarecrow Press, 1976. 2 vols.
A classified list of more than 9,700 items for the years 1929 to 1965, with some earlier references.

150. Hebblethwaite, Frank P. A Bibliographical Guide to the Spanish American Theater. Washington, D.C.: Pan American Union, 1969. viii, 84 pp.
Books and articles divided by country. Many items are annotated.

151. Index to Latin American Periodical Literature, 1929-1960. Boston: G. K. Hall & Co., 1962. 8 vols. 1961-65 Supplement (1967), 1966-1970 (1979). 2 vols.
Arranged alphabetically by author, title, and subject with coverage of around 1,700 periodicals. Some brief annotations.

152. Jackson, Richard L. The Afro-Spanish American Author: An Annotated Bibliography of Criticism. New York and London: Garland, 1980. xix, 129 pp.
Complements his Black Writers in Latin America (1979). Devoted to the works and criticism of 25

selected Afro-Spanish American authors, a major
part of the bibliography relates to Cuban writers
(60 percent of the citations) and especially Nicolás
Guillen (37 percent of the citations). Also contains
annotated lists of general bibliographies, studies,
and anthologies on Afro-American literature.

153. Leguizamón, Julio. Bibliografía general de la literatura hispanoamericana. Buenos Aires: Editoriales
Reunidas, 1954. 213 pp.
Anthologies of and studies on Spanish American
literature covering all countries and all genres. Author index. Not annotated.

154. Lohman Villena, Guillermo; Luis J. Cisneros; Julio
Ortega; and Horacio J. Becco. Bibliografía general
de la literatura latinoamericana. Paris: UNESCO,
1972. 187 pp.
Annotated bibliography (finished around 1967) that
covers the colonial period, the 19th century, and the
20th century. Contains bibliographies of bibliographies, critical studies, literary histories, collections
of essays, and proceedings of literary congresses.

155. Lozano, Stella. Selected Bibliography of Contemporary
Spanish-American Writers. (Latin America Bibliog-
raphy Series No. 8.) Los Angeles: California State
University, Latin American Studies Center, 1979. v,
149 pp.
This unannotated bibliography is mainly limited to
critical studies published between 1974 and 1978.
Borges is surprisingly omitted.

156. Lyday, Leon F., and George W. Woodyard. A Bibliography of Latin American Theater Criticism 1940-
1974. (Guides and Bibliographic Series, 10.) Austin: University of Texas, Institute of Latin American
Studies, 1976. xvii, 243 pp.
Includes 2,360 items, many of which are annotated.
This compilation continues their "Studies on the Latin
American Theatre, 1960-1969" (Theatre Documentation, 2 [Fall 1969-Spring 1970], 49-84), which has
694 items.

157. Matos, Antonio. Guía a las reseñas de libros de y
sobre Hispanoamérica. 1972- . Detroit: Blaine
Ethridge, 1976- . Volume for 1979 published in
1981.

The purpose of the Guide is to offer an index by
author of reviews that appear in over 633 periodicals
(1979 ed., p. vii).

158. Medina, José Toribio. Biblioteca hispanoamericana
(1493-1810). Facsimile ed., Santiago de Chile,
1958-62 (1898-1907). 7 vols. Amsterdam: N.
Israel, 1968. 7 vols.
Includes works by Americans and Spaniards in
chronological order.

159. Mesa, Rosa Quintero, comp. Latin American Serial
Documents. Ann Arbor, Mich.: R. R. Bowker,
1971-72, vols. 1-2 (Argentina, Bolivia); Xerox Uni-
versity Microfilms, 1968-77, vols. 3-12 (Brazil,
Chile, Colombia, Cuba, Ecuador, México, Paraguay,
Perú, Uruguay, Venezuela).
Bibliographic data on thousands of serials from
each Latin American nation. Also indicates United
States library holdings.

160. Neglia, Erminio, and Luis Ordaz. Repertorio selecto
del teatro hispanoamericano contemporáneo. 2d ed.
Tempe: Center for Latin American Studies, Arizona
State University, 1980 (1974). 110 pp.
Alphabetical listing of contemporary Spanish American dramatists by country. Many anthologies are
included. It also contains "Lista parcial de fuentes
bibliográficas" and "Antología de teatro."

161. Ocampo de Gómez, Aurora M. Novelistas iberoamericanos contemporáneos: Obras y bibliografía crítica.
(Cuadernos del Centro de Estudios Literarios, 2, 4,
6, 10, 11.) México: UNAM, 1971-81, 5 parts.
Supplies nationality and dates of important contemporary authors, along with a listing of their books
and criticism about them.

162. Okinshevich, Leo. Latin America in Soviet Writings:
A Bibliography. Baltimore: Johns Hopkins Press,
1966. 2 vols.
Updates and expands earlier work, Latin America
in Soviet Writings, published by Library of Congress.
Covers total geographical area and all material.

163. Pan American Union, Columbus Memorial Library.
List of Books Accessioned and Periodical Articles
Indexed. Boston: G. K. Hall & Co., 1950-70.

Annual listing of cultural aspects of Latin American life.

164. Pascual Buxó, José, and Antonio Melis, comps. Apuntes para una bibliografía crítica de la literatura hispanoamericana. Florence: Valmartina Editores, 1973. 133 pp.
Contains an extensively annotated listing of 34 general histories of Spanish American literature arranged alphabetically and 100 books on the literatures of individual Spanish countries. Two indexes of works consulted but not included and also an author index.

165. Payró, Roberto P. Historias de la literatura americana: Guía bibliográfica. Washington, D.C.: Pan American Union, 1950. 59 pp.
Includes some journal articles.

166. Piedracueva, Haydée. A Bibliography of Latin American Bibliographies, 1975-1979: Humanities and Social Sciences. Metuchen, N.J.: Scarecrow Press, 1982. xiii, 313 pp.
Classified, unannotated bibliographies useful for sections on national bibliographies, biography, and literature and printing. Supplements the original work of Arthur E. Gropp. See Gropp (no. 148) and Cordeiro (no. 139) above.

167. Polibiblón: Bibliografía acumulativa argentina e hispanoamericana. Buenos Aires, 1947- .
Includes Argentine, Spanish American, and Spanish books and reviews. Entries are by subject and some are annotated.

168. Rela, Walter. Guía bibliográfica de la literatura hispanoamericana desde el siglo XIX hasta 1970. Buenos Aires: Casa Pardo, 1971. 613 pp.
Contains 6,023 items. Unannotated, well indexed, but still difficult to use because many sections are arranged by the author of the work, rather than by the author written about. No articles listed.

168a. _____. Spanish American Literature: A Selected Bibliography, 1970-1980. East Lansing: Michigan State University, Department of Romance and Classical Languages, 1982. 231 pp.
A classified list of 1,502 titles, mainly of books

but also some periodicals. Contains bibliographies, dictionaries, literary criticism and history, anthologies, and proceedings of congresses. Many of the items are not annotated.

169. Rodríguez, Mario, and Vincent C. Peloso. A Guide for the Study of Culture in Central America: Humanities and Social Sciences. Washington, D.C.: Pan American Union, Division of Philosophy and Letters, 1968. 88 pp.
Lists 934 reference works, documentary sets, cultural journals, and books and articles on the humanities and social sciences.

170. Sánchez, Luis Alberto. Repertorio bibliográfico de la literatura latinoamericana. Vol. 1, Santiago de Chile: Talleres Gráficos, Encuadernación Hispano Suiza, 1955. Vol. 2, Lima: Universidad Mayor de San Marcos, 1957. Vol. 3, Santiago de Chile: Universidad de Chile, 1962. Vol. 4, Cuba and Ecuador.
Includes literary history, criticism, and anthologies. Annotated entries and bibliographic information. Volume 1 covers Central America and Argentina, volume 2 includes Bolivia and Brazil, volume 3 is devoted to Chile and Colombia, and volume 4 is on Cuba and Ecuador.

171. Seminar on the Acquisition of Latin American Library Materials (SALALM). Madison: Memorial Library, University of Wisconsin-Madison. Irregular.
SALALM's annual publication is filled with useful reports and bibliographies on Latin American library materials. Publication began in 1969.

172. Watson, Alice G. H. A Guide to Reference Materials of Colombia, Ecuador, and Venezuela Useful in Social Science and Humanities. Metuchen, N.J.: Scarecrow Press, 1971. 279 pp.
Contains evaluations of 894 current and retrospective bibliographies and reference works.

173. Woodbridge, Hensley C. "Latin American National Bibliography." In Encyclopedia of Information and Library Science, 36 (New York: Marcel Dekker, 1983), 270-342.
This article is the fullest discussion of national bibliographies, both retrospective and current, that has yet been produced.

174. Woods, Richard D. Reference Materials on Latin
     America in English: The Humanities. Metuchen,
     N.J., and London: Scarecrow Press, 1980. xii,
     639 pp.
     Contains bibliographies, dictionaries, guidebooks,
     handbooks, directories, catalogs, literary histories,
     etc. Includes 1,252 annotated items on a broad range
     of topics, with an extensive subject index done by
     computer analysis.

175. Zimmerman, Irene. Current National Bibliographies of
     Latin America: A State of the Art Study. Gaines-
     ville: University of Florida, Center for Latin Amer-
     ican Studies, 1971. 139 pp.
     Covers the status of the current Latin American
     national bibliographies in descriptive form, with use-
     ful summaries for each country. Also has an appen-
     dix on the Seminar on the Acquisition of Latin Amer-
     ican Library Materials (SALALM) and a selective bib-
     liography on serials, books, articles, and papers.

176. Zubatsky, David S. "Annotated Bibliography of Latin
     American Author Bibliographies." In Chasqui, vols.
     6, 7, 8 (1976-79): "Mexico," 6, 1 (Nov. 1976), 43-
     70; "Central America and the Caribbean," 6, 2 (Feb.
     1977), 41-72; "Colombia, Ecuador and Venezuela,"
     6, 3 (May 1977), 45-68; "Brazil," 7, 1 (Nov. 1977),
     35-54; "Bolivia, Chile, Paraguay and Perú," 7, 3
     (May 1978), 34-79; "Argentina and Uruguay," 8, 2
     (Feb. 1979), 47-94.
     Annotated bibliography of Brazilian and Spanish
     American writers, linguists, and literary critics.

National

--Argentina

177. Becco, Horacio Jorge. Bibliografías de bibliografías
     literarias argentinas. Washington, D.C.: Secretaría
     General de la Organización de los Estados Ameri-
     canos, 1972. 89 pp.
     Annotated bibliography of literary Argentine bibli-
     ographies together with more than 300 bibliographies
     on individual authors, themes, genres, and related
     subjects, and also 18 general Latin American bibli-
     ographies.

178. _____. Fuentes para el estudio de la literatura argentina. Buenos Aires: Centro Editor de América
Latina, 1968. 62 pp.
   Divided into nine sections: bibliography, literary
   history, literary criticism, biographies, magazines
   and newspapers, theater, anthologies, reference works,
   and literary collections.

179. Bibliografía argentina de artes y letras. Directed by
Augusto Raúl Cortázar. Buenos Aires: Fondo Nacional de las Artes, 1959-1973. Cumulative index
for 1959-63 in no. 20 (1963). Cumulative alphabetical index for 1964-68 and cumulative subject index
for nos. 1-40 (1959-69) in no. 39/40 (1969).
   Literary and cultural cumulative bibliography.
   List includes books, scholarly publications, literary
   criticism, and the like. Special bibliographic numbers are often devoted to material on single authors
   or topics; for example, the issue corresponding to
   number 29/30 (1966) has a 48-page bibliography entitled, "Cuento fantástico argentino en el siglo XX."

180. Biblos. Directed by Gonzalo Losada. Buenos Aires:
Cámara Argentina del Libro, 1943- . Published bimonthly.
   Coverage of publications by main Argentine publishers. Bibliographic data and brief reviews.

181. Foster, David W. Research Guide to Argentine Literature. Revised edition of Foster and Foster, Research Guide to Argentine Literature (Scarecrow
Press, 1970, 146 pp.). New York: Garland, 1982.
778 pp.
   The revision includes 80 Argentine literary figures, with expanded emphasis on women writers,
   essayists, and dramatists. Approximately one-fourth
   of the compilation is a very detailed listing of general studies on Argentine literature in 30 classified
   sections.

182. Geoghegan, Abel Rodolfo. Bibliografía de bibliografías
argentinas (1807-1970). Preliminary ed. Buenos
Aires: Casa Pardo, 1970. 130 pp.
   A selective listing that includes 452 bibliographies,
   most of which are annotated. Contains sections on
   general works and works in such fields as philosophy,
   religion, and social sciences. There are 30 works
   listed for literature and 14 for linguistics.

183. Pepe, Luz E. A. La crítica teatral argentina (1880-
     1962). Buenos Aires: Fondo Nacional de las Artes,
     1966. 78 pp.
         Contains 782 entries, many of which are annotated.
     List of companies, friends of theater, and experi-
     mental theaters.

     Polibiblón. See no. 167.

184. Sabor, Josefa E., and Lydia H. Revello. Bibliografía
     básica de obras de referencia de artes y letras para
     la Argentina. Buenos Aires: Fondo Nacional de las
     Artes, 1968. 78 pp.
         Included in this annotated guide to bibliographies
     and other reference works are 248 items.

     --Bolivia

185. Bibliografía boliviana. Cochabamba: Los Amigos del
     Libro, 1962-74. Title changed to Bio-bibliografía
     boliviana in 1975. Annual. (See no. 186 below.)
         An alphabetical listing of books and pamphlets pub-
     lished in Bolivia. Contains a separate bibliography
     of books on Bolivia written abroad. Title and subject
     indexes and a list of publishers and printers. Dates
     and profession of each author are given and some-
     times a brief biographical sketch is provided. In-
     cludes essays on Bolivian publishing, literature, and
     culture. Includes data on Bolivian magazines.

186. Bio-bibliografía boliviana del año. Compiled by Werner
     Guttentag Tichauer. La Paz and Cochabamba: Los
     Amigos del Libro, 1975- (1976-). Formerly en-
     titled Bibliografía boliviana del año..., 1962-74. (See
     no. 185.)
         Chiefly a listing of books published in this country
     with occasional notes on the author or volume. Bib-
     liographies of various kinds are sometimes a special
     feature of an individual volume. Some issues provide
     data on books published on Bolivia outside of the coun-
     try. Well indexed.

187. Boletín bibliográfico boliviano. La Paz, 1965- .
         All areas covered but does contain a lot on litera-
     ture.

188. Costa de la Torre, Arturo. Catálogo de la bibliografía
     boliviana. La Paz: Universidad Mayor de San An-

drés, 1969-73. 2 vols. Vol. 1, 1,255 pp.; vol. 2,
1,250 pp.
    Lists books and pamphlets for 1900-1963. Includes
more than 3,000 Bolivian authors with some 8,700
bibliographic entries. Extensive introductory section
(1:1-237) provides a comprehensive survey of Bolivian
bibliography.

189. Ortega, José. "Manual de bibliografía de la literatura
      boliviana." In Letras bolivianas de hoy. Buenos
      Aires: Fernando García Cambeiro, 1973, pp. 89-
      115.
          Classified bibliography which contains general and
      specific bibliographies, literary histories, antholo-
      gies, journals, and indexes.

190. Siles Guevara, Juan. Bibliografía de bibliografías bo-
      livianas. La Paz: Ministerio de Cultura, Informa-
      ción y Turismo, Imprenta del Estado, 1969. 38 pp.
      2d ed., La Paz, 1970 (Estudios andinos 1, no. 1:149-
      70).
          The second edition contains 120 entries, 17 more
      than the first. Presents a fairly complete panorama
      of the current state of bibliographic activities in Bo-
      livia. No author index.

              --Central America

191. Doyle, Henry Grattan. A Tentative Bibliography of the
      Belles-Lettres of the Republics of Central America.
      Cambridge, Mass.: Harvard University Press, 1935.
      136 pp.
          Divided by country. A supplement on periodicals
      and newspapers is included.

192. Peraza Sarausa, Fermín. Bibliografía de Centroaméri-
      ca y del Caribe, 1956-1959. Habana: Agrupación
      Bibliográfica Cubana José Toribio Medina and Archivos
      y Bibliotecas de España, 1958-61. 4 vols.
          Books and pamphlets dealing with the cultures of
      Caribbean countries.

              --Chile

193. Anuario de la prensa chilena. Santiago de Chile?:
      Biblioteca Nacional. Volume that covers 1877-1885
      published in 1952. Annual for 1886-1916. Volumes

that cover 1917-1921, 1922-1926, and 1927-1931 were published in 1963. In 1964 there appeared the volumes that cover 1932-1934, 1935-1936, 1937-1941, 1942-1946, 1947-1951, 1952-1956; 1957-1961 was published in 1963. It has been annual since 1962. The Anuario is a catalog of books deposited in Chile's Biblioteca Nacional. Since 1891 it has included books by Chilean authors or works about Chile published outside of Chile. From time to time it has included other types of printed materials.

194. Castillo, Homero. La literatura chilena en los Estados Unidos de América. Santiago: Biblioteca Nacional, 1963. 127 pp.
 Covers publications in the United States of texts, anthologies, translations, and criticism of Chilean literature. About 1,500 entries.

195. _____, and Raúl Silva Castro. Historia bibliográfica de la novela chilena. México: Ediciones de Andrea, 1961. 214 pp. Charlottesville: Bibliographical Society of the University of Virginia, 1961. 214 pp.
 Authors are listed alphabetically, and titles are in chronological order.

196. Durán Cerda, Julio. Repertorio del teatro chileno: Bibliografía, obras inéditas y estrenos. Santiago: Instituto de Literatura Chilena, 1962. 247 pp.
 Covers theater in Chile since 1910.

197. Felíu Cruz, Guillermo. Historia de las fuentes de la bibliografía chilena: Ensayo crítico. Santiago: Editorial Universidad Católica, 1966-68. 3 vols.
 First scholarly study on the history of Chilean bibliography. Covers such outstanding 19th-century bibliographers as Medina, Bello, and Vicuña Mackenna. Valuable for national and subject Chilean bibliography.

198. Foster, David William. Chilean Literature: A Working Bibliography of Secondary Sources. Boston: G. K. Hall, 1978. xxii, 236 pp.
 The first part, "General References," has 28 subject headings covering a broad range of areas and the second part concentrates on 46 major authors listed alphabetically. The cutoff date is 1975. Unannotated.

199. Goič, Cedomil. Bibliografía de la novela chilena del

siglo XX. Santiago: Editorial Universitaria, 1962.
168 pp.
The Chilean novel from 1910 to 1961, arranged
chronologically.

200. Lastra, Pedro. "Registro bibliográfico de antologías
del cuento chileno: 1876-1976." Revista crítica li-
teraría latinoamericana (Lima), 3:5, 1 (1977), 89-111.
Chronologically arranged. Gives contents of anthologies.

201. Referencias críticas sobre autores chilenos. Santiago:
Biblioteca Nacional, 1968- .
Arranged by author and also by critic. It is an
indispensable source for the criticism of Chilean au-
thors in Chilean books, newspapers, and periodicals.
Volume 11 for 1975 was published in 1979.

202. Rela, Walter. Contribución a la bibliografía del teatro
chileno, 1804-1960. Montevideo: Universidad de la
República, 1960. 51 pp.
Lists 895 items with author and title index.

203. Servicio bibliográfico chileno. Santiago: Zamorano y
Caperan, 1940-71. Published monthly at the begin-
ning, and then quarterly.
Unannotated listing of books published in Chile.

--Colombia

204. Anuario bibliográfico colombiano "Rubén Pérez Ortiz."
Bogotá: Instituto Caro y Cuervo, Departamento de
Bibliografía, 1958- . Published annually. Title
was Anuario bibliográfico colombiano through 1965.
A publication containing articles, books, pamphlets,
periodicals, and government publications. Indexes of
authors, translations, publishers, and bookstores.
Coverage from 1951 onward.

205. Anuario bibliográfico colombiano "Rubén Pérez Ortiz."
Compiled by José Romero Rojas. Bogotá: Instituto
Caro y Cuervo, 1963- (1966-). Formerly Anuario
bibliográfico colombiano, 1951/1956-1962 (1958-1964).
Classified bibliography of international publications
published by Colombians or by others writing about
the country.

206.   Bibliografía colombiana.   Directed by Fermín Peraza
       Sarausa.   Gainesville, Fla., 1961-68.   13 vols.
       Alphabetical listing of books published in Colombia
       and also books on Colombia published abroad.

207.   Florén Lozano, Luis.   Obras de referencia y generales
       de la bibliografía colombiana.   Medellín: Editorial
       de la Universidad de Antioquia, 1960.   72 pp.
       Bibliography of bibliographies and also has section
       on Colombian literature.

208.   Giraldo Jaramillo, Gabriel.   Bibliografía de bibliografías
       colombianas.   2d ed., revised by Rubén Pérez Ortiz.
       Bogotá: Instituto Caro y Cuervo, 1960.   20 pp.
       Annotated bibliography of general bibliographies,
       catalogs of libraries, biographies of individuals, and
       a short bibliography of Colombian literature.

209.   Orjuela, Héctor H.   Las antologías poéticas de Colom-
       bia: Estudio y bibliografía.   Bogotá: Instituto Caro
       y Cuervo, 1966.   514 pp.
       Study of 147 anthologies published in Chile and 242
       foreign anthologies.

210.   _____.   Bibliografía de la poesía colombiana.   Bo-
       gotá: Instituto Caro y Cuervo, 1971.   486 pp.
       Alphabetical arrangement of principal editions and
       pamphlets up to 1970.

211.   _____.   Bibliografía del teatro colombiano.   Bogotá:
       Publicaciones del Instituto Caro y Cuervo, 1974.
       xxvii, 313 pp.
       Compiles titles of Colombia's plays and also pro-
       vides selected sources for the study of Colombian the-
       ater and that of Spanish America.

212.   _____.   Fuentes generales para el estudio de la li-
       teratura colombiana: Guía bibliográfica.   Bogotá: In-
       stituto Caro y Cuervo, 1968.   xl, 863 pp.
       Several thousand items.   Division by subject and
       then listing by author.   Indicates location of items.

213.   Porras Collantes, Ernesto.   Bibliografía de la novela
       en Colombia.   Bogotá: Publicaciones del Instituto
       Caro y Cuervo.   Serie Bibliográfica XI, 1976.   xix,
       888 pp.
       Covers 2,326 novels published through 1974.   Con-

tains notes on the criticism of the novels included
and indexes of pseudonyms, of titles and a chronological index. Incorporates and completes (up to 1974)
Curcio Altamar's Evolución de la novela en Colombia (see no. 606).

--Costa Rica

214. Anuario bibliográfico costarricense. San José: Aso-
ciación Costarricense de Bibliotecarios. 1958- .
Published every few years. (Continues no. 215.)
Cumulative and national bibliography.

215. Boletín bibliográfico. San José: Imprenta Nacional,
1946-55.
Continued by the Anuario bibliográfico costarricense (see entry above).

216. Kargleder, Charles L., and Warren H. Mory. Bibliografía selectiva de la literatura costarricense. San
José: Editorial Costa Rica, 1978.
Covers the years 1869 to 1976. Unannotated listing of works written by Costa Rican authors and a
listing of 26 general anthologies.

217. Menton, Seymour. El cuento costarricense: Estudio,
antología y bibliografía. México: Ediciones de Andrea, 1964. 184 pp.
Bibliography until 1960 (pp. 161-82).

--Cuba

218. Bibliografía cubana. La Habana: Biblioteca Nacional
"José Martí," 1967- . Annual in recent years.
Bibliography for the period 1959-62, published in
1968. Books, pamphlets, and periodicals are among
the items listed. Subject, title, and name indexes.

219. Fernández Robaina, Tomás. Bibliografía de bibliografías
cubanas: 1859-1972. La Habana: Biblioteca Nacional
José Martí, Departamento de Hemeroteca e Información de Humanidades, 1973. 340 pp.
Classified annotated bibliography with author-subject
and periodical title index. Data on more than 1,300
items.

220. Montes Huidobro, Matías, and Yara González. Biblio-

grafía crítica de la poesía cubana.   Madrid: Plaza
Mayor Ediciones, 1973.   136 pp.
Covers the years 1959 to 1971.   Poets listed in
alphabetical order with their works and comments on
them.

221. Orta Varoni, Lesbia.   Bibliografía de bibliografías cu-
      banas (1970-78).   SALALM, Working Paper No. C-
      11, 1979.   68 pp.
      Includes bibliographies not found in Fernández Ro-
      baina and updates his compilation through 1978.   (See
      no. 219 above.)

222. Peraza Sarausa, Fermin, ed.   Anuario bibliográfico
      cubano, 1937-1965.   La Habana: Ediciones Anuario
      Bibliográfico Cubano, 1938-59; Medellín, Colombia:
      By the editor, 1960; Gainesville, Fla.:   By the edi-
      tor, 1963-66.
      Original national bibliography for Cuba.   With the
      1956 volume, the title became Bibliografia cubana.
      Includes books and pamphlets.   In early volumes
      there are separate author and subject lists and in
      later volumes the lists are arranged by author only,
      with a subject index.   Succeeded by Revolutionary
      Cuba: A Bibliographical Guide (see no. 225 below),
      when the editor fled Castro Cuba.

223. _____.   Bibliografía cubana, complementos 1937-
      1961.   Gainesville: University of Florida Libraries,
      1966.   viii, 233 pp.
      Alphabetical listing of the addenda to the first 25
      volumes of the Anuario bibliográfico cubano (see en-
      try above).   Includes subject index of the nearly 4,000
      items.

224. _____.   Bibliografías cubanas.   Washington, D.C.:
      Library of Congress Hispanic Foundation, 1945.   xiv,
      58 pp.
      Contains 485 entries, divided into general, subject,
      and personal bibliographies.   Index of authors and
      works.

225. _____.   Revolutionary Cuba: A Bibliographical Guide.
      Coral Gables, Fla.:   University of Miami Press,
      1967-1970.   Covers years 1966-68.
      An alphabetical listing of books, pamphlets, serials,
      and government publications.   Has an author-subject
      index.

226. Verez Peraza, Elena, ed. Cuban Bibliography, 1969.
      Coral Gables, Fla.: University of Miami, 1977.
      vii, 106 pp.
      Cuban bibliographic annual. Includes index.

      --Dominican Republic

227. Anuario bibliográfico dominicano. Ciudad Trujillo:
      Luis Sánchez Adújar, 1947- . Published irregu-
      larly.
      Listing of books with author index.

228. Anuario bibliográfico dominicano. Santo Domingo: Bi-
      blioteca Nacional, 1978. 325 pp.
      Describes 3,413 Dominican imprints found in the
      Biblioteca Nacional.

229. Florén Lozano, Luis. Bibliografía de la bibliografía
      dominicana. Ciudad Trujillo: Roques Román, 1948.
      viii, 66 pp.
      General and specific bibliographies. Author-subject
      index.

      --Ecuador

230. Anuario bibliográfico ecuatoriano. Quito: Universidad
      Central del Ecuador. Biblioteca General. 1975- .
      Classified list of books. Published as the sixth
      issue of Bibliografía ecuatoriana, which is a classi-
      fied bibliography of material published in periodicals.
      Author, title, subject index.

231. Bibliografía ecuatoriana. Quito: Universidad Central
      del Ecuador, 1967- . Bimonthly since 1975.
      Also publishes specialized bibliographies.

232. Chaves, Alfredo. Fuentes principales de la bibliografía
      ecuatoriana. Quito: Casa de la Cultura Ecuatoriana,
      1958. 24 pp.
      Treats primarily fields of literature, criticism,
      and journalism.

233. Norris, Robert E. Guía bibliográfica para el estudio
      de la historia ecuatoriana. Austin: Institute of Latin
      American Studies, University of Texas, 1978. viii,
      295 pp.
      Especially useful are "Bibliografías y estudios bi-

bliográficos" (pp. 8-12) and "El periodismo y la imprenta" (pp. 139-43).

--El Salvador

234. Bibliografía salvadoreña: Lista preliminar por autores. San Salvador: Biblioteca Nacional, 1953. 430 pp. Occasional brief annotations.

235. Boletín bibliográfico: Lista de obras incorporadas, autores y materias.... San Salvador: Administración de Bibliotecas y Archivo Nacionales, 1968- .

--Guatemala

236. Anuario bibliográfico guatemalteco. Guatemala: Biblioteca Nacional, 1960- . Published annually. Listing of books, pamphlets, and periodicals; also contains a list of principal presses and publishing houses.

237. Valenzuela Reyna, Gilberto, director. Bibliografía guatemalteca y catálogo general de libros, folletos, periódicos, revistas, etc.... Guatemala: Tipografía Nacional, 1960-64. 10 vols. Chronological listing of Guatemalan publications from 1660 to 1960. Vol. 1 covers 17th and 18th centuries; vol. 2 covers 1660-1821; vols. 3-5 cover 1821-60; and vols. 6-10 cover 1861-1960.

--Honduras

238. García, Miguel Angel. Anuario bibliográfico hondureño, 1961-1971. Tegucigalpa: Banco Central de Honduras, 1973. 512 pp. List of publications for each year arranged by subject, followed by a list of government documents for that year. Data are also provided on Honduran newspapers and periodicals.

239. _____ . Bibliografía hondureña: 1620-1930, 1931-1960. Tegucigalpa: Banco Central de Honduras, 1971-72. 203 pp. each vol. Items arranged chronologically.

--Mexico

240. Bibliografía mexicana. México: Biblioteca Nacional,

1967-   . Published six times a year.
Classified bibliography of current Mexican books.

241. Boletín bibliográfico mexicano. México: Porrúa,
     1940- . Published bimonthly.
     Cumulative bibliography arranged alphabetically
     by subject. Contains book reviews, new notes, and
     publishers' advertisements.

242. Foster, David William. Mexican Literature: A Bib-
     liography of Secondary Sources. Metuchen, N.J.:
     Scarecrow Press, 1981. xxv, 386 pp.
     Contains about 6,000 unannotated items for 50 au-
     thors. Includes 27 sections of general references
     (bibliographies, references on genres and special
     topics). Some major figures omitted, e.g. Reyes
     and Vasconcelos. Index of critics.

243. Hoffman, Herbert H. Cuento mexicano Index. New-
     port Beach, Calif.: Headway Publications, 1978.
     600 pp.
     Covers 7,230 short stories by 400 Mexican authors
     born after 1870 or so. Only books published since
     1945 have been analyzed.

244. Lamb, Ruth S. Mexican Theatre of the Twentieth Cen-
     tury: Bibliography and Study. Claremont, Calif.:
     Ocelot Press, 1975. 143 pp.
     Most of the book (pp. 19-141) seems to be fac-
     simile of her Bibliografía del teatro mexicano del
     siglo XX (México: Ediciones de Andrea, 1962. 143
     pp.). A brief history of the Mexican theater together
     with critical bibliography.

245. Leal, Luis. Bibliografía del cuento mexicano. México:
     Ediciones de Andrea, 1958. 162 pp.
     Alphabetical author listing of the short story since
     the 18th century. Includes titles of books as well as
     short stories published in newspapers and magazines.

246. Martínez, José Luis. Literatura mexicana siglo XX,
     1910-1949. México: Robredo, 1949-50. 2 vols.
     Volume 2 contains a general bibliography and bib-
     liographies of Mexican literature, anthologies, criti-
     cal studies, literary journals, and Spanish poetry in
     Mexico (1939-49).

247. Millares Carlo, Agustín, and José Ignacio Mantecón.

Ensayo de una bibliografía de bibliografías mexicanas (la imprenta, el libro, las bibliotecas,...). México: Panamericana, 1943. xvi, 224 pp. Adiciones I, 1944, 46 pp. Partially annotated. Includes publications in the United States, Europe, and Latin America.

248. Ocampo de Gómez, Aurora Maura. Literatura mexicana contemporánea: Biobibliografía crítica. México: Universidad Nacional Autónoma de México, 1965. xxiii, 329 pp. Covers the principal figures in criticism, poetry, prose fiction, and drama. Evaluative notes on each writer's works.

249. Recent Books in Mexico: Bulletin of the Centro Mexicano de Escritores. México, 1954- . Bimonthly. Reviews and listings of recent books.

--Nicaragua

250. Arellano, Jorge Eduardo, ed. Boletín nicaragüense de bibliografía y documentación, 1975- .

251. _____ . Panorama de la literatura nicaragüense. 3d ed., resumida y aumentada. Managua: Ediciones Nacionales, 1977. 195 pp. Contains a bibliography by and about 30 contemporary authors.

--Panama

252. Doyle, Henry Grattan. A Tentative Bibliography of the Belles-Lettres of Panama. Cambridge, Mass.: Harvard University Press, 1934. 21 pp. General works plus listing by authors.

253. King, Charles A. "Apuntes para una bibliografía de la literatura de Panamá." Revista Interamericana de Bibliografía 14 (July-September 1964): 262-302. Sections arranged by genres.

254. Susto, Juan Antonio. "Panorama de la bibliografía en Panamá," Revista Interamericana de Bibliografía 18 (1968), 3-27. Also published as Panorama de la bibliografía en Panamá (1619-1967). Panamá: Editorial Universitaria, 1971. 102 pp. A useful introduction to Panamanian bibliography.

--Paraguay

255. Fernández-Caballero, Carlos F. S. Araduká ha kuatiañeé
     paraguai rembiapocué. The Paraguayan Bibliography:
     A Retrospective and Enumerative Bibliography of
     Printed Works of Paraguayan Authors. Washington,
     D. C.: Paraguay Arandú Books, 1970. 143 pp. Vol.
     2, 1975 (No. 3 of SALALM bibliography series), 221
     pp.
          Vol. 1 lists 1,423 titles published between 1724 and
     1969, most of which are monographs. Vol. 2 has
     2,363 entries, which include additional authors and
     titles and works from the 18th century to 1974.

256. Jones, David Lewis. "XII. Literature." Paraguay:
     A Bibliography. New York: Garland, 1979. 499 pp.
          Section "XII: Literature" (pp. 372-415) has sub-
     sections of general studies and the pre- and post-
     1935 periods.

--Peru

257. Anuario bibliográfico peruano. Lima: Instituto Nacional
     de Cultura, Biblioteca Nacional, Centro Bibliográfico
     Nacional, 1943- (1945-).
          First several volumes covered a single year; later
     volumes have covered two or three years. The vol-
     ume for 1970-1972 was published in 1979. Includes
     publications of all kinds (books, pamphlets, news-
     papers, periodicals). Bibliographies are included of
     authors who had died during the period covered.
     These are extremely comprehensive.

258. Bibliografía nacional: Libros, artículos de revistas y
     periódicos. Lima: Biblioteca Nacional, 1978- .
     11 times per year.
          The first part of each issue is devoted to new
     books published in or about Peru. The second part
     is a classified list of articles published in newspapers
     and periodicals. Each issue has an author and a sub-
     ject index.

259. Cabel, Jesús. Bibliografía de la poesía peruana 65/79.
     [Lima]: Amaru [1980]. 143 pp.
          An author listing of works published either in Peru
     or abroad by Peruvians. Covers books and antholo-
     gies.

48   Bibliographies of Hispanic Literature

260. Foster, David William. Peruvian Literature: A Bib-
     liography of Secondary Sources, Westport, Conn.:
     Greenwood Press, 1981. xxix, 324 pp.
     Twenty-four sections of general references are
     followed by coverage for thirty-eight authors; same
     format as Mexico. Coverage is essentially complete
     for all important and emerging authors.

261. Puccinelli, Elsa Villanueva de. Bibliografía de la no-
     vela peruana. Lima: Ediciones de la Biblioteca Uni-
     versitaria, 1969. 90 pp.
     Bibliography and chronology.

262. Vargas Ugarte, Rubén. Biblioteca peruana. Lima:
     Tall. Tip. de la Empresa Periodística La Prensa,
     1935-57. 12 vols. Vols. 1-5 have half-title: Manu-
     scritos peruanos; vol. 4 has imprint: Buenos Aires:
     A. Baiocco; vol. 5, Buenos Aires: Tall. Gráf. "San
     Pablo"; vol. 6, Lima: Compañía de Impresiones y
     Publicidad; vols. 7-8, Lima: Editorial San Marcos;
     vols. 9-12, Lima: Tip. Peruana.
     Broad coverage of manuscripts and printed books
     from the colonial period to 1825.

--Puerto Rico

263. Anuario bibliográfico puertorriqueño: Indice alfabético
     de libros, folletos, revistas y periódicos publicados
     en Puerto Rico. Río Piedras: Biblioteca de la Uni-
     versidad, 1948- . Published irregularly.
     Alphabetical author listing. Also contains index
     of publishers and book dealers.

264. Bravo, Enrique R., comp. An Annotated Selected
     Puerto Rican Bibliography; Bibliografía puertorri-
     queña selecta anotada. New York: Urban Center
     of Columbia University, 1972. 115 pp. (Spanish
     section); 114 pp. (English section).
     The English section is a translation of the Spanish
     one. Besides literature and linguistics, this book in-
     cludes works on anthropology and sociology, politics,
     economics, education, culture, and reference works.
     Despite the title, many works mentioned are not anno-
     tated, and many annotations do not give a clear idea
     of the books contents.

265. Foster, David W. Puerto Rican Literature: A Bibli-

ography of Secondary Sources. Westport, Conn.:
Greenwood Press, 1982.
A classified index of general studies on Puerto
Rican literature, followed by listings of critical references on 75 Puerto Rican literary figures. The
first comprehensive bibliography of literary criticism
on Puerto Rican literature.

266. González, Nilda. Bibliografía de teatro puertorriqueño
(siglos XIX y XX). Río Piedras: Universidad de
Puerto Rico, Editorial Universitaria, 1979. 223 pp.
Includes list by author as well as criticism of published and unpublished Puerto Rican plays of the 19th
and 20th centuries. Also contains a general bibliography.

267. Pedriera, Antonio Salvador. Bibliografía puertorriqueña (1493-1930). Madrid: Hernando, 1932. xxxii,
707 pp. Rpt. New York: Burt Franklin, 1974.
Includes some 10,000 titles on Puerto Rico or by
Puerto Ricans of all professions. The reprint has
checklist of recent bibliography.

--Uruguay

268. Anuario bibliográfico uruguayo. Montevideo: Biblioteca
Nacional, 1946-1949, 1968- (1947-1951, 1969-).
Classified bibliography of books and pamphlets.

269. Bibliografía uruguaya. Montevideo: Biblioteca del
Poder Legislativo, 1962-68, 1971. 2 vols.
Covers all publications except periodicals. Gives
addresses of publishers. Published irregularly.

270. Englekirk, John Eugene, and Margaret M. Ramos. La
narrativa uruguaya; estudio crítico-bibliográfico.
Berkeley and Los Angeles: University of California
Press, 1967. 388 pp.
Part 1 is a survey of Uruguayan prose. Part 2
includes more than 400 writers and their works.
Part 3 has bibliographical and author indexes.

271. Musso Ambrosi, Luis Alberto. Bibliografía de bibliografías uruguayas, con aportes a la historia del periodismo en el Uruguay. Montevideo: Agrupación Bi-
bliotecológica, 1964. 102 pp.
Contains 637 entries on literature and other fields,

including bibliographies from periodicals and newspapers.

272.   Rela, Walter.   Fuentes para el estudio de la literatura
uruguaya, 1835-1962.   Montevideo: Editores de la
Banda Oriental, 1969.   134 pp.
A comprehensive bibliographic guide that updates
the previous entry.   Contains 900 references to books,
pamphlets, and journal articles, with bibliographies,
histories of literature, biographies, criticism, and
anthologies.   Not annotated.

--Venezuela

273.   Anuario bibliográfico venezolano.   Caracas: Tipografía
Americana, 1945-60.   3 vols.
Books and pamphlets by Venezuelan writers, Venezuelan periodicals, indexes of publishers, and author-
subject-title index.

274.   Anuario bibliográfico venezolano, prepared by Centro
Bibliográfico Venezolano.   Caracas: Imprenta del
Congreso, 1977- .
Starts with the year 1967.

275.   Becco, Horacio Jorge.   Bibliografía de bibliografías
venezolanas: Literatura (1968-1978).   Caracas: La
Casa de Bello, 1979.   62 pp.
Contains 250 annotated items of general sources,
Venezuelan bibliographies, bibliographies in periodicals, list of reviews and addenda for 1979.   Index of
names.

276.   _____.   Fuentes para el estudio de la literatura
venezolana.   Prólogo de Pedro Grases.   Caracas:
Ediciones Centauro, 1978.   2 vols.
Includes 1,860 entries, most of which are briefly
described, that cover general and Venezuelan bibliographies; universal, Spanish American, and Venezuelan biographies; and history and criticism of literature.   Also includes anthologies of Spanish America and Venezuela as well as information on newspapers and magazines.   Useful indexes of names and
of addenda.

277-   Carrera, Gustavo Luis.   Bibliografía de la novela vene-
8.

zolana. Caracas: Universidad Central de Venezuela, Centro de Estudios Literarios, 1963. 69 pp. Alphabetical listing of 187 novelists of the 19th and 20th centuries.

279. Hirshbein, Cesia Ziona. Hemerografía venezolana, 1890-1930. Caracas: Ediciones de la Facultad de Humanidades y Educacion, Instituto de Estudios Hispanoamericanos, Universidad Central de Venezuela, 1978. 574 pp.
Covers mainly newspaper and magazine articles written by Venezuelan authors. Authors are listed alphabetically by genres. One chapter (pp. 433-61) is by author-subject. Pages 463 to 565 contain articles by foreign writers that appeared in Venezuelan periodicals, arranged alphabetically. Short bibliography.

280. Larrazábal Henríquez, Osvaldo, et al. Bibliografía del cuento venezolano. Caracas: Universidad Central de Venezuela, Facultad de Humanidades y Educación, Instituto de Investigaciones Literarias, 1975. 315 pp.
Covers 3,311 short stories by 332 authors. Well indexed.

281. Sambrano Urdaneta, Oscar. Contribución a una bibliografía general de la poesía venezolana en el siglo XX. Caracas: Universidad Central de Venezuela, Facultad de Humanidades y Educación, Escuela de Letras, 1979. 367 pp.
Lists 747 authors and 2,068 works and includes information on anthologies, selected works, and critical evaluations. An important compilation.

282. Villasana, Angel Raúl. Ensayo de un repertorio bibliográfico venezolano, años 1808-1950. Caracas: Banco Central de Venezuela, 1969-79. 6 vols.
Annotated bibliography for years 1808 to 1950 of books and pamphlets; stresses authors and not subjects.
Many descriptive notes.

283. Waxman, Samuel M. A Bibliography of the Belles-Lettres of Venezuela. Cambridge, Mass.: Harvard University Press, 1935. xii, 145 pp.

Lists bibliographies, collections, critical works, and periodicals.

5. LITERARY DICTIONARIES AND ENCYCLOPEDIAS

SPAIN AND SPANISH AMERICA

284. Bleiberg, Germán, and Julián Marías, eds. Diccionario de la literatura española. 4th ed. Madrid: Revista de Occidente, 1972 (1949). 1,261 pp. New ed. in preparation.
Excellent work dealing with Spanish and Spanish American writers. Also has articles on such topics as literary terms, genres, and movements. Articles are written by well-known specialists in literature and language. Title index and also chronology of historical-political events synchronized with the evolution of letters, arts, and science.

285. Dizionario letterario Bompiani delle opere e dei personaggi di tutti i tempi e di tutte le letterature. Milan: Bompiani, 1947-52. 9 vols. Spanish edition by Martín de Riquer: Diccionario literario de obras y personajes de todos los tiempos y de todos los países. Barcelona: Montaner y Simón, 1959-60. 12 vols.
A dictionary that lists and describes the works of all times and all countries in literature, art, and music, with emphasis on literature.

286. Dizionario universale delle letteratura contemporanea. Milan: Mondadori, 1959-63. 5 vols.
Encyclopedia of world literature covering 1870-1960 and supplements Bompiani (see entry above). Includes authors, literary movements, periodicals, national literatures, and the like.

287. Foster, David William, editor. A Dictionary of Contemporary Latin American Authors. Tempe: Center

for Latin American Studies, Arizona State University,
1975. 110 pp.
Includes 290 articles averaging 400 words in length.

288. Herdeck, Donald E., et al. "Spanish Language Literature from the Caribbean." In their Caribbean Writers: A Bio-Bibliographical Encyclopedia. Washington, D.C.: Three Continents Press, 1979. pp. 599-
943.
A biobibliographical dictionary of the writers of
Cuba, Dominican Republic, and Puerto Rico, which
focuses on the important works of the authors represented. Also has sections on critical studies, bibliographies, and anthologies.

289. Jara, René; Juan C. Lértora; Juan Vargas; and Patricia
R. de Lértora. Diccionario de términos e "ismos"
literarios. Madrid: Porrúa Turanzas, 1977. 192
pp.
Helpful compilation which treats the pre-New Criticism and pre-Structuralism point of view.

290. Sáinz de Robles, Federico. Ensayo de un diccionario
de la literatura. 4th ed. Madrid: Aguilar, 1973
(1953-56). 3 vols.
Volume 1 covers literary terms, concepts, and
"isms"; volume 2, Spanish and Spanish American
writers; and the final volume, foreign writers. Much
of his literary judgment should be taken with a grain
of salt.

SPAIN

291. Ríos Ruiz, Manuel. Diccionario de escritores gaditanos. Cádiz: Instituto de Estudios Gaditanos, Di-
putación Provincial, 1973. 217 pp.
Alphabetic listing virtually limited to biobibliographies. Author index.

292. Rogers, Paul P., and Felipe A. Lapuente. Diccionario
de seudónimos literarios españoles. Madrid: Gredos,
1977. 610 pp.
Contains about 11,500 identified pseudonyms and
about 475 unidentified ones. Includes selected bibliography and onomastic index of more than 100 pages.

SPANISH AMERICA

General

293. Coll, Edna. Índice informativo de la novela hispano-
      americana. Río Piedras: Editorial Universitaria,
      Universidad de Puerto Rico, 1974-80. 4 vols. I,
      Las Antillas; II, Centroamérica; III, Venezuela; IV,
      Colombia.
          Very useful guide to the literature of Spanish
      America. Abundant biographical and bibliographical
      data for a vast number of individual writers of prose
      fiction, who appear by countries, together with ex-
      tensive bibliographies for each republic and the areas
      in general. This dictionary covers writers from Cu-
      ba, Puerto Rico, the Dominican Republic and Central
      America.

National

--Argentina

294. Becco, H. J.; R. F. Giusti; A. Correia Pacheco; A.
      A. Roggiano; and others. Diccionario de la litera-
      tura latinoamericana: Argentina. Washington, D.C.:
      Pan American Union, 1960-61. 2 vols. (See no.
      299 for format.)

295. Orgambide, Pedro G., and Roberto Yahni. Enciclo-
      pedia de la literatura argentina. Buenos Aires: Su-
      damericana, 1970. 639 pp.
          An alphabetical listing of Argentine writers, works,
      movements, and literary genres that provides usually
      brief biobibliographic material and some critical stud-
      ies. Contains about 1,000 entries.

296. Prieto, Adolfo. Diccionario básico de literatura argen-
      tina. Buenos Aires: Centro Editor de América La-
      tina, 1968. 160 pp.
          Contains brief biobibliographic sketches of Argen-
      tine writers born no later than 1930, as well as dis-
      cussions of important works, literary movements,
      and tendencies or groups that have been significant
      in the development of Argentine letters.

--Bolivia

297. Guzmán, Augusto. Diccionario de la literatura latino-
     americana: Bolivia. Washington, D.C.: Pan Amer-
     ican Union, 1957. ix, 121 pp. (See no. 299 for for-
     mat.)

298. Ortega, José, and Adolfo Cáceres Romero. Diccio-
     nario de la literatura boliviana. La Paz: Editorial
     Los Amigos del Libro, 1977. 337 pp.
     Bibliographical data on about 280 Bolivian authors.

--Central America

299. Hebblethwaite, Frank P. Diccionario de la literatura
     latinoamericana: América Central. 2d ed. Wash-
     ington, D.C.: Pan American Union, 1963 (1951).
     Vol. 1, 136 pp.; vol. 2, 154 pp.
     Volume 1--Costa Rica, El Salvador, and Guate-
     mala; volume 2--Honduras, Nicaragua, and Panama.
     Each volume in this series follows a similar format.
     Data on each author include biographical sketches and
     a bibliography of the author's works and of material
     about him and his works.

--Chile

300. Silva Castro, Raúl. Diccionario de la literatura latino-
     americana: Chile. Washington, D.C.: Pan Ameri-
     can Union, 1958. ix, 234 pp. (See no. 299 for for-
     mat.)

301. Smulewicz, Efrain. Diccionario de la literatura chilena.
     Santiago de Chile: Selecciones Lautaro, 1977. 563
     pp.
     Although useful, its utility is marred by insuffi-
     cient biobibliographic data and the virtual absence of
     critical comments in the dictionary of Chilean authors
     as well as in the "Bibliografía general sobre litera-
     tura chilena" and "Bibliografía básica."

--Colombia

302. Diccionario de escritores colombianos. Esplugas de
     Llobregat (Barcelona): Plaza y Janes Editores Colom-
     bia, 1978. 547 pp.
     Contains a bibliography, an alphabetical listing of

authors together with their works and commentaries
on them, a list of poets who won awards, a list of
Colombian fabulistas, and a list of pseudonyms.

303. García Prada, Carlos. Diccionario de la literatura
latinoamericana: Colombia. Washington, D. C.:
Pan American Union, 1959. ix, 179 pp. (See no.
299 for format.)

--Cuba

304. Instituto de Literatura y Lingüística de la Academia de
Ciencias de Cuba. Diccionario de la literatura cubana. La Habana: Editorial Letras Cubanas, 1980- .
1-(A-Ll).
Important tool for information on Cuban authors,
journals, and institutions. Stresses mainly work of
Cuban authors living in Cuba.

--Ecuador

305. Barrera, Isaac J., and Alejandro Carrión. Diccionario
de la literatura latinoamericana: Ecuador. Washington, D. C.: Pan American Union, 1962. xi, 172 pp.
(See no. 299 for format.)

306. Barriga López, Franklin, and Leonardo Barriga López.
Diccionario de la literatura ecuatoriana. Quito: Edi-
torial Casa de la Cultura Ecuatoriana, 1973. 590 pp.
Detailed listings of writers' works.

--Mexico

307. Montejano y Aguiñaga, Rafael, comp. Bibliografía de
los escritores de San Luis Potosí. Mexico: Universidad Nacional Autónoma de México, 1979. xxx, 438
pp.
The introduction contains a panorama of literature
of San Luis Potosí (1550-1975) together with listings
of bibliographies and anthologies. Includes a general
index of authors, an index arranged by genre, and an
index of pseudonyms and anagrams.

308. Ocampo de Gómez, Aurora, and Ernesto Prado Velázquez. Diccionario de escritores mexicanos. México:
Universidad Nacional Autónoma de México, 1967.
xxviii, 422, xlvii pp.

Biobibliographic dictionary which deals with 542
authors and critics.

--Peru

309.   Arriola Grande, F. Maurilio. Diccionario literario del
        Perú; nomenclatura por autores. Barcelona: Comer-
        cial y Artes Gráficas, 1968. 546 pp.
        Biographical sketches of around 1,500 Peruvian
        authors and authors who have resided in Peru, de-
        ceased and living.

310.   Romero de Valle, Emilia. Diccionario manual de lite-
        ratura peruana y materia afines. Lima: Universi-
        dad Nacional Mayor de San Marcos. Departamento
        de Publicaciones, 1966. 356 pp.
        Guide to past and contemporary Peruvian authors
        and their works. Alphabetical arrangement by author
        or subject. Some attention to literary genres and
        periodicals.

        --Puerto Rico

311.   Rivera de Alvarez, Josefina. Diccionario de literatura
        puertorriqueña. 2d ed., revised and updated until
        1967. San Juan, Puerto Rico: Instituto de Cultura
        Puertorriqueña, 1970 (1955). 499 pp.
        Alphabetical listing of writers and their works to-
        gether with a history of Puerto Rican literature and
        a general bibliography. A revision of the author's
        dissertation, Madrid, 1954.

        --Venezuela

312.   Diccionario general de la literatura venezolana (autores).
        Mérida, Venezuela: Universidad de los Andes, Cen-
        tro de Investigaciones Literarias, Facultad de Hu-
        manidades y Educación, 1974. xiv, 829 pp.
        A biobibliographical dictionary of Venezuelan au-
        thors. Contains biographical and critical data to-
        gether with a list of each author's published books
        and a list of references about the individual. The
        cutoff year is 1971.

6. HISTORIES OF HISPANIC LITERATURES

SPAIN AND SPANISH AMERICA

313. Cejador y Frauca, Julio. <u>Historia de la lengua y lite-ratura castellana, comprendidos los autores hispano-americanos</u>. Madrid: Revista de Archivos, Biblio-tecas y Museos, 1915-22. 14 vols. New printing, Madrid: Gredos, 1973. 7 vols.
    Detailed account from origins to 1920. Bibliogra-phies are arranged chronologically.

314. Díaz-Plaja, Guillermo, ed. <u>Historia general de las literaturas hispánicas</u>. Barcelona: Vergara, 1949-68. 7 vols.
    From the earliest times to the contemporary pe-riod. Contains chapters devoted to the literature of Spanish America, the Philippines, and Spain including Castilian, Basque, Catalonian, and Galician. The work was written by a large number of contributors. The introduction by Menéndez Pidal is of particular interest. Extensive bibliographies for most chapters.

315. _____, and Francisco Monterde. <u>Historia de la lite-ratura española e historia de la literatura mexicana</u>. 9th ed. México: Porrúa, 1971 (1955). 625 pp.
    Concise and useful overview.

316. Díez-Echarri, Emiliano, and José María Roca Fran-quesa. <u>Historia de la literatura española e hispano-americana</u>. 3d ed. Madrid: Aguilar, 1982 (1960). 2 vols.
    From the Middle Ages to the present. General bibliography as well as specific bibliographies for each section.

317. Ford, Jeremiah D. M.   Main Currents of Spanish Lit-
     erature. New York: Biblo and Tannen, 1968 (1919).
     vii, 284 pp.
          Covers important aspects of Spanish and Spanish
     American literature. A series of lectures by a
     highly respected American Hispanist delivered at the
     Lowell Institute in Boston, 1918. Bibliographical
     note.

318. Fox-Lockert, Lucía. Women Novelists in Spain and
     Spanish America. Metuchen, N. J.: Scarecrow
     Press, 1979. 347 pp.
          Divided into "Spanish Novelists" and "Spanish
     American Novelists." Studies 22 novelists from
     1630 to the present.

SPAIN

General

319. Alborg, Juan Luis. Historia de la literatura española.
     2d ed., 3d reprint. Madrid: Gredos, 1977-1980.
     5 vols. projected.
          To date, four large volumes have appeared. These
     cover the Middle Ages and the Renaissance (see no.
     337), the 17th century (see no. 343), the 18th cen-
     tury (see no. 349), and Romanticism (see no. 450a).
     Extensive bibliographic information in footnotes. Al-
     borg's ample studies of writers, periods, and genres
     utilize many recent scholarly contributions.

320. Bell, Aubrey F. G. Castilian Literature. Rpt., Ox-
     ford: Clarendon Press, 1976 (1938). xiv, 261 pp.
          From El Cid to 1936. Bell aims to demonstrate
     fundamental characteristics of Castilian literature.

321. Blanco Aguinaga, Carlos; Julio Rodríguez Puértolas; and
     Iris M. Zavala. Historia social de la literatura es-
     pañola (en lengua castellana). 2d ed. Madrid: Cas-
     talia, 1981 (1978). 3 vols.
          A Marxist approach that interprets Spanish litera-
     ture from a socioeconomic perspective. The epic is
     considered as propaganda of the dominant feudal class,
     more attention is paid to two sonnets of Cervantes
     than to the Quijote, the 18th and 19th centuries are

briefly treated, only 23 lines are devoted to Ortega;
Pedro Lain Entralgo and Julián Marias are ignored.
Extensive bibliography.

322. Brenan, Gerald. The Literature of the Spanish People
      from Roman Times to the Present Day. 2d ed.
      Cambridge: At the University Press, 1976 (1951).
      xxii, 496 pp.
          A very subjective treatment. Brenan's value judg-
      ments are sometimes controversial but always of in-
      terest. This book omits much that the author con-
      siders inferior. First paperback edition. Includes
      index.

      Cejador y Frauca. Historia de la lengua y literatura
      castellana. See no. 313.

323. Chandler, Richard E., and Kessel Schwartz. A New
      History of Spanish Literature. Baton Rouge: Loui-
      siana State University Press, 1961. 696 pp.
          Spanish literature arranged by genres. Extensive
      bibliography. Appendixes on first things in Spanish
      literature, common places of Spanish literature, and
      general historical chronology. Index of authors and
      titles.

324. Del Río, Angel. Historia de la literatura española.
      2d ed. New York: Holt, Rinehart & Winston, 1963
      (1948). 2 vols.
          Excellent work of synthesis. Reveals a familiarity
      with a wide range of scholarship. Contains a bibli-
      ography at the end of each chapter, an index which
      includes a glossary of literary terms, and appendixes
      providing brief surveys of Galician and Catalonian lit-
      eratures.

      Díaz-Plaja. Historia general de las literaturas his-
      pánicas. See no. 314.

325. Diez Borque, José María, general editor. Historia de
      la literatura española. Madrid: Taurus, 1980. 4
      vols. Companion volume: Historia de las literaturas
      hispánicas no castellanas, 995 pp.
          Covers from the Middle Ages to the present. Con-
      tains 30 chapters written by 33 different authors.
      There are general introductions to the Middle Ages
      (I), Renaissance and Baroque periods (II), 18th and

19th centuries (III), and the 20th century (IV), and
then discussions by literary genres (generally prose,
poetry and theater). Multiple authorship of this work
naturally causes unevenness in content and bibliography.

Díez-Echarri and Roca Franquesa. Historia general
de la literatura española e hispanoamericana. See
no. 316.

326. Fitzmaurice-Kelly, James. A History of Spanish Literature. Rev. ed. New York: G. E. Stechert,
1926 (1898). xvi, 551 pp. Reprint, New York:
Russell & Russell, 1968.
From early Spanish verse to the beginning of the
20th century.

Ford. Main Currents of Spanish Literature. See no.
317.

327. García López, José. Historia de la literatura española.
19th ed. Barcelona: Vicens-Vives, 1978 (1948).
viii, 789 pp.
Probably the best one-volume history of Spanish
literature. Contains concise but thorough treatment
of periods and authors. Well-organized sections on
authors include biographies and cogent analyses of
their works. Bibliographies at ends of chapters are
brief but current.

328. González López, Emilio. Historia de la literatura española. New York: Las Americas, 1962-65. 2 vols.
From the Middle Ages to 1900. Adequate bibliography for each chapter. Very clear, well-organized
presentation.

329. Hurtado y Jiménez de la Serna, Juan, and Angel González Palencia. Historia de la literatura española.
6th ed. Madrid: Seata, 1977 (1921). 1,106 pp.
Extensive bibliographic material, much of which
is rarely found in other manuals of literature.

330. A Literary History of Spain. London: Ernest Benn;
and New York: Barnes & Noble, 1971-72. 6 vols.
Vol. 1, The Middle Ages (1972), by A. D. Deyermond, 244 pp. (see no. 339); Vol. 2, The Golden
Age: Prose and Poetry--The 16th and 17th Centu-

ries (1971), by R. O. Jones, 233 pp. (see no. 345); Vol. 3, The Golden Age: Drama, 1492-1700 (1971), by Edward M. Wilson and Duncan Moir, 171 pp. (see no. 421); Vol. 4, The Eighteenth Century (1972) by Nigel Glendinning, 160 pp. (see no. 353); Vol. 5, The Nineteenth Century (1972), by Donald L. Shaw, 200 pp. (see no. 354); Vol. 6, The Twentieth Century (1972), by G. G. Brown, 176 pp. (see no. 358). Spanish versions: Barcelona: Ariel, 1981. La Edad Media by A. D. Deyermond; Siglo de Oro: Prosa y Poesía by R. O. Jones; Siglo de Oro: Teatro by Edward M. Wilson and Duncan Moir; El Siglo XVIII by Nigel Glendinning; El Siglo XIX by Donald L. Shaw; El Siglo XX by Gerald G. Brown.

331. Marín, Diego, and Angel del Río. Breve historia de la literatura española. New York: Holt, Rinehart & Winston, 1966. xvii, 394 pp.
An introductory manual based on the longer history of Del Río (see no. 324). From the Middle Ages to the present. Essential bibliographic information together with an index-glossary with definitions of literary terms.

332. Mérimée, Ernest. A History of Spanish Literature (Précis d'histoire de la littérature espagnole). Translated by S. Griswold Morley. New York: Holt, 1930 (1st French ed., 1908). xv, 635 pp.
Morley revised and enlarged the original French version. Lengthy bibliography. A well-known and often cited history.

333. Northup, George T., and Nicholson B. Adams. An Introduction to Spanish Literature. 3d rev. ed. Chicago: University of Chicago Press, 1960 (1925). xi, 473 pp.
An easy-to-read outline of Spanish literature.

334. Romera Navarro, Miguel. Historia de la literatura española. 2d ed. New York: D. C. Heath & Co., 1948 (1928). xvii, 701 pp.
From Iberians and Celts to the 20th century. Good background information on historical, political, and artistic developments. More than usual emphasis on plot summaries and includes many passages from works studied.

335. Ticknor, George. History of Spanish Literature. 6th
      ed. Boston: Houghton Mifflin Co., 1891 (1849). 3
      vols.
           A classic study that is still valuable.

336. Valbuena Prat, Angel. Historia de la literatura es-
      pañola. Expanded and updated by Antonio Prieto.
      9th ed. Barcelona: Gustavo Gili, 1980-82. 4 vols.
      (through Romanticism). Vols. 5 and 6 (19th and 20th
      centuries) are being reprinted.
           This extensive history is one of the most useful.
      Frequent quotations are given from literary texts.
      Ample bibliography is provided. Less important
      works and writers are also included.

Period

           --Medieval

337. Alborg, Juan Luis. Historia de la literatura española.
      Vol. 1, Edad media y renacimiento. 2d ed., 3rd
      print, 1979. 1,082 pp. (See no. 319.)
           Covers Spanish literature from the Middle Ages
      through the 16th century. A preliminary chapter
      deals with the general characteristics and periods
      of Spanish literature. Alborg includes such topics
      as the mester de juglaría, the mester de clerecía,
      Alfonso X, Juan Ruiz, characteristics of the Spanish
      Renaissance, the theater before Lope de Vega, La-
      zarillo de Tormes and the genesis of the picaresque
      novel, the mystics, and didactic writers. Index of
      authors and works.

338. Barja, César. Libros y autores clásicos. 4th ed.,
      reprint. New York: Las Americas Publishing Co.,
      1964 (1922). xii, 557 pp.
           Covers both the Middle Ages and the Golden Age,
      with more space given to the latter period. Studies
      important writers in depth. Bibliographies.

339. Deyermond, A. D. The Middle Ages. Vol. 1 of A
      Literary History of Spain. New York: Barnes &
      Noble, 1972. 244 pp. Spanish version: La edad
      media. Barcelona: Ariel, 1980. 419 pp.
           Begins with the earliest lyric poetry and studies
      the epic, the ballad, the novel, didactic literature,

the cancionero, and liturgic drama. The Cid and the Celestina are among the important works analyzed.

340. Green, Otis H. Spain and the Western Tradition: The Castilian Mind in Literature from El Cid to Calderón. Madison: University of Wisconsin Press, 1963-66. 4 vols. Spanish translation, España y la tradición occidental (Madrid: Gredos, 1969. 4 vols.).
Green interprets the essential ideas of Spanish literary texts from the 12th to the 17th century. Among the topics treated are love, reason, free will, fortune and fate, death, and religion. Good bibliography and useful index for each volume, and an extensive cumulative index at the end of volume 4.

341. López Estrada, Francisco. Introducción a la literatura medieval española. 4th ed. Madrid: Gredos, 1979 (1952). 606 pp.
Covers all aspects of medieval Spanish literature and language.

342. Millares Carlo, Agustín. Literatura española hasta fines del siglo XV. Mexico: Antigua Librería Robredo, 1950. 352 pp.
Includes a lengthy bibliography at the end of each chapter. The author makes use of many studies in this student manual.

--Renaissance and Golden Age

343. Alborg, Juan Luis. Historia de la literatura española. Vol. 2, Epoca barroca. 2d ed., 1981. 996 pp. (See no. 319.)
Covers the 17th century. After a general introduction to the baroque period, Alborg treats such topics as Cervantes (170 pages), the theater from Lope de Vega to Calderón, Góngora and culteranismo, Quevedo and conceptismo, the picaresque novel, Gracián and other didactic prose writers. Index of authors and works.

Barja. Libros y autores clásicos. See no. 338.

344. Bell, Aubrey F. G. El renacimiento español. Translated by E. Juliá. Zaragoza: Ebro, 1944. xxviii, 402 pp.
A clear, sound historical and literary introduction to the period. Bibliography.

Green. Spain and the Western Tradition. See no. 340.

345.   Jones, R. O.   The Golden Age: Prose and Poetry--
       The 16th and 17th Centuries.   Vol. 2 of A Literary
       History of Spain.   New York: Barnes & Noble, 1971.
       233 pp.   Spanish version: Siglo de oro: Prosa y
       poesía.   Barcelona: Ariel, 1980.   344 pp.
       Covers the humanism of the Valdés brothers and
       Guevara, Garcilaso's poetry, the chivalresque, pas-
       toral and picaresque novels, conceptismo and culte-
       ranismo, and such important writers as Cervantes,
       Góngora, Lope, Quevedo, and Gracián.

346.   Montolíu y de Togores, Manuel de.   El alma de España
       y sus reflejos en la literatura del Siglo de Oro.   Bar-
       celona: Cervantes, 1942.   752 pp.
       Interrelates Spanish history, spirit, and literature.

347.   Pfandl, Ludwig.   Historia de la literatura nacional es-
       pañola en la Edad de Oro.   Translated by Jorge Ru-
       bió Balaguer.   Rpt., Barcelona: Gustavo Gili, 1952
       (original German ed., 1924).   740 pp.
       A classic scholarly study of the period from 1550
       to 1700.   Lengthy bibliographies on authors and sub-
       jects.

348.   Vossler, Karl.   Introducción a la literatura española
       del Siglo de Oro: Seis lecciones.   Translated by Fe-
       lipe González Vicén.   3d Spanish ed.   México:
       Espasa-Calpe, 1961 (1934).   151 pp.
       Emphasis on the Spaniards' spiritual attitudes as
       revealed in their literature and language.

--Eighteenth and Nineteenth Centuries

349.   Alborg, Juan Luis.   Historia de la literatura española.
       Vol. 3, Siglo XVIII.   4th printing.   Madrid: Gredos,
       1977-80, 979 pp.
       Deals with the cultural and literary institutions and
       contains detailed studies of 18th-century writers in
       all genres, including such areas as erudition, history,
       and criticism.

350.   Barja, César.   Libros y autores modernos.   Rpt., New
       York: Las Americas, 1964 (1924).   xxvi, 466 pp.
       Perceptive, detailed analyses of works by major
       authors of the 18th and 19th centuries.   Bibliography.

351. Blanco García, P. Francisco. La literatura española
      en el siglo XIX. 3d ed. Madrid: Sáenz de Jubera,
      1909-12 (1891-94). 3 vols.
          Extensive treatment, including minor figures. Vol-
      ume 3 deals with regional literature of Spain and Span-
      ish America.

352. Cox, R. Merritt. Eighteenth-Century Spanish Litera-
      ture. Boston: Twayne, 1979. 161 pp.
          Helpful plot summaries and attention given to in-
      fluences.

353. Glendinning, Nigel. The Eighteenth Century. Vol. 4
      of A Literary History of Spain. New York: Barnes
      & Noble, 1972. 160 pp. Spanish version: El Siglo
      XVIII. Barcelona: Ariel, 1980. 304 pp.
          A reevaluation of the prose, poetry, and theater
      of the 18th century. Among the authors studied are
      Jovellanos, Cadalso, Meléndez Valdés, and Nicolás
      and Leandro Fernández de Moratín.

354. Shaw, Donald L. The Nineteenth Century. Vol. 5 of
      A Literary History of Spain. New York: Barnes &
      Noble, 1972. 200 pp. Spanish version: El Siglo
      XIX. Barcelona: Ariel, 1980. 296 pp.
          Deals with romanticism, bourgeois high drama, the
      poetry of Bécquer and Rosalía de Castro, costum-
      brismo, modernismo, and the Generation of 1898.

355. Warren, L. A. Modern Spanish Literature: A Com-
      prehensive Survey of the Novelists, Poets, Drama-
      tists, and Essayists from the Eighteenth Century to
      the Present Day. London: Brentano's, 1929. 2
      vols.
          Also includes Portuguese and other authors of the
      Iberian Peninsula. Stresses cultural and literary
      characteristics of the various provinces.

      --Twentieth Century

356. Barja, César. Libros y autores contemporáneos. New
      York: Las Americas Publishing Co., 1964 (1925).
      vii, 493 pp.
          Studies major writers at the turn of the century:
      Ganivet, Unamuno, Ortega, Azorín, Baroja, Valle-
      Inclán, A. Machado, and Pérez de Ayala. Originally
      written as a continuation of Libros y autores clásicos
      and Libros y autores modernos.

357. Bell, Aubrey F. G. Contemporary Spanish Literature.
     Reprint of 3d ed. London: Russell & Russell, 1966
     (1925). 313 pp.
     Covers literature of second half of the 19th cen-
     tury and early part of the 20th.

358. Brown, G. G. The Twentieth Century. Vol. 6 of A
     Literary History of Spain. New York: Barnes &
     Noble, 1972. 176 pp. Spanish version: El Siglo
     XX. Barcelona: Ariel, 1980. 276 pp.
     Studies the novel and poetry against the social and
     political events. Authors included are Unamuno,
     Valle-Inclán, Baroja, A. Machado, García Lorca,
     Guillén, Jiménez, Alberti, and Cernuda.

359. Chabás, Juan. Literatura española contemporánea,
     1898-1950. La Habana: Cultural, 1952. 702 pp.
     Comprehensive coverage of the first half of the
     20th century. Separate chapters are dedicated to
     major figures in all genres.

360. Lázaro Carreter, Fernando, and E. Correa Calderón.
     Literatura española contemporánea. 2d ed. Sala-
     manca: Anaya, 1969. 348 pp.
     An introductory manual which also includes a view
     of Catalan, Galician, Basque, and Spanish American
     literatures. Contains a short bibliography at the end
     of each chapter and a general bibliography at the end
     of the book. Author and subject indexes.

361. Madariaga, Salvador de. De Galdós a Lorca. Buenos
     Aires: Sudamericana, 1960 (1923). 223 pp. Ex-
     panded version of The Genius of Spain and Other Es-
     says on Spanish Contemporary Literature (Oxford:
     Clarendon Press, 1923).
     Suggestive essays on 11 authors. Among the au-
     thors included are Baroja, Azorín, Pérez de Ayala,
     Miró, and Unamuno.

362. Salinas, Pedro. Literatura española: Siglo XX. 3d
     ed., reprint. Madrid: Alianza Editorial, 1979 (1941).
     223 pp.
     Valuable collection of essays on various authors
     and general themes. The comments on modernism
     and the Generation of 1898 are of special interest.

363. Torre, Guillermo de. La aventura estética de nuestra

edad y otros ensayos. Barcelona: Seix Barral,
1962. 350 pp.
Analyzes the essence of literature as well as various Spanish and other European figures of the 20th
century.

364. Torrente Ballester, Gonzalo. Literatura española con-
temporánea (1898-1936). 4th ed. Madrid: Ediciones
Guadarrama, 1969 (1949). 2 vols.
Studies ideas and themes of 20th-century literature.
Critical examination of movements and representative
authors.

365. _____. Panorama de la literatura española contemporánea. 3d ed. Madrid: Guadarrama, 1965 (1956).
2 vols.
Volume 1 is a historical and critical study, and
volume 2 is an anthology primarily devoted to the
20th century. Volume 1 treats many writers of the
previous century. There is an extremely useful bibliography of some 132 pages by J. Campos in volume
2.

Genres

--Novel

366. Alborg, Juan Luis. Hora actual de la novela española.
Madrid: Taurus, 1968 (1958-62). 2 vols.
General introduction to the Spanish novel and also
contains studies devoted to 29 contemporary novelists.

367. Avalle Arce, Juan. La novela pastoril española. 2d
ed. Madrid: Ediciones Istmo, 1974 (1959). 286 pp.
Surveys critical studies devoted to the pastoral
novel and presents the author's own analysis of this
genre.

368. Balseiro, José A. Novelistas españoles modernos. 8th
ed. Río Piedras: Editorial Universitaria, 1977
(1933). 403 pp.
Detailed studies of the major works of realists
and naturalists of the 19th century. Includes such
authors as Valera, Pereda, Galdós, and Pardo Bazán.

369. Bjornson, Richard. The Picaresque Hero in European

Fiction. Madison: University of Wisconsin Press,
1977. x, 308 pp.
The author presents a broad definition of the picaresque novel and analyzes the important European works of this genre. He is more concerned
with social factors than the aesthetic or literary qualities of the works studied. The Spanish novels included are Lazarillo de Tormes, Guzmán de Alfa-
rache, El Buscón, El diablo cojuelo, Estebanillo González, and several minor novels. The book ends
with about 40 pages of notes on critical studies and
also contains name and subject indexes. This intelli-
gent study is very useful in understanding the picaresque novel.

370. Bosch, Rafael. La novela española del siglo XX. New
York: Las Americas, 1970-71. 2 vols.
Volume 1 deals with the generations of 1898 and
1914, and volume 2 with the generations of 1930 and
1960. Uses political, social, and historical matters
to study the development of the novel with a view to
showing how it contributed to the progress of contemporary life. Index of names in volume 2.

371. Chandler, Frank Wadleigh. Romances of Roguery: The
Picaresque Novel in Spain. Rpt., New York: Burt
Franklin Reprints, 1974 (1899). 483 pp.
The picaresque novel in Spain and the social and
literary reasons behind its development. Also concerned with translations of picaresque novels and
their incorporation into other literatures.

372. Dendel, Brian John. The Spanish Novel of Religious
Thesis, 1876-1936. Princeton, N.J.: Princeton
University, Department of Romance Languages; Ma-
drid: Castalia, 1968. 169 pp.
Mainly discusses the historical and religious prob-
lems found in the novels of such writers as Galdós,
Alarcón, Pereda, Blasco Ibáñez, Baroja, and Miró.

373. Dunn, Peter N. The Spanish Picaresque Novel. Boston: Twayne, 1980. 182 pp.
Analysis of the genre from Lazarillo de Tormes
to Estabanillo Gonzalez. Bibliography.

374. Eoff, Sherman H. The Modern Spanish Novel: Comparative Essays Examining the Philosophical Impact

of Science on Fiction. New York: New York University Press, 1961. 280 pp. Spanish version, El pensamiento moderno y la novela española (Barcelona: Seix Barral, 1980).
Studies Spanish and other European novelists of the 19th and 20th centuries in light of their common intellectual background. Analyzes such authors as Pereda and Dickens; Flaubert and Alas; Pardo Bazán, Galdós, and Zola; Blasco Ibáñez, Baroja, and Gorky; Unamuno; and Sender and Sartre.

375.   Ferreras, Juan Ignacio. La novela por entregas: 1840-1900. Madrid: Taurus, 1972. 314 pp.
Catalogues 130 feuilletonists and emphasizes 28 specialists, e.g., Ayguals de Izco, disciple of Eugène Sue; Fernández y González, who wrote romantic adventure novels; Pérez Escrich; and Blasco Ibáñez. Deals with themes and structures of serial novels.

376.   _____. Los orígenes de la novela decimonónica (1800-1830). Madrid: Taurus, 1973. 334 pp.
Holds the view that the modern Spanish novel was born in the first 30 years of the 19th century from three tendencies: novela sensible y quizá sentimental, novela anticlerical, and the novela histórica.

377.   _____. El triunfo del liberalismo y de la novela histórica (1830-1870). Madrid: Taurus, 1976. 233 pp.
Sociological and bibliographical method.

378.   Francis, Alán. Picaresca, decadencia, historia: Aproximación a una realidad histórico-literaria. Madrid: Gredos, 1978. 230 pp.
Studies 15 picaresque novels to redefine and reevaluate chronology, themes, and techniques of this genre.

379.   Gil Casado, Pablo. La novela social española (1920-1971). 2d ed. Barcelona: Seix Barral, 1975. 598 pp.
A consideration of social realism interpreted as a continuation of the social novel of the 1930s that was influenced by Brecht and Lukacs. Takes the view that novels which began with a treatment of social problems now reveal national consciousness.

380.   Gómez de Baquero, Eduardo.   El renacimiento de la
       novela en el siglo XIX.   Madrid: Mundo Latino,
       1924.   274 pp.
       The Spanish novel of the 19th century from the
       costumbristas to the Generation of 1898.

381.   Marra-López, José R.   Narrativa española fuera de
       España: 1939-1961.   Madrid: Guadarrama, 1963.
       539 pp.
       Studies the contemporary Spanish authors living
       outside of Spain, such as Francisco Ayala, Max Aub,
       Rosa Chacel, Segundo Serrano Poncela, and Arturo
       Barea.   Selected bibliography at the end of each chap-
       ter.

382.   Martínez Cachero, José María.   La novela española
       entre 1939 y 1975.   2d ed.   Madrid: Castalia, 1979
       (1973).   501 pp.
       Useful work which is more historical than critical
       in approach.   Also includes a critically annotated bib-
       liography of 235 items.

383.   Menéndez Pelayo, Marcelino.   Orígenes de la novela.
       2d ed.   Buenos Aires: Espasa-Calpe, 1961 (1905).
       3 vols.   Also published as vols. 13-16 of the Edición
       Nacional of his Obras completas (Madrid: Consejo
       Superior de Investigaciones Científicas, 1962).
       An extensive study of the novel in Spain.   Treats
       the classical influence and the cycles of the chivalric,
       sentimental, historical, and pastoral novels; novels
       of the 15th and 16th centuries; dialogued novels; and
       imitations of La Celestina and Apuleius's Golden Ass.
       Footnotes but no bibliography.

384.   Montesinos, José F.   Introducción a una historia de la
       novela en España en el siglo XIX, seguida del esbozo
       de una bibliografía de traducciones de novelas (1800-
       1850).   4th ed.   Madrid: Castalia, 1980 (1955).   xxii,
       297 pp.
       A useful introduction to the development of the 19th-
       century Spanish novel.

385.   Parker, Alexander A.   Literature and the Delinquent:
       The Picaresque Novel in Spain and Europe, 1599-1753.
       Edinburgh: University Press, 1977.   195 pp.   Span-
       ish version, Los pícaros en la literatura: La novela
       picaresca en España y Europa, 1599-1753.   2d ed.
       Madrid: Gredos, 1975.   215 pp.

Assesses the value of certain Spanish and German novels in the period before Defoe and Lesage. It is not a complete survey but offers new insights into the history of the genre.

386. Pérez Minik, Domingo. Novelistas españoles de los siglos XIX y XX. Madrid: Guadarrama, 1957. 352 pp.
Studies many authors of the modern period but also includes studies of the picaresque novels of Mateo Alemán and Quevedo.

387. Rennert, Hugo A. The Spanish Pastoral Romances. New York: Biblo & Tannen, 1968 (1892). 206 pp. Reprint of the 1912 rev. ed.
A brief review of 22 pastoral romances that appeared in Spain for nearly a century after the publication of Montemayor's Diana (ca. 1559).

388. Sáinz de Robles, Federico. La novela española en el siglo XX. Madrid: Pegaso, 1957. 302 pp.
Mainly biobibliographic material on 20th-century novelists. Includes a general as well as an author bibliography.

389. Siles Artés, José. El arte de la novela pastoril. Valencia: Albatros, 1972. 172 pp.
The evolution of the Spanish pastoral novel with most emphasis on Montemayor's Diana. Bibliography.

390. Sobejano, Gonzalo. Novela española de nuestro tiempo (en busca del pueblo perdido). 2d ed. Madrid: Prensa Española, 1975. 655 pp.
Studies the return of the Spanish novel to realism after the Civil War. Among the selected novelists examined are: Cela, Laforet, and Delibes, writers who illustrate existential realism; and Sánchez Ferlosio, Fernández Santos, and Juan Goytisolo, novelists who are social realists.

391. Soldevilla Durante, Ignacio. La novela desde 1936: Historia de la literatura española actual. Madrid: Alhambra, 1980. 482 pp.
A comprehensive study of the postwar Spanish novel. It follows a generational approach. The author begins with the Generation of 1898 and includes the latest writers. Contains a name index and useful bibliographic data.

392. Solé-Leris, Amadeu. The Spanish Pastoral Novel.
      Boston: Twayne, 1980. 171 pp.
      Contains introduction to pastoral tradition in
      Greece, Rome and Italy. Exhaustive analyses of
      Montemayor's Los siete libros de la Diana, Gil Po-
      lo's Diana enamorada, Cervantes' Galatea, and Lope
      de Vega's Arcadia. Brief, annotated bibliography
      (45 items).

393. Spires, Robert C. La novela española de posguerra.
      Madrid: Planeta/Universidad de Kansas, 1978. 365
      pp.
      Analytical study of 12 novels from Pascual Duarte
      to Reivindicación del Conde don Julián and La saga/
      fuga, with 13-page unannotated bibliography. The au-
      thor's "internal criticism" uses such concepts as nar-
      rative structure, point of view, and space and time.

394. Zamora Vicente, Alonso. ¿Qué es la novela picaresca?
      2d ed. Buenos Aires: Columba, 1970 (1962). 68
      pp.
      Concise introduction to this genre, with plot sum-
      maries.

      --Theater

395. Arias, Ricardo. The Spanish Sacramental Plays. Bos-
      ton: Twayne, 1980. 178 pp.
      The auto sacramental from its beginnings in early
      16th century to Valdivielso and Calderón. Emphasis
      on theological content.

396. Aubrun, Charles V. La comedia española (1600-1680).
      Translation of La comédie espagnole (1600-1680).
      Madrid: Taurus, 1981 (1966). 320 pp.
      Social, historical background is presented along
      with studies of individual dramatists of the Golden
      Age.

397. Borel, Jean Paul. El teatro de lo imposible: Ensayo
      sobre una de las dimensiones fundamentales del tea-
      tro español contemporáneo. Translated from the
      French by G. Torrente Ballester. 2d Spanish ed.
      Madrid: Guadarrama, 1966 (1963). 304 pp.
      Descriptive-critical study of the feeling of frustra-
      tion (the unattainable) in the contemporary Spanish
      theater through the works of its most established
      dramatists.

398. Campos, Jorge. Teatro y sociedad de España (1780-
     1820). Madrid: Editorial Moneda y Crédito, 1969.
     215 pp.
     Studies the Spanish theater in the period between
     neoclassicism and romanticism. Bibliographic foot-
     notes.

399. Cook, John A. Neo-Classic Drama in Spain: Theory
     and Practice. Reprint. Westport, Conn.: Green-
     wood Press, 1974 (1959). xvii, 576 pp.
     Detailed and well-documented analysis of neoclassic
     drama from the time of Luzán's Poetics through the
     failures of romanticism. Contains general and play
     indexes.

400. Crawford, James P. W. Spanish Drama Before Lope
     de Vega. Rpt., Westport, Conn.: Greenwood Press,
     1975 (1922). vii, 223 pp.
     Traces the development of drama from pre-Encina
     times to the religious drama and the tragedy and com-
     edy of the late 16th century. This is a reprint of the
     1967 edition.

401. _____. The Spanish Pastoral Drama. Rpt., Phil-
     adelphia: R. West, 1977 (1915). 126 pp.
     Pastoral plays from the period before Juan del
     Encina until the 17th century, including those by Lope
     de Vega and Calderón.

402. Díaz de Escobar, Narciso, and Francisco P. Lasso de
     la Vega. Historia del teatro español: Comediantes,
     escritores, curiosidades escénicas. Barcelona: Mon-
     taner y Simón, 1924. 2 vols.
     In addition, this study includes J. Bernat Durán's
     examination of the theater of Catalonia and Valencia.

403. Donovan, Richard B. Liturgical Drama in Medieval
     Spain. Toronto: Pontifical Institute of Medieval
     Studies, 1958. 229 pp.
     Studies the liturgical drama in Spain and its pos-
     sible relationship with the development of Spanish
     medieval drama and the liturgical drama of France.
     It presents for the first time texts uncovered by the
     author, primarily in Catalonia. Bibliography and de-
     tailed index of the new texts.

404. Guerrero Zamora, Juan. Historia del teatro contem-
     poráneo. Barcelona: Juan Flors, 1961-1967. 4 vols.

Extensive treatment of contemporary playwrights
of Spain and the world, taking into account not only
the literary aspects of theater but also the importance
of scenario and of contemporary thought. Discusses
such writers as García Lorca, Valle-Inclán, Galdós,
and Echegaray.

405. Hermenegildo, Alfredo. Los trágicos españoles del
siglo XVI. Madrid: Fundación Universitaria Española, 1961. 617 pp.
Reevaluation of previous criticism and presentation
of new insights into Spanish tragedy. Bibliography of
and about each author as well as an appendix of characters, plots, and verse forms of the many tragedies
studied in the text.

406. Lázaro Carreter, Fernando. Teatro medieval. 4th ed.
Madrid: Castalia, 1976 (1958). 287 pp.
From the Auto de los Reyes Magos to Comendador
Escrivá. Excellent introduction to the medieval the-
ater together with an anthology.

407. Leavitt, Sturgis E. Golden Age Drama in Spain: General Considerations and Unusual Features. Chapel
Hill: University of North Carolina Press, 1972. 128
pp.
Seventeen essays that emphasize the role of the
public in shaping the Spanish comedia. The first two
essays are general.

408. López Morales, Humberto. Tradición y creación en
los orígenes del teatro castellano. Madrid: Alcalá,
1968. 259 pp.
A study of the medieval tradition found in the early
16th-century theater and of the attempts to introduce
changes. The author finds it difficult to defend the
existence of a medieval liturgical theater.

409. McClelland, I. L. Spanish Drama of Pathos, 1750-
1808. Liverpool: University Press; Toronto: University of Toronto Press, 1970. 2 vols.
Major work on the drama of the Enlightenment
with special reference to its European context.
Treats translations, opera, parody, and experimen-
tation in new dramatic methods.

410. Muñoz, Matilde. Historia del teatro en España. Madrid: Tesora, 1965. 3 vols.

Volume 1 reviews highlights of the Spanish drama and comedy, volume 2 treats the opera and the Teatro Real, and volume 3 is a history of the zarzuela and the género chico. No bibliography or index.

411. Olson, E., and Wardropper, B. W. Teoría de la comedia: La comedia española del Siglo de Oro. Barcelona: Ariel, 1978. 243 pp.
Two stimulating essays that attempt to define the comedia.

412. Parker, Jack Horace. Breve historia del teatro español. México: Ediciones de Andrea, 1957. 213 pp.
General overview of the Spanish theater from the Middle Ages to the 1950s. Includes index of dramatists and dramas anónimos and ample bibliography.

413. Rennert, Hugo A. The Spanish Stage in the Time of Lope de Vega. Rpt., New York: Kraus Reprint, 1967 (1909). 635 pp.
Reprint of the first edition except for the omission of "List of Spanish Actors and Actresses, 1560-1680." Discusses major playwrights, origins of the comedia and other types of plays, famous theaters, staging of plays, notable actors, and the like. A classic study of the Spanish stage.

414. Ruiz Ramón, Francisco. Historia del teatro español. 4th ed. Madrid: Cátedra, 1979-80 (1967-71). 2 vols.
Volume 1 treats major writers from the Auto de los Reyes Magos to Galdós. Appendixes on the Celestina and the classification of the theater of major dramatists of the 17th century. Volume 2 covers the period from Benavente to the present.

415. Sánchez Escribano, F., and A. Porqueras Mayo. Preceptiva dramática española del renacimiento y el barroco. 2d rev. ed. Madrid: Gredos, 1972 (1965). 408 pp.
A useful compilation of passages on dramatic theory taken from writers of the Golden Age.

416. Shergold, N. D. A History of the Spanish Stage from Medieval Times Until the End of the Seventeenth Century. Oxford: Clarendon Press, 1967. xxx, 624 pp.

An extensive study of the staging of theatrical pro-
ductions. Numerous illustrations, glossary, and bibliography.

417. Torrente Ballester, Gonzalo. Teatro español contemporáneo. 2d ed. Madrid: Guadarrama, 1968 (1957).
606 pp.
Examines general themes in contemporary Spanish
drama and includes a chapter on the most important
authors (García Lorca, Casona, Sastre, Buero). It
treats such themes as teatro de evasión, the soltera
insatisfecha, and Don Juan.

418. Valbuena Prat, Angel. Historia del teatro español.
Barcelona: Noguer, 1956. 708 pp.
Stresses themes of the Spanish theater from the
beginnings to the middle of this century. Contains
indexes but little bibliography. Illustrations of dramatists and scenes from plays.

419. _____. Teatro moderno español. 2d ed. Zaragoza:
Partenón, 1954 (1944). 184 pp.
Studies the principal motifs of the Spanish theater
from the decline of the Golden Age to the 20th century.

420. Wardropper, Bruce. Introducción al teatro religioso
del Siglo de Oro: Evolución del auto sacramental
antes de Calderón. 2d ed. Salamanca: Anaya, 1967
(1953). 339 pp.
Treats the development of an important Spanish
dramatic form in all its aspects as well as the works
of some of the authors.

421. Wilson, E. M., and Duncan Moir. The Golden Age:
Drama, 1492-1700. Vol. 3 of A Literary History of
Spain. London: E. Benn; New York: Barnes and
Noble, 1972. xviii, 171 pp. Spanish version: Siglo
de Oro: Teatro. Barcelona: Ariel, 1980. 268 pp.
Begins with the églogas of Encina and studies the
development of the drama through Rueda, Cervantes,
Lope de Vega, Tirso, and Calderón.

422. Wilson, Margaret. Spanish Drama of the Golden Age.
Oxford: Pergamon, 1969. 211 pp.
Introduction to the dramatists and the social and
historical background of the Golden Age theater. Ample bibliography.

--Short Story

423. Anderson-Imbert, Enrique. El cuento español. 3d ed.
Buenos Aires: Columba, 1974 (1955). 47 pp.
Defines the term "cuento" and briefly relates its
development in Spain from the Middle Ages to the
present. The appendix is a guide to 20 significant
writers of this century.

424. Baquero Goyanes, Mariano. El cuento español en el
siglo XIX. Madrid: Consejo Superior de Investigaciones Científicas, 1949. 699 pp.
Studies the various kinds of short stories in the
19th century, such as historical, fantastic, humorous,
and religious.

425. Bourland, Caroline Brown. The Short Story in Spain
in the Seventeenth Century. Rpt., New York: B.
Franklin, 1973 (1927). xi, 217 pp.
Brief essay on the characteristics of the Spanish
short story in the 17th century and the Italian influence upon it. Bibliography of editions of novels,
1576-1700.

--Essay

426. Bleznick, Donald W. El ensayo español del siglo XVI
al XX. Mexico: Ediciones de Andrea, 1964. 140
pp. New York: Ronald Press Co., 1964. viii, 294
pp.
Covers development of the essay from the 16th
century to 1960, with most emphasis on the 20th century. Ample bibliographies.

427. Marichal, Juan. La voluntad de estilo. Rpt., Madrid:
Revista de Occidente, 1971 (1957). 271 pp.
Synthesizes the representative traits of Spanish essayists from Pulgar to Castro and Salinas. Points
out their individuality, indicating at the same time
the fitness of their styles to their historical epochs.
The 19th century is omitted. Bibliography.

--Poetry

428. Alonso, Dámaso. Poetas españoles contemporáneos.
3d ed. Madrid: Gredos, 1976 (1952). 424 pp.
Studies Bécquer, the Machado brothers, Salinas,

Guillén, García Lorca, Aleixandre, Panero, Rosales, and others.

429. Aub, Max. Poesía española contemporánea. México: Era, 1969. 239 pp.
Survey of Spanish poetry from the Generation of 1898 to the 1950s, with emphasis on the social, economic, and political background.

430. Cano, José Luis. Poesía española contemporánea: Generaciones de posguerra. Madrid: Guadarrama, 1974. 244 pp.
Covers the generation of the 1940s (Blas de Otero, Vicente Gaos, José Hierro, Carlos Bousoño, among others) and that of the 1950s (José Ángel Valente, Claudio Rodríguez, Gloria Fuertes, among others).

431. Cobb, Carl W. Contemporary Spanish Poetry (1898-1963). New York: Twayne, 1976. 160 pp.
A useful introduction to 20th-century Spanish poetry.

432. Debicki, Andrew P. Estudios sobre poesía española contemporánea (la generación de 1924-1925). Madrid: Gredos, 1968. 333 pp.
A panoramic view of the attitudes and theories of this group of poets. Detailed analyses of certain aspects of the works of Salinas, Guillén, Dámaso Alonso, García Lorca, Alberti, G. Diego, Cernuda, and Prados.

433. Díaz-Plaja, Guillermo. Historia de la poesía lírica española. 2d ed. Barcelona: Labor, 1976 (1937). xxiv, 456 pp.
Comprehensive overview of lyric poetry.

434. Frenk de Alatorre, Margarit. Las jarchas mozárabes y los comienzos de la lírica románica. México: El Colegio de México, 1975. 178 pp.
A sound, clearly written introduction to the jarchas. Abundant references to scholarly studies and a useful ten-page bibliography.

435. García Gómez, Emilio. Las jarchas romances de la serie árabe en su marco. 2d ed. Barcelona: Seix Barral, 1975.
Study and anthology of 43 Andalusian muwassahas in Roman alphabet, and also their Spanish versions.

Appendixes on Hebrew jarchas, metrics of the muwassahas, and information on the authors of these poems.
Also contains glossary for the jarchas included in the
book.

436. Menéndez Pidal, Ramón. La epopeya castellana a
través de la literatura española. 1st Spanish ed.
Buenos Aires: Espasa-Calpe, 1959 (1910). 245 pp.
Indispensable study. Traces the ever present influence of the epic throughout Spanish literature from
the Cid to modern poetry, stressing the wealth of national tradition which the epic embraces.

437. _____. Los godos y la epopeya española: Chansons
de gestes y baladas nórdicas. 2d ed. Madrid:
Espasa-Calpe, 1969 (1956). 255 pp.
Origins of the epic and its relation with Gothic
culture. Subject index and footnotes.

438. _____. Poesía juglaresca y orígenes de las literaturas hispánicas. 6th ed. Madrid: Instituto de Estudios Políticos, 1957 (1924). viii, 413 pp.
The nature of the juglar, and his role and influence upon narrative verse. More extensive than the
first edition. Contains abundant footnotes, author
and subject indexes, and an appendix on the juglares
of the courts of Sancho IV and Jaime I of Aragon.

439. _____. El romancero español. Reprint of 2d ed.
Madrid: Consejo Superior de Investigaciones Cien-
tíficas, 1973 (1910). 237 pp.
Studies the nature and evolution of the romancero.

440. Milá y Fontanals, Manuel. De la poesía heroico-
popular castellana. Barcelona: Consejo Superior
de Investigaciones Científicas, 1959. 623 pp.
From the epics of Rodrigo through the Carolingian
and Breton cycles. Contains a wealth of footnotes,
author and subject indexes, and a new classification
of the romances and their themes. This is an indispensable source.

441. Morris, C. B. A Generation of Spanish Poets (1920-
1936). Cambridge: Cambridge University Press,
1969. 301 pp.
Analysis of this generation, indicating attitudes of
each poet toward the various artistic experiments and
showing how each matures to gain an original style.

442. Nykl, Alois R. Hispano-Arabic Poetry and Its Relation
      with the Old Provenzal Troubadours. Geneva: Slat-
      kine Reprints, 1974 (1946). xxvii, 416 pp.
      Author's thesis is that Islamic civilization influ-
      enced the medieval lyricism of Moorish Spain.

443. Pierce, Francis William. La poesía épica del Siglo
      de Oro. 2d ed. Madrid: Gredos, 1968 (1961). 396
      pp.
      A survey of criticism of past centuries and an
      analysis of some epic poems. Appendixes include
      catalogs of published epic poems, translations, and
      editions of the 18th through 20th centuries.

444. Siebenmann, Gustav. Los estilos poéticos en España
      desde 1900. Spanish translation by Angel San Miguel.
      Madrid: Gredos, 1973. 582 pp.
      Studies the poetry of modernismo and the Genera-
      tion of 1898; "pure poetry," "neopopularism," sur-
      realism, and other "isms" of "dehumanized" poetry
      that began around 1920; and the "rehumanized" poetry
      that began around 1940. Includes two extensive bibli-
      ographies: a chronological listing of books of poetry
      (1883-1971), and a list of books consulted.

445. Stern, Samuel M. Les chansons mozarabes. 2d ed.
      London: Bruno Cassirer Oxford, 1964 (1953). 62 pp.
      Study of more than 40 jarchas of Arabic and He-
      brew muwassahas by the discoverer of this earliest
      lyric poetry in Spain.

446. _____. Hispano-Arabic Strophic Poetry. Studies
      by Stern, selected and edited by L. P. Harvey. Ox-
      ford: Oxford University Press, 1974. 252 pp.
      Studies on the sources, form, role, origins and
      history of the muwassaha with analysis of many po-
      ems. Chronological bibliography of Stern's writings,
      index of subjects, and index of authors and poets.

447. Vivanco, Luis Felipe. Introducción a la poesía es-
      pañola contemporánea. 2d ed. Madrid: Guadarra-
      ma, 1971 (1957). 2 vols.
      Studies the poetry of Juan Ramón Jiménez, Guillén,
      Salinas, León Felipe, Gerardo Diego, Alberti, Cer-
      nuda, García Lorca, Dámaso Alonso, Ridruejo, and
      others. Bibliographic notes on each poet represented
      and an introduction on the meaning of lyric poetry.

448. Wardropper, Bruce. Historia de la poesía lírica a lo
      divino en la cristiandad occidental. Madrid: Re-
      vista de Occidente, 1958. 344 pp.
          An examination of the poetic phenomenon of con-
      verting profane works into sacred ones.

449. Zardoya, Concha. Poesía española contemporánea:
      Estudios temáticos y estilísticos. Madrid: Guada-
      rrama, 1961. 724 pp.
          Detailed and thought-provoking study of the most
      distinguished modern Spanish poets: Bécquer, Una-
      muno, A. Machado, Salinas, Jiménez, Guillén, Gar-
      cía Lorca, Hernández, Aleixandre, and others. Bib-
      liography and general index.

450. _____. Poesía española del 98 y del 27: Estudios
      temáticos y estilísticos. Madrid: Gredos, 1968.
      346 pp.
          Another collection of essays that complete Zar-
      doya's book listed immediately above. About half of
      these perceptive essays deal with the Generation of
      1898 (especially Machado, Unamuno, Valle-Inclán,
      and Jiménez) and the rest treat León Felipe, Gui-
      llén, García Lorca, and Alberti.

Literary Movements

450a. Alborg, Juan Luis. Historia de la literatura española.
      Vol. 4, El Romanticismo. Madrid: Gredos, 1980,
      934 pp.
          Follows the format of previous volumes. Contains
      detailed studies of Romantic writers in all genres.
      Includes an index of names and works.

451. Cotarelo y Mori, Emilio. Iriarte y su época. Madrid:
      Sucesores de Rivadeneyra, 1897. 588 pp. Micro-
      film. Princeton, N.J.: Princeton University, 1980.
          Despite the use of Iriarte as a focal point, this
      book is a history of the entire neoclassical move-
      ment in the 18th century.

452. Díaz-Plaja, Guillermo. El espíritu del barroco: Tres
      interpretaciones. Barcelona: Apolo, 1940. 129 pp.
          Suggestive introduction to the baroque. Claims
      that Quevedo's La hora de todos is the key work of
      the period.

453. _____. Introducción al estudio del romanticismo
español. 2d ed. Madrid: Espasa-Calpe, 1967
(1936). 204 pp.
Helpful in pointing out characteristics of the romantic period. General schematic overview.

454. Ferreres, Rafael. Los límites del modernismo y del
98. 2d ed., corrected and expanded. Madrid:
Taurus Ediciones, 1981 (1964). 242 pp.
Besides three general essays on modernismo and
the Generation of '98, the author also studies Una-
muno's poetry, Baroja as literary critic, Antonio
Machado's poetry, Miró, the Generation of '27, and
Alexandre.

455. Granjel, Luis S. Panorama de la generación del 98.
Madrid: Guadarrama, 1959. 535 pp.
Thematic study of the writers of this generation.
Presents the ideology of these writers and also pro-
vides brief selections from their writings.

456. Gullón, Ricardo. Direcciones del modernismo. 2d ed.
Madrid: Gredos, 1971 (1963). 274 pp.
Describes the movement and contrasts it with other
styles. Juan Ramón Jiménez and the Machado brothers are some of the specific authors to whom considerable attention is given.

457. _____. La invención del '98 y otros ensayos. Madrid: Gredos, 1969. 199 pp.
Studies the period of the modernistas and the Generation of 1898 and relates these Spanish writers to
other European authors.

458. Hatzfeld, Helmut. Estudios literarios sobre mística
española. 2d ed. Madrid: Gredos, 1976 (1955).
460 pp.
Mysticism in Spain and its relationship to other
European writers and mystics.

459. _____. Estudios sobre el barroco. 2d ed. Madrid:
Gredos, 1973 (1964). 561 pp.
This study is based on earlier published articles.
Examines the baroque in Spain, Italy, France, and
Portugal. Concentrates on such Spanish writers as
Góngora, Gracián, Lope de Vega, and Cervantes.

460. Ilie, Paul. The Surrealist Mode in Spanish Literature:
      An Interpretation of Basic Trends from Post-
      Romanticism to the Spanish Vanguard. Ann Arbor:
      University of Michigan Press, 1968. 242 pp. Span-
      ish version, Los surrealistas españoles (Madrid:
      Taurus, 1972). 323 pp.
      A perceptive and comprehensive study of surreal-
      ism in Spanish literature.

461. Jeschke, Hans. La generación de 1898: Ensayo de
      una determinación de su esencia. Translated by Y.
      Pino Saavedra. Madrid Editora Nacional, 1954 (1934).
      177 pp.
      Traces the influences and origins of this genera-
      tion. Views this group of writers as a spiritual gen-
      eration.

462. Jiménez, Juan Ramón. El modernismo: Notas de un
      curso (1953). México: Aguilar, 1962. 369 pp.
      A sensitive study of modernismo by a major poet.
      Prologue and notes by Ricardo Gullón and E. Fernán-
      dez Méndez. Appendixes include prologue and index
      to Federico de Onís's Antología de la poesía española
      e hispanoamericana.

463. Laín Entralgo, Pedro. La generación del noventa y
      ocho. 9th ed. Madrid: Espasa-Calpe, 1979 (1947).
      259 pp.
      Perceptively analyzes the major writers of the
      Generation of 1898 and reveals that it was a genuine
      Spanish literary generation to which Laín's generation
      is indebted.

464. McClelland, I. L. The Origins of the Romantic Move-
      ment in Spain. 2d ed. Liverpool: University Press,
      1975 (1937). 402 pp.
      Takes the point of view that Spanish literature is
      essentially romantic in nature. Follows the trend of
      national instinctive romanticism during the classical
      18th century to the self-conscious romanticism of the
      19th century. This edition is almost identical to the
      first.

465. Morris, C. B. Surrealism and Spain, 1920-1936. Cam-
      bridge: Cambridge University Press, 1972. 291 pp.
      Deals with French surrealist influences on Spanish
      writers and artists and with the themes, motifs,

moods, and techniques used by Spanish and Catalan authors. Contains several appendixes of documentary materials, poems, lectures, and other writings in French, Spanish, and Catalan. Select critical bibliography.

466. Navas-Ruiz, Ricardo. El romanticismo español: Historia y crítica. 3d rev. ed. Madrid: Cátedra, 1982 (1970). 477 pp.
Studies the development of Spanish romanticism from its beginnings in the 18th century.

467. Pattison, Walter T. El naturalismo español: Historia externa de un movimiento literario. Madrid: Gredos, 1969. 190 pp.
Contains important writings dealing with naturalism in Spain; and critical studies, book reviews, and the like. Based primarily on periodicals published from 1875 to 1897.

468. Peers, E. Allison. Historia del movimiento romántico español. 2d Spanish ed. Madrid: Gredos, 1973 (1954). 2 vols. Translation by J. M. Gimeno of A History of the Romantic Movement in Spain (Cambridge, 1940).
Extensive data on the origins, influences, literary battles, and rise and fall of romanticism. Peers's condensed work (230 pp.) on the subject is The Romantic Movement in Spain: A Short History (Liverpool: University Press, 1968).

469. _____. Studies of the Spanish Mystics. 2d rev. ed. London: S. P. C. K. ; New York: Macmillan, 1951 (1927-30). 2 vols.
Extensive study from Saint Ignatius of Loyola to post-Teresan mysticism. Lengthy bibliography.

470. Piñeyro, Enrique, and E. Allison Peers (trans.). The Romantics of Spain. Liverpool: Institute of Hispanic Studies, 1934. 256 pp.
Biographical and critical essays on the chief and some minor writers of the romantic period. Select bibliography and index.

471. Ramsden, H. The 1898 Movement in Spain: Towards a Reinterpretation. Manchester: Manchester University Press, 1974. 212 pp.

His critical position is that an organic determinism, coming from the influence of 19th-century natural sciences and reflected in the thought mainly of Unamuno and Ganivet, was the determining trait of the Generation of 1898.

472. Sender, Ramón. Examen de ingenios: Los noventayochos: Ensayos críticos. Prologue by Eduardo Naval. 2d ed. México: Aguilar, 1967 (1961). 446 pp.
A very personal evaluation of such writers as Unamuno, Valle-Inclán, Baroja, Azorín, Maeztu, and Machado. Sender minimizes Unamuno's literary contributions. Covers Spanish literature of the 19th century, its history and criticism, and includes addresses, essays, and lectures.

473. Shaw, Donald L. The Generation of 1898 in Spain. New York: Barnes and Noble, 1975. 246 pp.
Concludes that the writers of the Generation of 1898 mistakenly relied on abstract and philosophical perspectives in treating the practical and concrete problems of the time in which they wrote.

474. Torre, Guilermo de. Historia de las literaturas de vanguardia. 3d ed. Madrid: Guadarrama, 1974 (1965). 3 vols.
Basic works on literary movements of the 20th century. A survey of an extremely wide range of authors from the Italian futurists and German expressionism to concretism, the "angry young men," and the "beatniks."

475. _____. Ultraísmo, existencialismo y objectivismo en literatura. Madrid: Guadarrama, 1968. 320 pp.
Studies the three vanguardist movements that have most influenced Spanish and Spanish American literature from 1920 to the present.

476. Videla, Gloria. El ultraísmo. 2d ed. Madrid: Gredos, 1971 (1963). 246 pp.
Introduction to vanguardist literary movements of the 20th century in Spain.

SPANISH AMERICA

General

477. Alegría, Fernando. Historia de la novela hispanoameri-
      cana. 4th ed. México: Ediciones de Andrea, 1974
      (1959). 319 pp.
      Comprehensive coverage of the Spanish American
      novel that begins with Fernández de Lizardi and comes
      up to the 1970s. General bibliography and bibliogra-
      phies for specific novelists.

478. Amorós, Andrés. Introducción a la novela hispano-
      americana actual. 2d ed. Salamanca: Anaya, 1973
      (1971). 181 pp.
      Essays on such contemporary authors as Carpen-
      tier, Sábato, Cortázar, Rulfo, Fuentes, and García
      Márquez.

479. Anderson-Imbert, Enrique. Historia de la literatura
      hispanoamericana. 6th ed. México: Fondo de Cul-
      tura Económica, 1974 (1954). 2 vols. English trans-
      lation by John F. Falconieri, Spanish American Lit-
      erature: A History. 2d ed., revised and updated by
      Elaine Malley. Detroit: Wayne State University
      Press, 1969 (1963).
      Follows the generational approach in organization.
      A vast number of authors and works are given brief
      presentations. Vol. 1 covers the colonial period and
      100 years of Republic. Vol. 2 includes contemporary
      works.

480. Arrom, José Juan. Esquema generacional de las letras
      hispanoamericanas. 2d ed. Bogotá: Instituto Caro
      y Cuervo, 1977 (1963). 261 pp.
      Studies from a generational point of view. The
      19th-century political, or regional, approach is re-
      jected in favor of a continental and chronological one.
      The opening chapter is a review of the attempts to
      bring order out of the apparent chaos of names and
      dates pertaining to Spanish American literature.

481. _____. Historia del teatro hispanoamericano (época
      colonial). México: Ediciones de Andrea, 1967. 151
      pp. Published originally as El teatro de Hispano-
      américa en la época colonial (La Habana: Anuario
      Bibliográfico Cubano, 1956). 237 pp.

Valuable handbook that goes from indigenous theater to costumbrismo.

482. Ashhurst, Anna Wayne. La literatura hispanoamericana
en la crítica española. Madrid: Gredos, 1980. 643
pp.
    Part 1 deals mainly with 19th-century attitudes
toward Spanish-American literature and Part 2 treats
Spanish critical reactions to Darío and modernismo
as well as non-modernista and post-modernista authors through and including Paz. Problems in organization of the material used have been pointed out
in several reviews of the work.

483. Aubrun, Charles V. Histoire des lettres hispanoaméri-
caines. Paris: Armand Colin, 1954. 224 pp.
    Concise, general introduction. Bibliographies.

484. Bazin, Robert. Histoire de la littérature américaine
de langue espagnole. Paris: Firmin-Didot, 1953.
354 pp. Spanish version edited by Raúl H. Castagnino; translated by Josefina A. de Vázquez. Buenos
Aires: Editorial Nova, 1958. 412 pp.
    From 1800 to the 1950s. Appendixes treat con-
temporary literary trends and national literature.

485. Blanco-Fombona, Rufino. Grandes escritores de América (Siglo XIX). Madrid: Renacimiento, 1917. 343
pp.
    Comments on five major writers of the 19th cen-
tury: Bello, Sarmiento, Hostos, Montalvo, and González Prada. No bibliography.

486. Brotherston, Gordon. The Emergence of the Latin
American Novel. Cambridge: Cambridge University
Press, 1977. 164 pp.
    Introduction to the Latin American novel in eight
chapters on individual novelists: Asturias, Carpentier, Onetti, Rulfo, Cortázar, Arguedas, Vargas
Llosa, and García Márquez. Extensive notes and
selective bibliography.

487. _____. Latin American Poetry: Origins and Presence. Cambridge: Cambridge University Press,
1975. 228 pp.
    Fresh interpretations, with attention to social and
political considerations.

488. Brushwood, John S.   Genteel Barbarism: New Read-
      ings of Nineteenth-Century Spanish-American Novels.
      Lincoln & London: University of Nebraska Press,
      1981. 241 pp.
          A structural analysis of eight 19th-century novels,
      e.g. Mármol's Amalia, Isaac's María, Gamboa's
      Suprema Ley, and Blest Gana's Martín Rivas.

489. _____. The Spanish American Novel: A Twentieth-
      Century Survey. Austin: University of Texas Press,
      1975. xiv, 390 pp.
          Covers the years 1900 to 1970. A serious study
      of the evolution of the novel from Los de abajo to
      Conversación en la catedral. Alternate chapters are
      organized around the specific publication years of a
      dozen novels while the other chapters fill in the gaps.
      Includes comments on many of the belatedly recog-
      nized earlier novels and the most recent ones.

490. Carvalho, Joaquim de Montezuma de. Panorama das
      literaturas das Américas (de 1900 à actualidade).
      Angola: Edição do Município de Nova Lisboa, 1958-
      65. 4 vols.
          Collection of 35 studies by individual writers on
      Brazil, North America, and South America. Volume
      4 has articles by Fernando Alegría on Chile, Luis
      Leal on Mexico, and José Ramón Medina on Vene-
      zuela.

491. Castagnaro, R. Anthony. The Early Spanish American
      Novel. New York: Las Americas, 1971. 208 pp.
          From the colonial beginnings through the 19th cen-
      tury, with emphasis on 19th-century Mexican and Ar-
      gentine novels. Also includes indianista, antislavery,
      realistic, and historical novels. Short bibliography.

      Cejador y Frauca. Historia de la lengua y literatura
      castellana. See no. 313.

492. Chang-Rodríguez, Raquel. Prosa hispanoamericana
      virreinal. Barcelona: Borrás Ediciones, 1978. 175
      pp.
          The editor's introductory essay discusses major
      prose writers of viceregal Spanish America. Other
      essays include the following: E. Pupo-Walker on the
      Comentarios reales; R. Chang-Rodríguez on La en-
      diablada, a 17th-century Peruvian tale; J. J. Arrom

on a relato by Fray Agustín de la Calancha and Fray
Bernardo de Torres in Lima; A. Roggiano on Juan
de Espinosa Medrano; L. Leal on the Cautiverio
feliz; a listing of Spanish-American colonial manuscripts in the Hispanic Society of America by T. J.
Beardsley, Jr.; and a Bibliography of some 250 items
on Spanish American colonial prose by the editor.

493. Coester, Alfred. The Literary History of Spanish
      America. Rpt., New York: Macmillan, 1970 (1916).
      xii, 522 pp.
         Emphasis is on facts and plot summaries. First
      literary history of Spanish America. Judgments often
      differ from those of today.

494. Dauster, Frank. Historia del teatro hispanoamericano
      (siglos XIX y XX). 2d ed. México: Ediciones de
      Andrea, 1973 (1966). 167 pp.
         A comprehensive survey with ample bibliography.

495. Debicki, Andrew P. Poetas hispanoamericanos. Ma-
      drid: Gredos, 1976. 266 pp.
         The ten poets studied are Martí, Vallejo, Borges,
      Pellicer, Neruda, Villaurrutia, Paz, Parra, Sabines,
      and Pachero.

      Díaz Plaja. Historia general de las literaturas his-
      pánicas. See no. 314.

496. Díez Canedo, Enrique. Letras de América: Estudios
      sobre las literaturas continentales. México: Fondo
      de Cultura Económica, 1944. 426 pp.
         Studies in depth of writers of the 19th and 20th
      centuries.

      Díez-Echarri and Roca Franquesa. Historia general
      de la literatura española e hispanoamericana. See
      no. 316.

497. Earle, Peter G., and Robert G. Mead, Jr. Historia
      del ensayo hispanoamericano. México: Ediciones de
      Andrea, 1973. 173 pp. Earlier version by Mead,
      Breve historia del ensayo hispanoamericano (México:
      Ediciones de Andrea, 1956). 144 pp.
         A biobibliographic study from the colonial period
      to the present. Extensive bibliographies.

498.   Englekirk, John E.; Irving A. Leonard; John T. Reid;
       and John A. Crow. An Outline History of Spanish
       American Literature. 4th ed. New York: Irvington
       Publishers, 1979 (1941). xii, 252 pp.
       Excellent outline history intended for students.
       Brief introductions to periods and authors, including
       bibliographies. Bibliographies on history, antholo-
       gies, literary history, and criticism.

499.   Eyzaguirre, Luis B. El héroe en la novela hispano-
       americana. Santiago de Chile: Editorial Universi-
       taria, 1973. 359 pp.
       Archetypal criticism applied to exemplary novels
       of the generations of 1894 (Gallegos, Rivera, Azuela),
       1924 (Cortázar, Onetti, Sábato), and 1954 (Donoso,
       Fuentes, Vargas Llosa, Cabrera Infante, and García
       Márquez).

500.   Fernández Moreno, César; Ivan A. Schulman; and Julio
       Ortega, eds. Latin America in Its Literature. Tr.
       from Spanish by Mary G. Berg. New York & Lon-
       don: Holmes and Meier, 1980. 356 pp. Original
       title: América latina en su literatura (1972).
       Fifteen essays on various aspects of Latin Ameri-
       can literary history and criticism, written by Schul-
       man, Rodríguez Monegal, Alegría, Fernández Reta-
       mar, Portuondo, Lezama Lima, and others. Useful
       contribution to the understanding of 20th-century Latin
       American literature.

501.   Ferro, Hellén. Historia de la poesía hispanoamericana.
       New York: Las Américas, 1964. 428 pp.
       Outline history of Spanish American poetry from
       colonial period to present. Not a penetrating study
       but contains important names and facts.

502.   Forster, Merlin. Historia de la poesía hispanoameri-
       cana. Clear Creek, Ind.: The American Hispanist,
       1981. 329 pp.
       Studies Spanish American poetry from the pre-
       Hispanic period to contemporary writers. Includes
       a very useful extensive bibliography (pp. 110-324).

503.   Foster, David William, and Virginia Ramos Foster,
       comps. Modern Latin American Literature. New
       York: Frederick Ungar, 1975. 2 vols.
       Collection of critical evaluations of 137 major au-
       thors (including Brazilian).

504. Franco, Jean. An Introduction to Spanish American
      Literature. Reprint, Cambridge: Cambridge
      University Press, 1975 (1969). xiv, 306 pp.
      Deals mainly with literature of Spanish America
      from time of Independence. Author attempts to cover
      common characteristics as well as national differ-
      ences.

505. _____. Spanish American Literature Since Inde-
      pendence. London: Ernest Benn, 1973. xiv, 306
      pp.
      Covers but does not duplicate the periods and au-
      thors studied in An Introduction to Spanish-American
      Literature (1969), listed immediately above.

506. Fuentes, Carlos. La nueva novela hispanoamericana.
      5th ed. México: Joaquín Mortiz, 1976. 98 pp.
      Personal study on most outstanding contemporary
      writers, such as Borges, Vargas Llosa, Carpentier,
      García Márquez, Cortázar, and Juan Goytisolo.

507. Gallagher, D. P. Modern Latin American Literature.
      London: Oxford University Press, 1973. 197 pp.
      Individual chapters on Vallejo, Neruda, Paz, Bor-
      ges, Vargas Llosa, García Márquez, and Cabrera
      Infante, with background chapters on poetry and fic-
      tion.

508. Gallo, Ugo, and Giuseppe Bellini. Storia della lettera-
      tura ispano-americana. 2d ed. Milan: Nuova Aca-
      demia Editrice, 1958 (1954). 482 pp.
      Divided into four parts: from colonial period to
      Independence, the romantic period, modernism, and
      the 20th century. Extensive bibliography of antholo-
      gies and critical studies. In the attempt to cover
      many authors of all the Spanish American countries,
      most writers are given scant individual attention, es-
      pecially in the last part.

509. Gertel, Zunilda. La novela hispanoamericana contempo-
      ránea. Buenos Aires: Columba-Nuevos Esquemas,
      1970. 200 pp.
      Studies the outstanding novels from the beginning
      of the 20th century to the 1960s. Romanticism, re-
      alism, regionalism, modernism, and the new novel
      are covered.

510. Goič, Cedomil. Historia de la novela hispanoamericana.

Valparaíso: Universidad Católica de Valparaíso,
1972. 304 pp.
The best organized and most coherent history of
the Spanish American novel. The chapters are based
on fifteen-year generations with relatively long analyses of the key works.

511. Gómez-Gil, Orlando. Historia crítica de la literatura
hispanoamericana. New York: Holt, Rinehart &
Winston, 1968. xiv, 768 pp.
Studies major authors as well as secondary ones
who have importance in literary developments of their
period. Discussions by regions or countries are
avoided. Some errors of factual information. Good
bibliographies.

512. Hamilton, Carlos. Historia de la literatura hispanoamericana. New York: Las Americas, 1960-61. 2
vols. 2d ed., Madrid: Ediciones y Publicaciones
Españolas, 1966. 397 pp.
Highlights of Spanish American literary production
with background information on various periods. First
part covers the colonial period and the 19th century,
and the second includes modernism and the 20th century.

513. Harss, Luis, and Barbara Dohmann. Into the Main-
stream: Conversations with Latin American Writers.
New York: Harper & Row, 1969. 385 pp. Spanish
version, Los nuestros, 4th ed. (Buenos Aires: Su-
damericana, 1978 [1966]). 465 pp.
Studies the literary styles of Carpentier, Asturias,
Borges, Onetti, Cortázar, Fuentes, Rulfo, García
Márquez, and Vargas Llosa.

514. Henríquez-Ureña, Pedro. Literary Currents in Hispanic America. Cambridge, Mass.: Harvard University Press, 1949. vi, 345 pp. Spanish title,
Las corrientes literarias en la América hispánica.
2d ed. 3d print. Translation by Joaquín Díaz Ca-
ñedo. México: Fondo de Cultura Económica, 1969
(1949). 340 pp.
Introduction to the important men, ideas, and
epochs of Latin American literature. Follows rigor-
ous chronological scheme, dividing material (1492-
1940) into seven stages of development. Lengthy bibliography.

515. Jackson, Richard L. The Black Image in Latin Amer-
      ican Literature. Albuquerque: University of New
      Mexico Press, 1976. 174 pp.
          Shows that the black and the mulatto are shown to
      be victims of white prejudice in Latin American lit-
      erature. Extensive bibliography.

516. _____. Black Writers in Latin America. Albuquer-
      que: University of New Mexico Press, 1979. 224
      pp.
          Studies writings of Nicolás Guillén and lesser known
      authors among the relatively few writers of African
      or part-African descent in Spanish America. Con-
      cludes that "there is little black literature in Latin
      America that specifically supports black nationalism
      and a concomitant militancy."

517. Jones, Willis Knapp. Behind Spanish American Foot-
      lights. Austin: University of Texas Press, 1966.
      xvi, 609 pp.
          Very informative study of the theater from indige-
      nous to present. Lengthy bibliography including un-
      published theses.

518. _____. Breve historia del teatro latinoamericano.
      México: Ediciones de Andrea, 1956. 239 pp.
          Concise study with ample bibliography.

519. Jozef, Bella. O Espaço reconquistado. Linguagem e
      criação no romance hispanoamericano contemporâneo.
      Petrópolis: Editora Vozes, 1974. 151 pp.
          A well-documented series of essays in Portuguese
      on Spanish American prose fiction from Borges to
      Sarduy.

520. Lazo, Raimundo. Historia de la literatura hispano-
      americana. 3d ed. México: Porrúa, 1976 (1967).
      333 pp.
          From the colonial period to 1914.

521. _____. Historia de la literatura hispanoamericana,
      el período colonial: 1492-1780. 4th ed. México:
      Porrúa, 1979 (1969). xvii, 370 pp.

522. Leal, Luis. Breve historia de la literatura hispano-
      americana. New York: Alfred A. Knopf, 1971.
      392 pp.

Survey of Spanish American literature from pre-
Columbian times to 1970. Extensive bibliographies.

523. _____. Historia del cuento hispanoamericano. México: Ediciones de Andrea, 1971. 187 pp.
Cogent study with ample bibliography.

524. Leguizamón, Julio A. Historia de la literatura hispanoamericana. Buenos Aires: Editoriales Reunidas, 1945. 2 vols.
From colonial era to about 1900. Material is divided into four epochs within which the organization
is according to geographical regions or literary genres. Volume 2 contains index and bibliography by
country.

525. Luzuriaga, Gerardo. Popular Theater for Social Change
in Latin America. Los Angeles: UCLA Latin American Center Publications, 1978. 432 pp.
A collection of essays on the new popular and collective theater of Latin America. Authors include
Boal, Buenaventura, Monleón, and Suárez-Radillo.

526. Meléndez, Concha. La novela indianista en Hispanoamérica (1832-1889). Rpt., San Juan, P.R.: Editorial Cordillera, 1970 (1934). 227 pp.
Treats origins of the novela indianista (literature
of the conquest and foreign influences), historical and
poetic novels, and novels with the theme of social in-
justices. Good bibliography.

527. Menéndez Pelayo, Marcelino. Historia de la poesía
hispanoamericana. Rpt., Santander: Consejo Superior de Investigaciones Científicas, 1948 (1911). 2
vols.
One chapter devoted to each Spanish American
country. Covers poetry up to about 1875. Index at
end of each volume facilitates use of anthology compiled by same author.

528. Moreno-Durán, Rafael Humberto. De la barbarie a la
imaginación. Barcelona: Tusquets, 1976. 325 pp.
A solid historical introduction followed by essays
on the evolution of the 20th-century novel from criollismo to the boom. The author is one of the best
current Colombian critics.

529. Olivera, Otto. Breve historia de la literatura antillana.
     México: Ediciones de Andrea, 1957. 222 pp.
     Concise treatment of the literatures of Cuba, Do-
     minican Republic, and Puerto Rico from the 16th cen-
     tury to the middle of the 20th. Ample bibliography.

530. Orjuela, Héctor H. Poesía de la América indígena:
     Nahuatl, maya, quechua. Bogotá: Editorial Cos-
     mos, 1980. 130 pp.
     General introduction to pre-Columbian poetry based
     on 57 poems. Claims that Aztec poetry was more
     highly perfected than that of the other two. The bib-
     liography contains 87 items.

531. Ortega, Julio. La contemplación y la fiesta: Ensayos
     sobre la novela latinoamericana. Caracas: Monte
     Avila, 1969. 328 pp.
     Contains a detailed analysis of language as pro-
     tagonist in Lezama Lima's Paradiso. Also includes
     conquest of reality by poetry, metaphoric descriptions
     of speech, and initiation into poetry.

532. Pupo-Walker, Enrique, ed. El cuento hispanoamericano
     ante la crítica. Madrid: Castalia, 1980. 383 pp.
     Twenty-four articles by as many critics, some of
     them outstanding, that study well-known cuentistas
     and the cuento in Mexico, Chile, Peru, and contem-
     porary Cuba. Pupo-Walker provides a concise over-
     view of the Spanish American cuento.

533. Rivera Rodas, Oscar. Cinco momentos de la lírica
     hispanoamericana: Historia literaria de un género.
     La Paz: Instituto Boliviano de Cultura, 1978. 360
     pp.
     Studies Spanish American lyric poetry from 1880
     onward. This work won the Premio Centenario de
     la Academia Mexicana (1976).

534. Rodríguez Monegal, Emir. El arte de narrar: Diá-
     logos. 2d ed. Caracas: Monte Avila, 1977 (1968).
     311 pp.
     Interviews with 12 writers, all Latin Americans
     except for Max Aub and Juan Goytisolo. Among the
     others included are Homero Aridjis, Cabrera Infante,
     Fuentes, Sábato, and Sarduy. Brief biobibliographic
     introductions to each author.

535. _____. Narradores de esta América. Buenos Aires: Editorial Alfa Argentina, 1974-1977. 2 vols. Evaluates modern novelists of Latin America: Azuela, Quiroga, Gallegos, Borges, Marechal, Mallea, and others. Introductory analysis of the new novel.

536. Rosenbaum, Sidonia Carmen. Modern Women Poets of Spanish America. Rpt., Westport, Conn.: Greenwood Press, 1978 (1945). 273 pp. Study of women poets since the colonial period. Analyzes Delmira Agustini at length but also includes studies on Mistral, Storni, and Ibarbourou. Extensive bibliography.

537. Roy, Joaquín. Narrativa y crítica de nuestra América. Madrid: Editorial Castalia, 1978. 415 pp. A collection of seminal articles written by a variety of critics on the most important prose fiction writers from Borges to Sarduy.

538. Sánchez, Luis Alberto. Historia comparada de las literaturas americanas: Desde los orígenes hasta el barroco, Del naturalismo neoclásico al naturalismo romántico, Del naturalismo al posmodernismo, Del vanguardismo a nuestros días. Buenos Aires: Editorial Losada, 1973-1976. 4 vols. 401, 464, 371, 446 pp. A good reference for Latin and North American literatures. Most attention given to Latin American. This work's approach is like Sánchez's earlier studies.

539. _____. Proceso y contenido de la novela hispanoamericana. 3d ed. Madrid: Gredos, 1976 (1953). 625 pp. After a general discussion of the Spanish American novel, the author chronologically studies the novel from the colonial period to the 20th century.

540. Sánchez Trencado, José Luis. Literatura latinoamericana: Siglo XX. Buenos Aires: A. Peña Lillo, 1964. 138 pp. General view, with chapters treating specific authors.

541. Sanjuán, Pilar A. El ensayo hispánico: Estudio y antología. Madrid: Gredos, 1954. 412 pp.

Anthology as well as study of Spanish and Spanish American essayists. Good bibliography for each author as well as a general bibliography. Factual errors and poor introduction.

542. Saz Sánchez, Agustín del. Teatro hispanoamericano. Barcelona: Vergara, 1963-64. 2 vols. Comprehensive general history of the Spanish American theater. Uneven treatment of authors, occasional poor organization of material, and absence of indexes.

543. Schulman, Ivan; Manuel Pedro González; Juan Loveluck; and Fernando Alegría. Coloquio sobre la novela hispanoamericana. México: Fondo de Cultura Económica, 1967. 150 pp. Studies the origin and nature of the new Spanish American novel and its relation to the world novel.

544. Schwartz, Kessel. A New History of Spanish American Fiction. Coral Gables, Fla.: University of Miami Press, 1972. 2 vols. Volume 1 covers the literature from colonial times to the Mexican Revolution, and volume 2, which discusses social concern and universalism, is devoted largely to the study of the new novel. Contains copious notes, and extensive bibliography, and indexes of authors and titles. This is probably the most comprehensive historical-critical assessment of Spanish American fiction published to date.

545. Solórzano, Carlos. Teatro latinoamericano del siglo XX. Buenos Aires: Ediciones Nueva Visión, 1961. 105 pp. México: Pormaca, 1964. 200 pp. Guide to the 20th-century theater. Includes information on the development of the university theater.

546. Spell, Jefferson Rea. Contemporary Spanish American Fiction. Rpt., New York: Biblo and Tannen, 1968 (1944). ix, 323 pp. One chapter is devoted to fiction prior to 1914. Gives detailed treatment of the works of a limited number of writers.

547. Stabb, Martin S. In Quest of Identity: Patterns in the Spanish American Essay of Ideas. Chapel Hill: University of North Carolina Press, 1967. 244 pp.

Ideological tendencies studied in essayists and political publicists. Covers the humanist reaction
against science and the rediscovery of America from
1920 on. Final chapters are devoted to Argentina
and Mexico. Bibliography (pp. 221-33).

548.   Stimson, Frederick S. The New Schools of Spanish
American Poetry. Estudios de Hispanófila, vol. 13.
Chapel Hill: University of North Carolina Press,
1970. 217 pp.
History of literary movements in modern poetry
that attempts to define contemporary movements since
modernism. Bibliography.

549.   Suárez-Murias, Marguerite C. La novela romántica en
Hispanoamérica. New York: Hispanic Institute, 1963.
247 pp.
About 10 to 15 pages devoted to the novel of each
country. Emphasis on names, titles, dates, and plot
summaries. Lengthy bibliography.

550.   Torres-Ríoseco, Arturo. The Epic of Latin American
Literature. Reprint of 3d ed. Berkeley: University
of California Press, 1970 (1942). 277 pp. Spanish
version, La gran literatura iberoamericana, 2d ed.
(Buenos Aires, 1951 [1945]). 320 pp.
Popular, concise history. One chapter is devoted
to Brazilian literature. Major emphasis is on kinds
of literature and broad themes, for example, novels
of the city. Passages translated into English indicate
the intention of reaching non-Spanish-speaking persons.
Some errors of fact.

551.   _____. Grandes novelistas de la América hispana.
2d ed. Berkeley and Los Angeles: University of
California Press, 1949 (1941-43). 2 vols.
Basically the same work as Novelistas contemporáneos de América (see no. 553).

552.   _____. La novela en la América hispana. 2d ed.
Berkeley and Los Angeles: University of California
Press, 1949 (1939). 255 pp.
A survey. Most attention given to those novels
demonstrating local color.

553.   _____. Novelistas contemporáneos de América.
Santiago de Chile: Editorial Nascimiento, 1939.
422 pp.

Studies of the novels of 12 writers. Torres-
Ríoseco characteristically divides the novels according to their setting, countryside or city, with a third
category revealing the influence of modernismo.

554. _____. Nueva historia de la gran literatura ibero-
americana. 7th ed. Buenos Aires: Emecé, 1972
(1945). 337 pp.
From the colonial period to the 1950s on Latin
American culture, history, and criticism.

555. _____, ed. La novela iberoamericana: Memoria
del Quinto Congreso del Instituto Internacional de
Literatura Iberoamericana. Albuquerque: University of New Mexico Press, 1951. 212 pp.
A collection of 13 essays on the novel from colonial times to the present.

556. Ugarte, Manuel. Escritores iberoamericanos de 1900.
2d ed. México: Editorial Vértice, 1947 (1942). 269
pp.
Chapters on 12 writers with general commentary
on the literary scene.

557. Valbuena Briones, Angel. Literatura hispanoamericana.
Vol. 5 of Historia de la literatura española, by Angel
Valbuena Prat. 4th ed. Barcelona: Gustavo Gili,
1973 (1963). 668 pp.
An extensive overview of Spanish American litera-
ture from its beginnings to the contemporary period.
A sound introduction to this literature.

558. Vidal, Hernán. Literatura hispanoamericana e ideología
liberal: Surgimiento y crisis. Buenos Aires: Ediciones Hispamérica, 1976. 120 pp.
Marxist view. This slim volume is often sketchy
and contains controversial opinions based on the de-
pendency theory.

559. Vitier, Medardo. Del ensayo americano. México:
Fondo de Cultura Económica, 1945. 292 pp.
Considers 12 essayists of Spanish America. Stress-
es the political and cultural background. Useful study.

560. Yáñez, Mirta, ed. Recopilación de textos sobre la novela romantica latinoamericana. La Habana: Casa
de las Américas, 1978. 576 pp.
A collection of essays on the Spanish American

Romantic novel by such well-known critics as Pedro
Henríquez Ureña, Fernando Alegría, Luis Alberto
Sánchez, Alberto Zum Felde, Ezequiel Martínez Es-
trada, and Enrique Anderson-Imbert.

561. Zum Felde, Alberto. Los ensayistas. México: Gua-
      ranía, 1954. 606 pp.
      The first of a two-volume study under the title of
      Indice crítico de la literatura hispanoamericana. Very
      extensive study of the essay from colonial times to
      the present. Includes a wide variety of writers such
      as Cortés, Bello, Korn, and Anderson-Imbert.

562. _____. Indice crítico de la literatura hispanoameri-
      cana. 2 vols. Vol. 2, La narrativa. México:
      Guaranía, 1959.
      History of the novel in Spanish America. Excel-
      lent index indicates content of each chapter. The
      first volume treats the essay.

National

Consult chapter 7 (pp. 142-160) for anthologies
of Spanish America, since these books frequently have introductory studies, biobibliographic information, and notes.

--Argentina

563. Arrieta, Rafael Alberto. La literatura argentina y sus
      vínculos con España. Buenos Aires: Impresora
      Francisco A. Colombo, 1957. 205 pp.
      A concise history from the late 1770s to this cen-
      tury, interpreting the works as they relate to Argen-
      tine history, world events, and other literatures.

564. _____, ed. Historia de la literatura argentina.
      Buenos Aires: Peuser, 1958-60. 6 vols.
      Done in collaboration with many writers, some of
      them well-known critics. Comprehensive coverage of
      all genres and all periods from 1516 on, relating
      them to world literature and events. Detailed foot-
      notes.

565. Berenguer Carisomo, Arturo. Las ideas estéticas en

el teatro argentino. Buenos Aires: Comisión Nacional de Cultura, Instituto Nacional de Estudios de
Teatro, 1947. xv, 438 pp.
Somewhat nebulous discussion of the Argentine theater from pre-Columbian times to 1919.

566. Blanco Amores de Pagella, Angela. Nuevos temas en
el teatro argentino: La influencia europea. Buenos
Aires: Huemul, 1965. 185 pp.
Careful analysis of such influences as the sainete,
Pirandello, expressionism, Brecht, Beckett, Greek
myth.

567. Castagnino, Raúl H. Literatura dramática argentina
(1717-1967). Buenos Aires: Pleamar, 1968. 208
pp.
Outline history, which is, however, the best source
for up-to-date information on the Argentine theater.
This is a somewhat revised and substantially updated
version of Castagnino's Esquema de la literatura dramática argentina (1950).

568. Castellanos, Luis Arturo. El cuento en la Argentina.
Santa Fe: Editorial Colmegna, 1967. 64 pp.
A brief, superficial study of the modern short
story in Argentina. The work is designed to orient
the reader to a few of the general trends.

569. Foppa, Tito L. Diccionario teatral del Río de la Plata.
Buenos Aires: Ediciones Carro de Tespis, 1961.
1,046 pp.
Biographies of Argentine dramatists; history of
Argentine theater; and lists of associations of au-
thors, dramatists, composers, and artists.

570. García, Germán. La novela argentina: Un itinerario.
Buenos Aires: Sudamericana, 1952. 317 pp.
Guide to the development of Argentine prose fiction. Treats the cuento and the relato breve as well
as the novel.

571. Ghiano, Juan Carlos. Poesía argentina del siglo XX.
México: Fondo de Cultura Económica, 1957. 285
pp.
Ninety-two poets are treated succinctly. The last
80 to 90 pages are more a directory than a selective
study. The material is arranged according to three

main categories: modernism, imagism, and neoro-
manticism.

572. _____. Testimonio de la novela argentina. Buenos
Aires: Leviatán, 1956. 187 pp.
Payró, Güiraldes, and Arlt are among the authors
treated in this study.

573. Lichtblau, Myron I. The Argentine Novel in the Nineteenth Century. New York: Hispanic Institute, 1959.
225 pp.
Thorough coverage of material. Chronological list
of novels. Much bibliographic information.

574. Magis, Carlos Horacio. La literatura argentina. México: Editorial Pormaca, 1965. 307 pp.
In nine chapters the author traces briefly the development of Argentine literature from 1516 to 1960,
fixing attention on the most representative writers of
each period. He considers effects on literature of
political, educational, social, and economic changes.

575. Mastrángelo, Carlos. El cuento argentino: Contribución al conocimiento de su historia, teoría y prác-
tica. 2d ed. Buenos Aires: Editorial Nova, 1975
(1963). 188 pp.
An analysis of Argentine short-story anthologies
from Manuel Gálvez's Los mejores cuentos (1919) to
Mignon Domínguez's 16 cuentos argentinos (1957);
brief comments on unanthologized authors (at the
time) like Martínez Estrada and Borges; and some
theoretical considerations.

576. Ordaz, Luis. El teatro en el Río de la Plata desde
sus orígenes hasta nuestros días. 2d ed. Buenos
Aires: Leviatán, 1957 (1946). 233 pp.
From primitive Indian dances and festivities to
modern period.

577. Percas, Helena. La poesía femenina argentina (1810-
1950). Madrid: Cultura Hispánica, 1958. 738 pp.
Major emphasis on the poetesses since the generation of 1916, that is, since Alfonsina Storni. Extensive bibliography.

578. Pinto, Juan. Panorama de la literatura argentina contemporánea. Buenos Aires: Angel Estrada, 1955.
382 pp.

Brief treatment of each author with bibliography, commentary, and evaluations by other critics.

579. Rojas, Ricardo. Historia de la literatura argentina. 4th ed. Buenos Aires: Kraft, 1957 (1917). 9 vols. From the colonial era to the end of 19th century. Extensive coverage. A factual, historical approach to Argentine literature by an eminent critic.

580. Williams Alzaga, Enrique. La pampa en la novela argentina. Buenos Aires: Angel Estrada, 1955. 382 pp. Description of the pampa, travelers' impressions of the pampa, and its role in the novel and also the short story.

--Bolivia

581. Díez de Medina, Fernando. Literatura boliviana: Introducción al estudio de las letras nacionales del tiempo mítico a la producción contemporánea. Madrid: Aguilar, 1959. 416 pp. Gives social picture of each period. Concentrates on principal authors. From indigenous myths to contemporary period.

582. Finot, Enrique. Historia de la literatura boliviana (desde sus orígenes hasta 1942). 5th ed. La Paz: Gisbert, 1981 (1945). xv, 588 pp. Extensive study of Bolivian literature.

583. Guzmán, Augusto. La novela en Bolivia: Proceso, 1847-1954. La Paz: Juventud, 1955. 180 pp. Revision and enlargement of author's book by the same title published in 1938. Covers the romantics (1847-1905), the realists (1905-32), and the naturalists (1932-54).

584. Pastor Poppe, Ricardo. Escritores bolivianos contemporáneos. La Paz: Editorial Los Amigos del Libro, 1980. 197 pp. Studies 27 Bolivian writers of prose fiction during the 1960s and 1970s for the purpose of shedding light on the writings and biographies. Little analysis.

585. Rivera Rodas, Oscar. La nueva narrativa boliviana. La Paz: Ediciones Camarlinghis, 1972. 226 pp. Although all the new authors are covered, the

approach is formalistic. The formal characteristics of the new fiction are studied with examples from a variety of authors.

586. Soria, Mario T. Teatro boliviano en el siglo XX. Prólogo de S. M. Suárez Radillo. La Paz: Editorial Casa Municipal de la Cultura Franz Tamayo, 1980. 217 pp.
   The prologue treats Bolivian theater from around 1600 to the end of the 19th century. The second part covers theater from 1900 to 1979. The third part deals in detail with six outstanding Bolivian dramatists, and the last part contains a useful bibliography.

--Chile

587. Alegría, Fernando. La literatura chilena del siglo XX. 3d ed. Santiago: Zig-Zag, 1970 (1962). 287 pp.
   First part offers an overall view, while the second is divided into discussions of writings in prose and poetry.

588. _____. La poesía chilena: Orígenes y desarrollo del siglo XVI al XIX. México: Fondo de Cultura Económica: Berkeley and Los Angeles: University of California Press, 1954. xiii, 312 pp.
   Comprehensive study with bibliography.

589. Campbell, Margaret V. The Development of the National Theater in Chile to 1842. Rpt., New York: Kraus Reprint Co., 1972 (1958). 78 pp.
   Also includes a select bibliography on Chilean theater.

590. Cánepa Guzmán, Mario. El teatro en Chile: Desde los indios hasta los teatros universitarios. Santiago: Arancibia Hermanos Editores, 1966. 135 pp.
   The orientation is historical rather than aesthetic. The bibliography is brief, and there are no indexes. The "Epoca Actual" is devoted almost entirely to Acevedo Hernández, Moock, and lists of drama prizes.

591. Castillo, Homero. El criollismo en la novela chilena. México: Ediciones de Andrea, 1962. 110 pp.
   Study of an important aspect of the Chilean novel. Good bibliography.

592. Díaz Arrieta, Hernán ("Alone"). Los cuatro grandes
      de la literatura chilena del siglo XX. Santiago: Zig-
      Zag, 1963. 234 pp.
      Studies Augusto D'Halmar, Pedro Prado, Gabriela
      Mistral, and Pablo Neruda.

593. _____. Historia personal de la literatura chilena,
      desde don Alonso de Ercilla hasta Pablo Neruda. 2d
      ed. Santiago: Zig-Zag, 1962 (1954). 669 pp.
      Contains a biographical dictionary of authors and an
      anthology of 20th-century authors.

594. Goič, Cedomil. La novela chilena: Los mitos degra-
      dados. 4th ed. Santiago: Editorial Universitaria,
      1976 (1968). 214 pp.
      Among the eight 19th- and 20th-century novels
      analyzed are Blest Gana's Martín Rivas, M. Romas's
      Hijo de ladrón, M. L. Bombal's Última niebla, and
      J. Donoso's Coronación.

595. Medina, José Toribio. Historia de la literatura colonial
      de Chile. Santiago: Librería del Mercurio, 1878. 3
      vols.
      Classic study by an eminent scholar.

596. Rojas, Manuel. Historia breve de la literatura chilena.
      Santiago: Zig-Zag, 1965. 202 pp.
      A good general overview of Chilean literature.

597. _____. Manual de literatura chilena. México: Uni-
      versidad Nacional Autónoma de México, 1964. 152
      pp.
      A concise, elementary manual comprising five
      chapters that recount chronologically the evolution of
      Chilean letters.

598. Silva Castro, Raúl. Historia crítica de la novela chi-
      lena, 1843-1956. Madrid: Cultura Hispánica, 1960.
      425 pp. Previous version, Panorama de la novela
      chilena (1843-1953) (México: Fondo de Cultura Eco-
      nómica, 1955). 224 pp.
      From precursors to contemporaries, with compre-
      hensive introduction and critical bibliography at end
      of each chapter.

599. _____. Panorama literario de Chile. Santiago: Edi-
      torial Universitaria, 1961. 570 pp.

Comprehensive coverage. Much attention is given
to younger writers. Useful appendixes on such topics
as the literary world of 1842 and Rubén Darío's
presence in Chile.

600. Torres-Ríoseco, Arturo. Breve historia de la literatura chilena. México: Ediciones de Andrea, 1956.
175 pp.
Concise study that covers 16th through 20th centuries.

601. Urbistondo, Vicente. El naturalismo en la novela chilena. Santiago: Andrés Bello, 1966. 197 pp.
Useful contribution to the study of the Chilean
novel.

602. Villegas, Juan. Estudios sobre poesía chilena. Santiago: Editorial Nascimento, 1980. 246 pp.
Essays are grouped around the topics of literary
history, the poetic voice, and the use of myth.

603. _____. Interpretación de textos poéticos chilenos.
Santiago: Editorial Nascimento, 1977. 207 pp.
Interpretations of works by Pedro Prado, Cruchaga
Santa María, Mistral, Oscar Castro, Neruda, and
Parra.

--Colombia

604. Botero, Ebel. Cinco poetas colombianos: Estudios
sobre Silva, Valencia, Luis Carlos López, Rivera,
y Maya. Manizales: Imprenta Departamental, 1964.
270 pp.

605. Caparroso, Carlos Arturo. Dos ciclos de lirismo colombiano. Bogotá: Instituto Caro y Cuervo, 1961.
213 pp.
A history of Colombian poetry of the 19th and early
20th centuries which is marred by a lack of historical
sense. It contains biographical sketches and bibliographies.

606. Curcio Altamar, Antonio. Evolución de la novela en
Colombia. 2d ed. Bogotá: Instituto Colombiano de
Cultura, 1975 (1957). 255 pp.
Studies the novel from the colonial period to the
20th century. Relates Colombian novels to those of

other American countries and Europe.   Extensive bibliography.

607. Gómez Restrepo, Antonio.   Historia de la literatura colombiana.   4th ed.   Bogotá: Ministerio de Educación Nacional, Ediciones de la Revista Bolívar, 1956 (1953-54).   4 vols.
This history covers only the colonial period and poetry of the 19th century.   Author includes many passages from original works; for example, 75 pages are devoted to the writings of Madre Francisca Josefa del Castillo.

608. McGrady, Donald.   La novela histórica en Colombia.   Bogotá: Kelly, 1962.   189 pp.
Studies 29 historical novels, 25 of which have American themes.

609. Menton, Seymour.   La novela colombiana: Planetas y satélites.   Bogotá: Plaza y Janés, 1978.   395 pp.
Literary history of 100 years of the Colombian novel from María (1867) to the works of Garcia Márquez and Gustavo Alvarez Gardeazábal's El titiritero (1977).

610. Núñez Segura, José A.   Literatura colombiana: Sinopsis y comentarios de autores representativos.   7th ed.   Medellín: Bedout, 1964 (1961).   xii, 776 pp.
Synopsis of historical events; authors' biographies; accounts of literary movements; studies of novels, short stories, oratory, theater, journalism, and so forth.   Also includes catalog of writers and their works, and excerpts from many works and analyses of same.

611. Ortega Torres, José J.   Historia de la literatura colombiana.   2d ed.   Bogotá: Cromos, 1935 (1934).   xl, 1,214 pp.
From 1538 to 1934.   Many minor authors included. Passages from works of all authors.

612. Otero Muñoz, Gustavo.   Historia de la literatura colombiana.   5th ed.   Bogotá: Editorial Voluntad, 1943 (1935).   334 pp.
General treatment of Colombian literature.

613. Peña Gutiérrez, Isaías.   La generación del bloqueo y

del estado de sitio. Bogotá: Ediciones Punto Rojo,
1973. 253 pp.
  Biobibliographical information and interviews with
many of the well-known Colombian writers except for
García Márquez.

614. Sanín Cano, Baldomero. Letras colombianas. México:
Fondo de Cultura Económica, 1944. 213 pp.
  Concise reference to chief authors from the co-
lonial period to 1941.

615. Vergara y Vergara, José María. Historia de la literatura en Nueva Granada: Desde la conquista hasta
la independencia (1538-1820). 4th ed. Bogotá: Banco
Popular, 1974 (1867). 2 vols.
  Well-known work. Notes by A. Gómez Restrepo
and G. Otero Muñoz. Lengthy indexes of various
subject matter are very helpful.

616. Williams, Raymond L. La novela colombiana contemporánea. Bogotá: Plaza y Janés Editores Colombia,
1976. 93 pp.
  Very short critical account of the Colombian novel
from Cien años de soledad onward.

--Costa Rica

617. Bonilla, Abelardo. Historia de la literatura costarricense. San José: Editorial Costa Rica, 1967. 408
pp.
  Panoramic history of Costa Rican literature, which
acquired depth in the 20th century. The essay is
considered the most cultivated genre today.

--Cuba

618. Arrom, José Juan. Historia de la literatura dramática
cubana. Rpt., New York: AMS Press, 1973 (1944).
132 pp.
  Extensive coverage of Cuban theater from 1512 to
modern period. Good bibliography.

619. Benedetti, Mario, et al. Literatura y arte nuevo en
Cuba. Barcelona: Editorial Estela, 1971. 290 pp.
  Articles by a variety of writers on the role of the
intellectual or artist in Cuba's socialist society.

620. Bueno, Salvador. Historia de la literatura cubana
(1902-1952). 3d ed. La Habana: Ministerio de Educación, 1963 (1953). 459 pp.
Evolution of Cuban literature with reading selections.

621. González Freire, Natividad. Teatro cubano, 1928-1961.
La Habana: Ministerio de Relaciones Exteriores,
1961. 181 pp.
The author carefully studies each group, applying
Petersen's theory of generations and analyzing the
work of each author in some detail. References and
notes are included.

622. Henríquez Ureña, Max. Panorama histórico de la literatura cubana. La Habana: Editorial Arte y Literatura, 1978-79 (1963). 2 vols.
Cuban literature viewed against the background of
its history.

623. Jiménez, José O. Estudios sobre poesía cubana contemporánea. New York: Las Americas, 1967. 113
pp.
Studies Boti, Acosta, Florit, Gaztelu, and Fernández Retamar.

624. Lazo, Raimundo. Historia de la literatura cubana. 2d
ed. México: Universidad Nacional Autónoma de México, 1974 (1965). 313 pp.
Concise history from its beginnings to the 1950s.
Short bibliography.

625. Menton, Seymour. Prose Fiction of the Cuban Revolution. Austin: University of Texas Press, 1975.
xviii, 344 pp. Spanish version: Narrativa de la
Revolución cubana. Madrid: Editorial Playor, 1978.
312 pp.
The most complete study of the Cuban novel and
short story from 1959 to the present. Also includes
chapters on literature written by exiles and works
written by non-Cubans about the Revolution.

626. Miranda, Julio E. Nueva literatura cubana. Madrid:
Taurus, 1971. 145 pp.
Good survey of how the different literary genres
have fared in socialist Cuba.

627. Olivera, Otto. Cuba en su poesía. México: Ediciones
      de Andrea, 1965. 217 pp.
      Author limits himself to regionalistic and nation-
      alistic themes. Studies Cuban poetry from the Es-
      pejo de paciencia (1608) through the 19th century. A
      final chapter summarizes the first 60 years of the
      20th century.

628. Remos y Rubio, Juan J. Historia de la literatura cu-
      bana. Rpt., Miami: Mnemosyne, 1969 (1945). 3
      vols.
      From the 16th to the 20th century. V.1 Origins
      and classicism; v.2 Romanticism; v.3 Modernism.

629. Souza, Raymond D. Major Cuban Novelists: Innovation
      and Tradition. Columbia: University of Missouri
      Press, 1976. 120 pp.
      Starts with the avant-garde writings of the 1920s.
      Chapters on Lezama Lima, Carpentier, and Cabrera
      Infante.

      --Dominican Republic

630. Balaguer, Joaquín. Literatura dominicana. Buenos
      Aires: Editorial Americalee, 1950. 365 pp.
      Studies of 25 authors, all of whom were born in
      the 19th century.

631. Henríquez Ureña, Max. Panorama histórico de la li-
      teratura dominicana. 2d ed. Santo Domingo: Colec-
      ción Pensamiento Dominicano, 1965 (1945). 337 pp.
      Good introduction. From first literary manifesta-
      tions to contemporary period.

      --Ecuador

632. Barrera, Isaac J. Historia de la literatura ecuatoriana.
      2d ed. Rpt., Quito: Editorial Casa de la Cultura
      Ecuatoriana, 1960 (1944). 4 vols.
      Ecuadorian literature from pre-Columbian and co-
      lonial epochs to the middle of the 20th century. Abun-
      dant bibliographic sources.

633. Carrera Andrade, Jorge. Galería de místicos y de in-
      surgentes. Quito: Casa de la Cultura Ecuatoriana,
      1959. 190 pp.
      Ecuadorian intellectual and literary activity between
      1555 and 1955.

634. Descalzi, Ricardo. Historia crítica del teatro ecuato-
      riano. Quito: Casa de la Cultura Ecuatoriana, 1968.
      6 vols.
          Half of volume 1 (125 pp.) is a history of the
      Ecuadorian theater, and the remaining 5½ volumes
      treat individual authors chronologically by year of
      first play. Over 75 percent of the total is devoted
      to the 20th century. Evaluations of about 125 au-
      thors and close to 600 plays.

635. Rojas, Angel F. La novela ecuatoriana. Rpt., Guaya-
      quil: Publicaciones Educativas Ariel, 1970 (1948).
      238 pp.
          Provides a sociopolitical background for the history
      of the Ecuadorian novel. Brief consideration of au-
      thors and works. Bibliography.

      --El Salvador

636. Gallegos Valdés, Luis. Panorama de la literatura sal-
      vadoreña. 2d ed. San Salvador: Ministerio de Edu-
      cación, 1962 (1958). 238 pp.
          Lacks organization and perspective in attempting
      to cover the whole literary history of El Salvador.

637. Toruño, Juan Felipe. Desarrollo literario de El Sal-
      vador: Ensayo cronológico de generaciones y etapas
      de las letras salvadoreñas. San Salvador: Ministerio
      de Cultura, Departamento Editorial, 1957. 440 pp.
          Prolix panoramic view of Salvadorean literature
      which often degenerates into mere listings of authors
      and works.

      --Guatemala

638. Menton, Seymour. Historia crítica de la novela gua-
      temalteca. Guatemala: Editorial Universitaria, 1960.
      335 pp.
          General view of Guatemalan novel. Analyses of
      the works of the most important writers, for exam-
      ple, Milla, Asturias, and Monteforte Toledo.

639. Vela, David. Literatura guatemalteca. 3d ed. Guate-
      mala: Tipografía Nacional, 1948 (1943). 2 vols.
          Lengthy treatment of Guatemalan literature from
      indigenous period to the 20th century.

--Mexico

640. Azuela, Mariano. Cien años de novela mexicana.
      México: Botas, 1947. 226 pp.
      Study of the most important Mexican novelists be-
      tween the War of Independence and the Revolution.

641. Brushwood, John S. Mexico in Its Novel: A Nation's
      Search for Identity. Austin and London: University
      of Texas Press, 1966. 292 pp. Spanish version,
      México en su novela: Una nación en busca de su
      identidad. Translated by Francisco González Aram-
      buro. México: Fondo de Cultura Económica, 1973.
      437 pp.
      Mexican reality revealed through the nation's novel.
      Covers period 1521-1963. Also contains a chrono-
      logical list of Mexican novels (1832-1963) on which
      organization of book is based, a selected bibliogra-
      phy, and an index.

642. _____. The Romantic Novel in Mexico. Columbia:
      University of Missouri Press, 1954. 98 pp.
      A sound introductory study with bibliography.

643. _____, and José Rojas Garcidueñas. Breve historia
      de la novela mexicana. México: Ediciones de An-
      drea, 1959. 157 pp.
      This useful student manual provides a brief intro-
      duction to authors together with a bibliography. From
      origins to 1959.

644. Dauster, Frank. Breve historia de la poesía mexicana.
      México: Ediciones de Andrea, 1963. 198 pp.
      Covers all movements of Mexican poetry from pre-
      Hispanic times. Brief annotated bibliography.

645. Dessau, Adalbert. La novela de la Revolución mexicana.
      México: Fondo de Cultura Económica, 1972. 477 pp.
      Original edition in German (1967). A thorough
      Marxist interpretation ending with Al filo del agua
      and Azuela's last novels.

646. González, Manuel Pedro. Trayectoria de la novela en
      México. México: Botas, 1951. 418 pp.
      The evolution of the novel as revealed in its most
      prominent stages, schools, and individual works. The
      result is a rather comprehensive history.

647. González Peña, Carlos. Historia de la literatura me-
      xicana: Desde los orígenes hasta nuestros días. 13th
      ed. México: Porrúa, 1977 (1928). 362 pp. English
      translation, History of Mexican Literature, by Gusta
      Barfield Nance and Florence Johnson Dunstan, 3d ed.
      (Dallas, Tex.: Southern Methodist University Press,
      1968 [1943]). 398 pp.
          A standard study that provides general critical
      evaluation of important literary works and move-
      ments.

648. Haneffstengel, Renate von. El México de hoy en la
      novela y el cuento. México: Ediciones de Andrea,
      1966. 113 pp.
          Includes Yáñez, Fuentes, Castellanos, Rulfo, Ro-
      jas González, and Spota.

649. Jiménez Rueda, Julio. Historia de la literatura mexi-
      cana. 5th ed. México: Botas, 1960 (1928). 387
      pp.
          From the indigenous period to the present. Chron-
      ological table of literary events. Good bibliography.

650. _____. Letras mexicanas en el siglo XIX. México:
      Fondo de Cultura Económica, 1944. 189 pp.
          Emphasis on movements, history, and society.
      A clear presentation of trends, but there are no sharp
      analyses of literary works.

651. Langford, Walter M. The Mexican Novel Comes of Age.
      Notre Dame, Ind.: University of Notre Dame Press,
      1971. 229 pp. Spanish version translated by Luis
      Saúl Flores, La novela mexicana: Realidad y va-
      lores. México: Editorial Diana, 1975. 278 pp.
          Brief summary of the Mexican novel prior to the
      20th century. Covers Azuela and his disciples,
      Traven, Yáñez, Rulfo, Spota, Fuentes, and others.
      Selective general and special bibliographies for each
      chapter.

652. Larson, Ross. Fantasy and Imagination in the Mexican
      Narrative. Tempe: Arizona State University, 1977.
      xi, 154 pp.
          Concentrates mainly on the short story in his study
      of fantasy and imagination throughout different periods
      of Mexican fiction. Extensive bibliography and index
      of authors and works.

653. Leal, Luis. Breve historia del cuento mexicano. Mé-
      xico: Ediciones de Andrea, 1956. 163 pp.
      Covers all epochs from the pre-Hispanic to the
      middle of this century. Brief treatment of authors
      with essential bibliographic information.

654. Magaña Esquivel, Antonio, and Ruth S. Lamb. Breve
      historia del teatro mexicano. México: Ediciones de
      Andrea, 1958. 176 pp.
      Concise study with a good deal of bibliography.

655. María y Campos, Armando de. El teatro de género
      chico en la revolución mexicana. México: Biblio-
      teca del Instituto Nacional de Estudios Históricos de
      la Revolución Mexicana, 1956. 439 pp.
      Studies the género chico from 1901 to 1956.

656. Martínez, José Luis. Literatura mexicana, siglo XX.
      México: Robredo, 1949-50. 2 vols.
      Part 1 consists of a lengthy series of studies on
      a wide variety of topics. The second part constitutes
      a major contribution to a bibliography of Mexican let-
      ters and, in particular, to literary journals.

657. Morton, F. Rand. Los novelistas de la revolución
      mexicana. México: Editorial Cultura, 1949. 270
      pp.
      Very detailed, informative presentation of 13 nov-
      elists of the Mexican Revolution. Other authors are
      mentioned briefly.

658. Navarro, Joaquina. La novela realista mexicana. Mé-
      xico: Compañía General de Ediciones, 1955. 333 pp.
      Detailed study of Mexican society as seen in the
      works of major and minor novelists of the realistic
      period. Bibliography.

659. Olavarría y Ferrari, Enrique de. Reseña histórica del
      teatro en México. 3d ed. Prologue by Salvador Novo.
      México: Porrúa, 1968 (1961). 5 vols.
      It includes the author's unpublished manuscript for
      the years 1896 to 1911 as well as a month-by-month
      listing for 1911-61 prepared by David Arce. Mate-
      rial from two previous editions (1880 and 1895) is also
      included. A recent index to this work is Indices a la
      reseña histórica del teatro en México (1538-1911) de
      Enrique de Olavarría y Ferrari, Bibliografía mexi-
      cana, no. 4 (México: Porrúa, 1968).

660. Portal, Marta. Proceso narrativo de la Revolución
      Mexicana. Madrid: Ediciones Cultura Hispánica,
      1977. 329 pp.
          Structuralist and archetypal concepts and termi-
      nology are used to study the portrayal of the Revolu-
      tion in the works of twenty authors from Azuela to
      Poniatowska.

661. Read, John L. The Mexican Historical Novel, 1826-
      1910. Rpt., New York: Russell & Russell, 1973
      (1939). 337 pp.
          Provides information on literary trends and their
      influence on the historical novel. Bibliography of
      novels and critical studies.

662. Rojas Garcidueñas, José J. El teatro de Nueva Es-
      paña en el siglo XVI. 2d ed. México: Secretaría
      de Educación Pública, 1973 (1935). 191 pp.
          Outline history of early Mexican theater. Appen-
      dix contains some theatrical pieces.

663. Sommers, Joseph. After the Storm: Landmarks of
      the Modern Novel. Albuquerque: University of New
      Mexico Press, 1968. xii, 208 pp. Spanish version,
      Yáñez, Rulfo, Fuentes: La novela mexicana (Caracas:
      Monte Avila, 1970). 240 pp.
          Mainly studies Yáñez, Rulfo, and Fuentes. In-
      cludes bibliographic references.

664. Urbina, Luis Gonzaga. La vida literaria de México y
      la literatura mexicana durante la guerra de la Inde-
      pendencia. 2d ed. México: Porrúa, 1965 (1946).
      xv, 397 pp.
          Two major studies by Urbina which serve as a
      history of literature. The period of the War of In-
      dependence is well covered.

665. Valenzuela Rodarte, Alberto. Historia de la literatura
      en México. México: Editorial Jus, 1961. 623 pp.
          Development of Mexican literature from the indige-
      nous period to the 1950s.

666. Warner, Ralph E. Historia de la novela mexicana en
      el siglo XIX. México: Robredo, 1953. 130 pp.
          Work of synthesis which gives essential facts, crit-
      ical evaluations, and bibliography.

-- Nicaragua

667. Arellano, Jorge Eduardo. Panorama de la literatura
nicaragüense. 3d ed. Managua: Ediciones Nacionales, 1977 (1966). 197 pp.
Overview of Nicaraguan literature from its indigenous and Spanish origins to the present. Begins with
an 86-page panorama and has several chapters devoted to several genres: short narrative, novel, theater, and poetry. Basic bibliography and 30 semblanzas on 20th-century Nicaraguan authors.

668. Ycaza Tigerino, Julio César. La poesía y los poetas
de Nicaragua. Managua: Academia Nicaragüense de
la Lengua, 1958. 148 pp.

-- Panama

669. García S., Ismael. Historia de la literatura panameña.
2d ed. México: Universidad Nacional Autónoma de
México, 1972 (1964). 206 pp.
Manual for university students. Bibliography.

670. Miró, Rodrigo. La literatura panameña (origen y proceso). 3d ed. Panamá: Editorial Serviprensa, 1976.
336 pp.
The first part treats the literature of conquest
(1502-1821), the second extends from the colonial
period to the republic (1821-1903), and the third and
longest part covers Panamanian literature during the
years 1903-70. Bibliography.

-- Paraguay

671. Centurión, Carlos R. Historia de las letras paraguayas.
Buenos Aires: Ayacucho, 1947-51. 3 vols.
First serious attempt at a systematic study of Paraguayan letters from the colonial period to the middle
of the 20th century. Much politico-cultural history in
addition to literature.

672. Pérez-Maricevich, Francisco. La poesía y la narrativa
en el Paraguay. Asunción: Editorial del Centenario,
1969. 72 pp.
While this critical analysis of Paraguayan literature
rejects the notion of a literary tradition in Paraguay,
the author rightfully focuses on the better achieve-

ments of Gabriel Casaccia and Augusto Roa Bastos.
First part of this study is a reprint of Poesía y conciencia de la poesía en el Paraguay (Asunción: Ediciones Epoca, 1967).

673. Plá, Josefina. El teatro en el Paraguay: Primera
      parte, de la fundación a 1870. Asunción: Editorial
      Diálogo, 1967. 90 pp.
      Volume 1 of the second edition of the author's
      Cuatro siglos de teatro en el Paraguay (Asunción,
      1966). A careful and documented study. Contains
      bibliography.

674. Rodríguez Alcalá, Hugo. Historia de la literatura pa-
      raguaya. México: Ediciones de Andrea, 1970. 199
      pp.; Asunción: Colegio de San José, 1971. 202 pp.
      Concise history from the colonial period to the
      20th century. Ample bibliography.

675. Velázquez, Rafael Eladio. Breve historia de la cultura
      en el Paraguay. 6th ed. Asunción: The Author,
      1978 (1966). 313 pp.
      Textbook that deals chronologically with the educa-
      tion, culture, arts and letters, and sciences of Para-
      guay.

      --Peru

676. Aldrich, Earl M., Jr. The Modern Short Story in
      Peru. Madison: University of Wisconsin Press,
      1966. xi, 212 pp.
      Study of the 20th-century Peruvian short story.
      Stresses importance of the modernista movement in
      the development of this genre. Aldrich considers
      Alegría and J. M. Arguedas to be pivotal figures.
      Good bibliography.

677. Castro Arenas, Mario. La novela peruana y la evolu-
      ción social. 2d ed. Lima: J. Godard, 1967 (1965).
      288 pp.
      The development of the Peruvian novel as related
      to its society. Begins with El Lazarillo de ciegos
      caminantes and extends to the present. Much atten-
      tion given to 19th-century novelists, but too sketchy
      for the 20th century.

678. Monguió, Luis. La poesía postmodernista peruana.

Berkeley and Los Angeles: University of California
Press; México: Fondo de Cultura Económica, 1954.
253 pp.
Careful scholarship. Bibliography on Peruvian poetry from 1915 to 1950 covers 33 pages.

679. Nieto, Luis Carlos. Poetas y escritores peruanos.
Cuzco: Editorial Sol y Piedra, 1957. 72 pp.
Biocritical notes on nine of Peru's outstanding
writers, among whom are Santos Chocano, Clorinda
Matto de Turner, José Díaz Canseco, Ricardo Palma,
and César Vallejo.

680. Núñez, Estuardo. La literatura peruana en el siglo
XX. México: Editorial Pormaca, 1965. 256 pp.
Organized by literary genres with almost one half
the book devoted to different types of essays. Good
critical judgments.

681. Sánchez, Luis Alberto. La literatura del Perú. 2d
ed. Buenos Aires: Imprenta de Buenos Aires, 1943
(1939). 189 pp.
Volume 1 of a two-volume collection called Las
literaturas américas. Emphasis on sociological, historical background. Bibliography of basic titles of
Peruvian literature.

682. _____. La literatura peruana: Derrotero para una
historia espiritual del Perú. 5th ed. Lima: P. L.
Villanueva, 1981 (1950). 5 vols.
From the time of the Incas to 1979 as seen through
the influence of the geography and culture of the Indi-
ans and Spaniards. Literature is viewed as a spirit-
ual voice of the people. Much bibliographic information.

683. Tamayo Vargas, Augusto. Apuntes para un estudio de
la literatura peruana. 4th ed. Lima: Librería Stu-
dium, 1977 (1948). 2 vols.
From pre-Columbian literature to the present.
Useful bibliography.

--Puerto Rico

684. Manrique Cabrera, Francisco. Historia de la literatura puertorriqueña. Río Piedras, P. R.: Editorial
Cultural, 1973 (1956). 384 pp.

Panoramic view of Puerto Rican literature from
the 16th century to the present.

685. Pasarrel, Emilio J. Orígenes y desarrollo de la afi-
ción teatral en Puerto Rico. Reprint of pts. 1 (1951)
and 2 (1967). San Juan: Editorial Universitaria,
1970. 463 pp.
      The standard source on the subject. Important
for its facts and not its critical comments. Part 2
is a summary of activity on the stage from 1900 to
1962.

686. Phillips, Jordan B. Contemporary Puerto Rican Drama.
Madrid: Plaza Mayor Ediciones, 1973. 220 pp.
Covers the years 1938-68. Bibliography of books
and articles. Also includes an index of plays dis-
cussed.

687. Quiles de la Luz, Lillian. El cuento en la literatura
puertorriqueña. Río Piedras: Universidad de Puerto
Rico, Editorial U. P. R., 1968. 295 pp.
Spans the years 1843 to 1963. Bibliography on
pages 141-293.

688. Rivera de Alvarez, Josefina. Historia de la literatura
puertorriqueña. Santurce: Departamento de Instruc-
ción Pública, 1969. 2 vols.
Intended as a text for high school and university
students. Comprises eight chapters, each with a
historical-cultural introduction. Contains an end
vocabulary, notes, and bibliography.

689. Rosa-Nieves, Cesáreo. Aguinaldo lírico de la poesía
puertorriqueña. Rev. ed. Río Piedras: Edil, 1971
(1957). 3 vols.
Volume 1 covers romantics and Parnassians (1843-
1907), volume 2 the modernists (1907-21), and volume
3 the postmodernists and vanguardists (1921-56).
Brief bibliographic introduction to each author.

--Uruguay

690. Benedetti, Mario. Literatura uruguaya: Siglo XX. 2d
ed. Montevideo: Alfa, 1969 (1963). 364 pp.
A collection of essays on contemporary Uruguayan
letters. Most are concerned with specific authors
and aspects of their work. One essay comments on
recent literary trends in Uruguay.

691. Bollo, Sarah. Literatura uruguaya, 1807-1975. 2d
      ed. Montevideo: Universidad de la República, 1976
      (1965). 351 pp.
      Biobibliography of the literature of Uruguay.

      Englekirk and Ramos. La narrativa uruguaya. See
      no. 270.

692. Rela, Walter. Historia del teatro uruguayo, 1808-1968.
      Montevideo: Banda Oriental, 1969. 187 pp.
      A good overview of the Uruguayan theater. Bib-
      liography.

693. Reyles, Carlos, ed. Historia sintética de la literatura
      uruguaya. Montevideo: Alfredo Vila, 1931. 3 vols.
      A series of 26 essays by 25 critics covering Uru-
      guayan literature of all periods.

694. Roxlo, Carlos. Historia crítica de la literatura uru-
      guaya. Montevideo: A. Barreiro y Ramos, 1912-16.
      7 vols. Later ed., 1936.
      Very extensive coverage from the period of Inde-
      pendence to 1916.

695. Zum Felde, Alberto. La literatura del Uruguay. 2d
      ed. Vol. 2 of Las literaturas américas (2 vols.).
      Montevideo: Colorado, 1941 (1939).
      From colonial period to about 1935. Brief bibli-
      ography.

696. _____. Proceso intelectual del Uruguay y crítica
      de la literatura uruguaya. Montevideo: Editorial del
      Nuevo Mundo, 1967. 3 vols.
      From the end of the colonial period to the con-
      temporary period. Treats a vast number of authors
      but gives considerable attention to the few major ones.

      --Venezuela

697. Araujo, Orlando. Narrativa venezolana contemporánea.
      Caracas: Editorial Tiempo Nuevo, 1972. 355 pp.
      Treats best such writers as Gallegos, Meneses,
      Uslar Pietri, Otero Silva, and González León but in-
      sufficiently covers most of the newest writers. Some
      of the later chapters have some thematic unity: the
      novel of violence (chapter 7) and the narratives deal-
      ing with the problems of present-day Venezuelan youth
      (chapter 12).

698. Azparren, Leonardo. El teatro venezolano y otros tea-
      tros. Caracas: Monte Avila, 1979. 247 pp.
      This book treats the development of Venezuelan
      theater during the post-World War II period.

699. Díaz Siejas, Pedro. La antigua y la moderna litera-
      tura venezolana: Estudio histórico-crítico con an-
      tología. Caracas: Ediciones Armitano, 1966. 782
      pp.
      Evolution of Venezuelan letters with representative
      selections from many authors. Valuable bibliography
      for each chapter.

700. Medina, José Ramón. 50 años de literatura venezolana.
      Caracas: Monte Avila, 1972. 324 pp.
      Very general history from 1918 to 1968.

701. Picón-Febres, Gonzalo. La literatura venezolana en
      el siglo diez y nueve. 2d ed. Caracas: Presidencia
      de la República, 1972 (1906). 447 pp.
      Stresses historical setting, society, and reviews
      of the period.

702. Picón Salas, Mariano. Estudios de literatura venezo-
      lana. Caracas and Madrid: Edime, 1961. 320 pp.
      From the Spanish conquest to the present. Fo-
      cuses on the spirit of the Venezuelans as revealed
      through their literature. Emphasis on 20th-century
      authors.

703. _____. Formación y proceso de la literatura vene-
      zolana. Caracas: Cecilio Acosta, 1940. 271 pp.
      Outline history from conquest to 1940. Extensive
      bibliography of literature from 1930 to 1940. Brief
      general bibliography.

704. Ratcliff, Dillwyn F. Venezuelan Prose Fiction. New
      York: Instituto de las Españas, 1933. 286 pp.
      Spanish version, La prosa de ficción en Venezuela
      (Caracas: Universidad Central, 1966). 278 pp.
      History of the novel, sketch, and short story from
      the middle of the 19th century to the 1920s. Plots
      of some unattainable works summarized.

705. Rivera Silvestrini, José. El cuento moderno venezolano.
      Río Piedras: Editorial Cultura, 1967. 186 pp.
      The development of the Venezuelan short story from

the period of modernism (1890s) to around 1960.
General bibliography and extensive bibliography on
the writers included.

Literary Movements

Anderson. Spanish American Modernism. See no. 132.

706. Argüello, Santiago. Modernismo y modernistas. Guatemala: Tipografía Nacional, 1935. 2 vols.
Studies devoted mainly to Silva, Gutiérrez Nájera,
Blanco Fombona, Darío, Nervo, and Arévalo Martínez.

707. Blanco-Fombona, Rufino. El modernismo y los poetas
modernistas. Madrid: Editorial Mundo Latino, 1929.
364 pp.
Study of major poets of the various stages of the
modernist movement. Quotes rather extensively from
modernist poetry.

708. Bollo, Sarah. El modernismo en el Uruguay. 2d ed.
Montevideo: Universidad de la República, 1976 (1951).
116 pp.
Defines modernism and surveys criticism dealing
with the movement.

709. Carilla, Emilio. La literatura barroca en Hispanoamérica. New York: Anaya, 1972. 209 pp.
The literary and historical development of the
baroque in Latin America. Brief treatment of the
neobaroque in contemporary Spanish American narrative.

710. _____. El romanticismo en la América hispánica.
3d ed. Madrid: Gredos, 1975 (1958). 2 vols.
Covers all aspects of romanticism (political, social, economic, European influences, themes, and
language) in Spanish America and Brazil.

711. Castillo, Homero, ed. Estudios críticos sobre el modernismo. Madrid: Gredos, 1968. 416 pp.
A collection of essays by outstanding critics on
modernism in Spain and Spanish America. Introduction, selection, and general bibliography by Castillo.

712. Collazos, Oscar, ed. Los vanguardismos. 2d ed.
Barcelona: Ediciones Península, 1977 (1970). 234
pp.
Covers ultraísmo, martinfierrismo, futurismo,
creacionismo, estridentismo besides the vanguard
movements in Colombia, Cuba, and Brazil. Includes
some of the original manifestos.

713. Corvalán, Octavio. Modernismo y vanguardia: Coordi-
nadas de la literatura hispanoamericana del siglo XX.
New York: Las Americas, 1967. 263 pp.
Treats the poetry and novel of the "heirs" of modernism and the poetry, essay, and novel of the vanguardists.

714. _____. El postmodernismo. New York: Las Americas, 1961. 159 pp.
Focuses on major writers of the period between
the world wars. Some important writers are omitted.

715. Craig, George Dundas. The Modernist Trend in
Spanish-American Poetry. Berkeley and Los Angeles: University of California Press, 1934. 347
pp. Rpt., New York: Gordian Press, 1971.
Introductory chapter on the modernist trend in
Spanish American poetry, an anthology of representative poetry with English translations in verse, and
commentaries. Short bibliography.

716. Davison, Ned J. The Concept of Modernism in Hispanic Criticism. Boulder, Colo.: Pruett Press,
1966. 188 pp. Spanish version, El concepto de
modernismo en la crítica hispánica (Buenos Aires:
Nova, 1971). 107 pp.
Description of the concept of modernism with emphasis on poetry. Useful bibliography.

717. Fein, John M. Modernismo in Chilean Literature:
The Second Period. Durham, N.C.: Duke University Press, 1965. x, 167 pp.
The "second period" occurred after the departure
of Darío from Chile. Two journals are given extensive treatment: Revista cómica and Pluma y lápiz.
A chapter is devoted to the role of Francisco Contreras.

718. Fogelquist, Donald F. Españoles de América y amer-
      icanos de España. Madrid: Gredos, 1968. 348 pp.
      Modernism as a Hispanic phenomenon in poetry
      and prose. Attention is mostly given to Spanish
      American modernists.

719. Henríquez Ureña, Max. Breve historia del modernismo.
      2d ed. México: Fondo de Cultura Económica, 1962
      (1954). 559 pp.
      General view of modernism with chapters on more
      important writers. Good bibliography.

720. Loprete, Carlos. La literatura modernista en la Ar-
      gentina. 3d ed. Buenos Aires: Plus Ultra, 1976
      (1955). 179 pp.
      Brief survey. Includes journals, polemics, pre-
      cursors, and major figures of modernism in Argen-
      tina, especially Larreta and Lugones.

721. Schulman, Ivan A. Génesis del modernismo. 2d ed.
      St. Louis, Mo.: Washington University Press, 1971
      (1966). 224 pp.
      Studies on early manifestations of modernist lit-
      erature with special emphasis on Martí, Silva, and
      Casal.

722. _____, and Manuel Pedro González. Martí, Darío
      y el modernismo. Madrid: Gredos, 1974. 268 pp.
      Schulman contributes a chapter defining modernism,
      and the remaining chapters deal with works of Martí
      and Darío.

723. Torres-Ríoseco, Arturo. Precursores del modernismo.
      Rpt., New York: Las Americas, 1963 (1925). 221
      pp.
      Introduction to modernism and essays on four ma-
      jor writers: Casal, Gutiérrez Nájera, Martí, and
      Silva.

7. ANTHOLOGIES

SPAIN AND SPANISH AMERICA

724. Abreu Gómez, Ermilo, ed. Bellas, claras y sencillas páginas de la literatura castellana (España e Hispanoamérica). 2d ed. México: B. Costa-Amic, 1970 (1965). 198 pp.
Prose and verse of Spain and Spanish America from the 14th to the 20th century.

725. Cohen, J. M., ed. The Penguin Book of Spanish Verse. Harmondsworth, Middlesex: Penguin Books, 1972 (1956). xxxvi, 472 pp.
Original Spanish with prose translations from earliest to contemporary poetry.

726. Espina García, Antonio, ed. Las mejores escenas del teatro español e hispanoamericano (desde sus orígenes hasta la época actual). Madrid: Aguilar, 1959. 1,172 pp.
Works of 66 Spanish and eight Spanish American playwrights, with introductions to each.

727. Onís, Federico de, ed. Antología de la poesía española e hispanoamericana (1882-1932). Rpt., New York: Las Américas, 1961 (1934). xxxvi, 1,212 pp.
A classic collection which contains a wealth of bio-bibliographic information.

728. Sanjuán, Pilar A. El ensayo hispánico: Estudio y antología. Madrid: Gredos, 1954. 412 pp.
Anthology as well as study of Spanish and Spanish American essayists. Good bibliography for each author as well as a general bibliography. Factual errors and poor introduction.

729. Valverde, José M., ed. Antología de la poesía es-
     pañola e hispanoamericana. México: Renacimiento,
     1962. 2 vols.
     From the 10th century to the present.

                              SPAIN

General

730. Bleiberg, Germán, editor. Antología de la literatura
     española: Siglos XI al XVI (1976), Siglos XVI al
     XVII (1979), Siglos XVII al XVIII (1980). Madrid:
     Alianza Editorial, 1976-   .
     All genres covered. Brief introductions to the
     authors included.

731. Del Río, Angel, and Emilia A. de Del Río, eds. An-
     tología general de la literatura española. 2d ed.
     New York: Holt, Rinehart & Winston, 1960 (1954).
     2 vols.
     Excellent anthology from origins to the Civil War.

732. Díaz-Plaja, Guillermo, ed. Antología mayor de la
     literatura española. 2d ed. Barcelona: Labor,
     1969-70 (1958-62). 4 vols.
     From beginnings of Spanish literature (Seneca)
     through the 19th century.

733. _____. Tesoro breve de las letras hispánicas.
     Madrid: Magisterio Español, 1968-   .
     Fifteen volumes planned; from jarchas to con-
     temporary writers.

734. Franco, Dolores, ed. España como preocupación.
     Rpt., 2d ed. Barcelona: Aryos Vergara, 1980
     (1960). 445 pp.
     Very good headnotes. Selections from essayists
     of the 17th to the 20th century. Living essayists
     are excluded.

735. García Mercadal, José, ed. Antología de humoristas
     españoles del siglo I al XX. 3d ed. Madrid: Agui-
     lar, 1964 (1956). 1,773 pp.
     Biographical introduction to each author.

736. Pattison, Walter T., and Donald W. Bleznick, eds.
     Representative Spanish Authors. 3d ed. New York:
     Oxford University Press, 1971 (1942). 2 vols.
     From the jarchas to the late 1950s. Critical and
     historical essays and headnotes on the various literary
     schools and many authors. Abundant footnotes and
     extensive vocabulary.

737. Romera-Navarro, Miguel, ed. Antología de la litera-
     tura española desde los orígenes hasta principios del
     siglo XIX. Boston: D. C. Heath & Co., 1933. xi,
     425 pp.
     Still useful. From the Cantar de Mio Cid to El
     sí de las niñas. Good notes and glossary.

Period

738. Díaz-Plaja, Fernando, ed. Antología del romanticismo
     español. 2d ed. New York: McGraw-Hill, 1968
     (1959). 252 pp.
     Selections chosen to illustrate the idea and major
     themes of romanticism.

739. Ford, Jeremiah D. M. Old Spanish Readings. Rpt.,
     2d ed. New York: Kraus Reprint, 1966 (1906). 312
     pp.
     Detailed analysis of some early Spanish writings.
     Etymological vocabulary.

740. Fotitch, Tatiana, ed. An Anthology of Old Spanish.
     Washington, D. C.: Catholic University of America
     Press, 1969. vii, 253 pp.
     From oldest documents to the 15th century. Texts
     for study of Vulgar Latin.

741. Gifford, D. J., and F. W. Hodcroft, eds. Textos
     lingüísticos del medioevo español. 2d ed. corrected.
     Oxford: Dolphin, 1966 (1959). 327 pp.
     Texts from different provinces of Spain. Vocabu-
     lary and glossary.

742. Greenfield, Sumner N., ed. La generación de 1898
     ante España: Antología de literatura de temas nacio-
     nales y universales. Lincoln, Neb.: Society of
     Spanish and Spanish-American Studies, 1981. 223
     pp.

Good variety of selections on the Spanish people,
history, and literature written by Azorín, Baroja,
Ganivet, Machado, Maeztu, Unamuno, and Valle-Inclán.
Contains a general introduction, biographies of authors included, ample notes, and a selective bibliography.

743. Kohler, Eugene, ed. Antología de la literatura es-
      pañola de la Edad Media (1140-1500). 2d ed. Re-
      vised and corrected. Paris: C. Klincksieck, 1970
      (1957). 420 pp.
         Contains glossary and preliminary notes to vari-
      ous sections.

744. Romero, Mariana, ed. Paisaje y literatura de España:
      Antología de los escritores del 98. Madrid: Tecnos,
      1957. 430 pp.
         Seven writers treating the Spanish landscape.

Genres

   --Prose

745. Arco, Juan del, ed. Novelistas españoles contempo-
      ráneos. Madrid: Aldecoa, 1944. 439 pp.
         Selections from works written between the years
      1893 and 1943. Major authors from Valle-Inclán to
      Cela. Biographical data and bibliographies.

746. Blecua, José Manuel, ed. Escritores costumbristas.
      9th ed. Madrid: Ebro, 1978. 145 pp.
         Selections by Larra, Mesonero Romanos, and Es-
      tébanez Calderón.

747. Bleznick, Donald W. , ed. El ensayo español del siglo
      veinte. New York: Ronald Press, 1964. 294 pp.
         From Unamuno to Julián Marías. Brief history
      of the Spanish essay from the 16th century and head-
      notes on each of ten essayists represented.

748. Buckley, Ramón, and John Crispin, eds. Los van-
      guardistas españoles (1925-1935). Madrid: Alianza
      Editorial, 1973. 438 pp.
         A wide range of views on vanguardism with an ap-
      pendix of bibliographic notes on 30 vanguardistas.

749. Buendía, Felicidad, ed. Antología de la novela histórica española (1834-1844). Madrid: Aguilar, 1963. 1,803 pp.
     Biobibliographical data are included.

750. Correa Calderón, E., ed. Costumbristas españoles. 2d ed. Madrid: Aguilar, 1964 (1950). 2 vols.
     An extensive collection with introduction.

751. Del Río, Angel, and M. J. Benardete, eds. El concepto contemporáneo de España. New York: Las Americas, 1962 (1946). 741 pp.
     Very good anthology and headnotes. Includes essays written between 1895 and 1931. The long introduction is a mine of information on the origins and development of the Spanish essay.

752. Díaz-Plaja, Guillermo, ed. El poema en prosa en España: Estudio crítico y antología. Barcelona: G. Gili, 1956. 404 pp.
     Lengthy introduction. Eighty-four authors from modernism to mid-20th century.

753. Entrambasaguas, Joaquín de, and María del Pilar Palomo, eds. Las mejores novelas contemporáneas. 3d ed. Barcelona: Planeta, 1971 (1957). 9 vols.
     Five novels in each volume. Covers the years 1895-1939. Bibliographies of novels and authors as well as general bibliographies.

754. García Pavón, Francisco, ed. Antología de cuentistas españoles contemporáneos (1939-1966). 3d ed. Madrid: Gredos, 1976 (1959). 478 pp.
     Some 50 authors are represented. Biobibliographic headnotes.

755. Herrero García, Miguel, ed. Cuentos de los siglos XVI y XVII. Madrid: Instituto-Escuela Junta para Ampliación de Estudios, 1926. 285 pp.
     Twenty-two cuentistas from Guevara to Francisco Santos.

756. Maeztu, María de, ed. Antología siglo XX: Prosistas españoles; semblanzas y comentarios. 7th ed. Madrid: Espasa-Calpe, 1969 (1943). 248 pp.
     First half contains essays dealing with the Quijote. Good anthology and cogent semblanzas.

757. Menéndez Pidal, Ramón, ed. Antología de prosistas
      españoles. 9th ed. Madrid: Espasa-Calpe, 1969
      (1899). 261 pp.
          Biographical notes and comments on works. From
      Alfonso "el Sabio" to the beginning of the 19th cen-
      tury.

758. Sáinz de Robles, Federico, ed. La novela corta es-
      pañola: Promoción de "El cuento semanal" (1901-
      1920). Madrid: Aguilar, 1959. 1,804 pp.
          Introduction treats the novel of the early 20th cen-
      tury. Brief sketch of each author.

759. Valbuena Prat, Angel, ed. La novela picaresca es-
      pañola. 7th ed. Madrid: Aguilar, 1974 (1943). 2
      vols.
          Lengthy study of picaresque novel and texts of
      many important picaresque novels. Useful indexes.

--Theater

760. Alpern, Hymen, José Martel, and Leonard Mades, eds.
      Diez comedias del Siglo de Oro. 2d ed. New York:
      Harper & Row, 1968 (1939). xxx, 865 pp.
          Many helpful features such as bibliographies, met-
      rical schemes, and extensive notes.

761. Brett, Lewis E., ed. Nineteenth-Century Spanish Plays.
      New York: Appleton-Century, 1963 (1935). ix, 889
      pp.
          Fifteen plays by as many playwrights from Moratín
      to Benavente.

762. Díaz-Plaja, Fernando, ed. Teatro español de hoy:
      Antología (1939-1966). 2d ed. Madrid: Alfil, 1967
      (1958). 414 pp.
          Some 15 writers are represented.

763. González Ruiz, Nicolás, ed. Piezas maestras del te-
      atro teológico español. 3d ed. Madrid: Editorial
      Católica, 1968 (1958). 2 vols.
          Autos sacramentales and comedias written primar-
      ily by major figures of the Golden Age. Vol. 1 Autos
      sacramentales. Vol. 2 Comedias.

764. Lázaro Carreter, Fernando, ed. Teatro medieval. 4th
      ed. Madrid: Editorial Castalia, 1976 (1958). 285
      pp.

Contains a good introduction to the medieval theater.

765. Sáinz de Robles, Federico, ed. Teatro español. Ma-
      drid: Aguilar, 1951- . Published annually.
      Selection of the five best plays of each theatrical
      season since 1949-50. Includes comments by critics
      and authors.

766. _____. El teatro español: Historia y antología
      desde el siglo XIV al XIX. Madrid: Aguilar, 1942-
      43. 7 vols.
      Also contains studies of periods and authors as
      well as notes and bibliographies.

767. Valencia, Antonio, ed. El género chico: Antología
      de textos completos. Madrid: Taurus, 1962. 619
      pp.
      Fifteen plays of the 19th century.

      --Poetry

768. Alonso, Dámaso, ed. Poesia de la Edad Media y poesía
      de tipo tradicional. 2d ed. Buenos Aires: Losada,
      1942 (1935). 558 pp.
      From the Cid to 1550.

769. _____, and José Manuel Blecua, eds. Antología de
      la poesía española: Lírica de tipo tradicional. 2d
      print, 2d ed. Madrid: Gredos, 1975 (1956). lxxxvi,
      265 pp.
      Basic sholarly anthology of traditional poetry.
      Good introduction and notes.

770. Altolaguirre, Manuel, ed. Antología de la poesía ro-
      mántica española. Buenos Aires: Espasa-Calpe Ar-
      gentina, 1965 (1954). 208 pp.
      Twenty-one poets from Arjona to Rosalía de Cas-
      tro. Brief biographies.

771. Barnstone, Willis, ed. Spanish Poetry: From Its Be-
      ginnings Through the Nineteenth Century. New York:
      Oxford University Press, 1970. xxi, 526 pp.
      Introduction, headnotes, notes, and bibliography.
      Many poets are well represented.

772. Blecua, José M., ed. Floresta de lírica española. 3d
      ed. Madrid: Gredos, 1972 (1957). 2 vols.

Volume 1 extends from jarchas to San Juan, and
volume 2 from the 18th century to Miguel Hernández
and José Luis Hidalgo.

773. Buchanan, Milton A., ed. Spanish Poetry of the Golden
Age. Rpt., Toronto: University of Toronto Press,
1970 (1942). 149 pp.
Notes to each selection. Covers years 1500-1700.

774. Cano, José Luis, ed. Antología de la nueva poesía
española. 4th ed. Madrid: Gredos, 1978 (1958).
438 pp.
An extensive collection from Miguel Hernández to
the latest poets, with biobibliographic information on
each.

775. Correa, Gustavo, ed. Antología de la poesía española
(1900-1980). Madrid: Gredos, 1980. 2 vols. Expanded version of Poesía española del siglo veinte
(New York, 1972).
Contains a useful introduction to Spanish poetry
from end of last century to 1936 (Vol. I) and 1936 to
present (Vol. II). The first volume includes poems,
biographical sketches, lists of published works and
bibliography of critical materials for 17 writers and
the second tome does the same for 38 poets.

776. Cossío, José María de, ed. Los toros en la poesía
castellana. Madrid: Compañía Ibero-Americana de
Publicaciones, 1931. 2 vols.
Study and anthology from the Middle Ages to the
20th century.

777. Crow, John A., comp. and ed. An Anthology of Spanish Poetry: From the Beginnings to the Present Day,
Including Both Spain and Spanish America. Baton
Rouge: Louisiana State University Press, 1979.
xxxi, 220 pp.
Bilingual collection from the medieval period to
the present for the general English-reading public.

778. Cueto, Leopoldo Augusto de, ed. Poetas líricos del
siglo XVIII. Vols. 61, 63, 67 of Biblioteca de autores españoles. Madrid: Atlas, 1952. 3 vols.
Still the only useful and complete source of poetic
texts for the 18th century.

779. Cummins, John G., ed. The Spanish Traditional Lyric.
Oxford: Pergamon Press, 1977. 178 pp.
Part I is an anthology of traditional poetry from
the 11th century to the present. There are 241 texts
grouped by theme. Part II is a brief anthology of the
recreation of this type of poetry from the 11th century to Alberti.

780. Diego, Gerardo, ed. Poesía española contemporánea,
1901-1934. 4th ed. Madrid: Taurus Ediciones,
1979 (1932). 673 pp.
An influential anthology that represents some 30
poets.

781. Fitzmaurice-Kelly, James, and J. B. Trend, eds.
The Oxford Book of Spanish Verse. 2d ed. Ox-
ford: Clarendon Press, 1969 (1913). xl, 522 pp.
Poetry from the 13th to the 20th century.

782. Foulché-Delbosc, Raymond, ed. Cancionero castellano
del siglo XV. Vols. 19 and 22 of Nueva biblioteca
de autores españoles. Madrid: Casa Editorial Bailly-
Baillière, 1912-15. 2 vols.
Very informative introduction to each author.

783. Gullón, Germán, ed. Poesía de la vanguardia española.
Madrid: Taurus Ediciones, 1981. 383 pp.
Includes an introduction to "Ultraísmo creacionismo
y surrealismo" in addition to a good selection of poems by the poets who represent these "isms." Brief
biographies are provided for each poet and there is
a short bibliography.

784. Landínez, Luis, ed. Antología de la poesía española
en la Edad Media (castellana, catalana y gallega).
Barcelona: Iberia, 1948. 178 pp.
Notes include bibliography.

785. Marín, Diego, ed. Poesía española: Siglos XV al XX.
Chapel Hill, N.C.: Estudios de Hispanófila, 1971.
537 pp. Revised and enlarged edition of Lira es-
pañola (Toronto: Ryerson Press, 1954).
Good selection. Introduction, extensive notes (in
English), and vocabulary.

786. Menéndez Pelayo, Marcelino, ed. Antología de poetas

líricos castellanos desde la formación del idioma
hasta nuestros días. Madrid: Viuda de Hernandó,
1890-1916. 14 vols.

787. Menéndez Pidal, Ramón, ed. Flor nueva de romances
viejos. 4th ed. Madrid: Espasa-Calpe, 1980 (1928).
246 pp.
Romances on a variety of subjects by the foremost
authority in the field.

788. _____. Reliquias de la poesía épica española. Madrid: Espasa-Calpe, 1973 (1951). lxxviii, 293 pp.
Very informative introduction on various aspects
of the medieval epic.

789. _____, and María Goyri, eds. Romancero tradicional de las lenguas hispánicas (español-portugués-
catalán-sefardí). Madrid: Gredos, 1957. 2 vols.
The romancero and its relationship to Moorish-
Christian legends.

790. Peers, E. Allison, ed. A Critical Anthology of Spanish
Verse. Rpt., New York: Greenwood Press, 1968
(1949). 1, 741 pp.
Useful for its analyses of many poems by Spain's
finest poets.

791. Perry, Janet, ed. The Heath Anthology of Spanish Poetry. Boston: D. C. Heath & Co., 1953. 468 pp.
Good introduction on meter in Spanish poetry.

792. Rivers, Elias, ed. Renaissance and Baroque Poetry
of Spain. Reprint. New York: Charles Scribner's
Sons, 1973 (1966). 351 pp.
Nearly 200 poems from the works of 25 poets together with prose translations.

793. Rubio, Fanny, and José Luis Falcó, eds. Poesía española contemporánea (1939-1980). Madrid: Alhambra, 1981. 423 pp.
Contains an introductory study of the period covered (pp. 7-94). Broad coverage. Also includes
notes, short biobibliographic sketches of the poets
anthologized, and a bibliography.

794. Terry, Arthur, ed. An Anthology of Spanish Poetry,
1500-1700. Oxford; New York: Pergamon Press,
1965-68. 2 vols.

Introduction, headnotes, and many footnotes expli-
cating the poetry covered.

SPANISH AMERICA

General

795. Anderson-Imbert, Enrique, and Eugenio Florit, eds.
     Literatura hispanoamericana: Antología e introduc-
     ción histórica. 2d ed. New York: Holt, Rinehart
     & Winston, 1970 (1960). 2 vols.
     Works of all epochs with introductory comments.

796. Antología poética hispanoamericana. Buenos Aires:
     Fondo Editorial Bonaerense, 1978. 583 pp.
     Includes 190 contemporary poets of Spanish Amer-
     ica and Spain.

797. Caillet-Bois, Jules, comp. Antología de la poesía his-
     panoamericana. 3d ed. Madrid: Aguilar, 1978
     (1958). 2,092 pp.
     A good, comprehensive collection.

798. Caracciolo-Trejo, Enrique, ed. The Penguin Book of
     Latin American Verse. Harmondsworth and Balti-
     more: Penguin Books, 1971. xlv, 425 pp.
     Includes the best 19th- and 20th-century poets of
     practically every Latin American country. Contains
     English prose translations of every poem, an intro-
     duction, very brief biobibliographic notes, and an ex-
     planatory guide to movements in Latin American po-
     etry.

799. Castillo, Homero, ed. Antología de poetas modernistas
     hispanoamericanos. Englewood Cliffs, N.J.: Prentice-
     Hall, 1972. 505 pp.
     Contains brief introduction; bibliographies; vocabu-
     lary; and glossary of terms, places, historical and
     mythological characters, and so forth.

     Craig. Modernist Trend in Spanish-American Poetry.
     See no. 715.

800. Dauster, Frank; Leon Lyday; and George Woodyard, eds.
     Dramaturgos hispanoamericanos: Antología del teatro

hispanoamericano del siglo XX. Ottawa: GIROL
Books, 1979. 3 vols.
Each play with a brief critical introduction and a
bibliography on each individual author. Plays include
the following: Vol. I, Usigli, Corona de sombra;
Triana, La noche de los asesinos; Dragún, El ama-
sijo. Vol. 2, Villaurrutia, Invitación a la muerte;
Gambaro, Los siameses; Wolff, Flores de papel.
Vol. 3, Marqués, Los soles truncos; Díaz, El ce-
pillo de dientes; Carballido, Yo también hablo de la
rosa.

801. Englekirk, John; Irving Leonard; John Reid; and John
      Crow, eds. An Anthology of Spanish American Lit-
      erature. 3d ed. New York: Appleton-Century-
      Crofts, 1968 (1946). xiv, 772 pp.
      From Hernán Cortés to the present day. Very
      few excerpts from novels and plays. This is a com-
      panion volume to An Outline History of Spanish Amer-
      ican Literature (see no. 498).

802. Flores, Angel, ed. The Literature of Spanish Ame-
      rica: A Critical Anthology. New York: Las Amer-
      icas, 1966-67. 4 vols.
      From the colonial period to the 1960s. Texts in
      Spanish; notes and bibliography in English.

803. _____, ed. Narrativa hispanoamericana 1816-1981:
      Historia y antología. México: Siglo XXI, 1981-82.
      4 vols. Vol. 4: La generación de 1940-1969.
      Introductions to periods and authors, bibliography,
      and a large compilation of prose fiction works.

804. Florit, Eugenio, and José Olivio Jiménez, eds. La
      poesía hispanoamericana desde el modernismo. New
      York: Appleton-Century-Crofts, 1968. xvi, 482 pp.
      Selections of poetry from 72 different poets ar-
      ranged in five major sections: modernism, post-
      modernism, vanguardism, postvanguardism, and re-
      cent tendencies. Biographical sketches of each au-
      thor and selected critical bibliography.

805. García Prada, Carlos, ed. Poetas modernistas his-
      panoamericanos. 2d ed. Madrid: Cultura Hispánica,
      1968 (1956). 422 pp.
      Introductory study, critical and bibliographic notes,
      and selections from 15 poets.

806. Gómez-Gil, Orlando, ed.   Literatura hispanoamericana:
      Antología crítica.   New York: Holt, Rinehart & Win-
      ston, 1972. 2 vols.
          From pre-Hispanic period to present.   All genres
      represented except the novel.

807. Jiménez, José Olivio, ed.   Antología de la poesía his-
      panoamericana contemporánea, 1914-1970.   Madrid:
      Alianza Editorial, 1978. 511 pp.
          Numerous selections taken from 37 well-known
      poets.

808. _____, and Antonio R. de la Campa, eds.   Antología
      crítica de la prosa modernista hispanoamericana.
      New York: Eliseo Torres and Sons, 1976. 399 pp.
          There is a 32-page introduction to this four-part
      book: "El ensayo, " "La crónica y el artículo de
      viaje, " "El cuento, " and "El poema en prosa y la
      prosa poetica. "

809. Jones, Willis Knapp, ed.   Antología del teatro hispano-
      americano.   México: Ediciones de Andrea, 1958.
      254 pp.
          Modern dramatists as well as Sor Juana Inés de
      la Cruz.

810. Latcham, Ricardo, ed.   Antología del cuento hispano-
      americano contemporáneo, 1910-1956.   2d ed.   San-
      tiago de Chile: Zig-Zag, 1962 (1958).   450 pp.
          Sixty-six authors of every Spanish American coun-
      try are included.

811. Leal, Luis, and Frank Dauster, eds.   Literatura de
      Hispanoamérica.   New York: Harcourt, Brace &
      World, 1970. 560 pp.
          From pre-Columbian literature to the contempo-
      rary period.   Includes complete works of all genres
      except the novel.   Introduction, bibliographic infor-
      mation on authors, and notes.

812. Luzuriaga, Gerardo, and Richard Reeve, eds.   Los
      clásicos del teatro hispanoamericano.   México:
      Fondo de Cultura Económica, 1975.   908 pp.
          From colonial theater to the contemporary period.
      Reeve provides a brief introduction for the period to
      1900 and Luzuriaga for the 20th century.   Selected
      bibliography for each of dramatists included.

813. Mejía Sánchez, Ernesto, and Pedro Guillén, eds. El
      ensayo actual latinoamericano. México: Ediciones
      de Andrea, 1971. 288 pp.
           Contemporary essayists from 21 countries, in-
      cluding such authors as Arciniegas, Mañach, Aré-
      valo, Pedro Henríquez Ureña, Zum Felde, and Picón
      Salas.

814. Menéndez y Pelayo, Marcelino, ed. Antología de po-
      etas hispanoamericanos. 2d ed. Madrid: Real
      Academia Española, 1927-28 (1893-95). 4 vols.
      Lengthy introductory study. Includes writers
      from the colonial period to the late 19th century.

815. Menton, Seymour, ed. El cuento hispanoamericano:
      Antología crítico-histórica. 3d ed. México: Fondo
      de Cultura Económica, 1970 (1964), 2 vols. English
      version: The Spanish American Short Story. Berke-
      ley and Los Angeles: University of California Press,
      1980. 496 pp.
           Includes the best short-story writers from roman-
      ticism to the "boom" decade (1960-70). Studies on
      each story and bibliography on the short story (gen-
      eral and by countries).

816. Reyes Nevárez, Salvador, ed. Novelas selectas de
      Hispano-América, siglo XIX. México: Labor Me-
      xicana, 1959. 2 vols.
           Thirteen novels from various countries.

817. Ripoll, Carlos, ed. Conciencia intelectual de América:
      Antología del ensayo hispanoamericano. 3d ed. New
      York: E. Torres & Sons, 1974 (1966). 459 pp.
           General introduction, headnotes, and bibliography
      for each of the essayists included.

818. Rodríguez Sardiñas, Orlando, and Carlos Miguel Suárez
      Radillo, eds. Teatro contemporáneo hispanoameri-
      cano. Madrid: Escelicer, 1971. 2 vols.
           Country-by-country anthology containing mostly so-
      cial drama.

819. Silva Castro, Raúl, ed. Antología crítica del moder-
      nismo hispanoamericano. New York: Las Americas,
      1963. 376 pp.
           Selections from 43 modernista poets, who include
      such precursors as Rubén Darío. One critical bio-
      graphical paragraph for each writer represented.

820. Skirius, John. El ensayo hispanoamericano. México:
      Fondo de Cultura Económica, 1981. 407 pp.
          Wide selection of historical, sociopolitical and lit-
      erary essays from González Prada to Carlos Monsi-
      váis. Introductory essay, bibliography, and one-page
      biobibliography summary for each author.

821. Solórzano, Carlos, ed. El teatro actual latinoameri-
      cano. México: Ediciones de Andrea, 1972. 338 pp.
          Eight plays by as many playwrights. Some of the
      dramatists represented are Carlos Gorostiza (Argen-
      tina), Enrique Buenaventura (Colombia), Isidora
      Aguirre (Chile), and Demetrio Aguilera Malta (Ecua-
      dor).

822. _____. El teatro hispanoamericano contemporáneo.
      México: Fondo de Cultura Económica, 1976 (1964).
      2 vols.
          Plays by 14 dramatists from as many countries.
      Solórzano, Benedetti, Salazar Bondy, Marqués, and
      Aguilera Malta are among those included.

823. Stimson, Frederick S., and Ricardo Navas-Ruiz, eds.
      Literatura de la América hispánica: Antología e
      historia. I. La época colonial (1492-1825) (1971);
      II. El siglo diecinueve (1825-1910) (1971); III. La
      época contemporánea (1975). New York: Dodd,
      Mead, 1971-75. 3 vols.
          All volumes contain extensive introductory mate-
      rial written in Spanish. Only some 70 authors are
      included. The short story is almost totally excluded
      from volume 3. This anthology is primarily intended
      for undergraduates.

824. Verdevoye, Paul, editor. Antología de la narrativa
      hispanoamericana, 1940-1970. Madrid: Gredos,
      1979. 2 vols.
          Contains a 25-page introduction. Some of the au-
      thors represented are Borges, Asturias, Carpentier,
      Onetti, Cortázar, García Marquez, Vargas Llosa,
      Rulfo, and Fuentes.

825. Wieser, Nora Jacquez, ed. Open to the Sun: A Bilin-
      gual Anthology of Latin-American Women Poets. 3d
      printing. Van Nuys, Calif.: Perivale Press, 1982
      (1979). 279 pp.
          Twenty-five women poets of this century are an-
      thologized, with translations in English. There are

brief biobibliographic sketches for each poet and a
relatively short bibliography of studies on Spanish
American poetry and some critical studies on the
poets included.

826. Zanetti, Susana, ed. Costumbristas de América Latina:
Antología. Buenos Aires: Centro Editor de América
Latina, 1973. 162 pp.
A collection of articles by 19th-century costum-
bristas, many of whom are little known.

827. Zapata, Celia Correas de, and Lydia Johnson, eds.
Detrás de la reja. Caracas: Monte Avila, 1980.
400 pp.
Twenty-three short stories by Latin American
women from Carmen Lyra (1888) to Ana María Simó
(1944). Arranged thematically according to the different ages of the female protagonists.

National

--Argentina

828. Berenguer Carisomo, Arturo, ed. Antología argentina
contemporánea. 2d ed. Buenos Aires: Huemul,
1973 (1970). 417 pp.
Verse and prose of three literary movements of
this century: postmodernista, generation of 1922
(vanguardistas), and generation of 1940. Introduction, biobibliographic notes, textual commentaries,
and glossary.

829. _____. Teatro argentino contemporáneo. 2d ed.
Madrid: Aguilar, 1962. 475 pp.
Contains introductory study and notes on the dram-
atists and their works. Samuel Eichelbaum and Nalé
Roxlo are among the seven playwrights included.

830. Crogliano, María Eugenia, ed. Antología de la poesía
argentina: Siglos XIX y XX. Buenos Aires: Editorial Kapelusz, 1975. 181 pp.
Also includes a succinct introduction to Argentine
poetry.

831. Fernández Moreno, César, and Horacio Jorge Becco,
eds. Antología lineal de la poesía argentina. Madrid: Gredos, 1968. 384 pp.

From the colonial to the contemporary period.
Bibliography.

832. Ghiano, Juan, ed. Poesía argentina del siglo XX.
México: Fondo de Cultura Económica, 1957. 285
pp.
Ninety-three poets are represented.

833. Henríquez Ureña, Pedro, and Jorge Luis Borges, eds.
Antología clásica de la literatura argentina. Buenos
Aires: A. Kapelusz, 1937. 445 pp.
Thirty-six authors from the 16th century to the
20th. Each selection is preceded by a biobiblio-
graphic sketch.

834. Martini Real, Juan Carlos. Los mejores poemas de
la poesía argentina. 3d ed. Buenos Aires: Ediciones Corregidor, 1977. 384 pp.
Good variety of poetry from 19th century to the
contemporary period.

835. Mastrángelo, Carlos. 25 cuentos argentinos magistrales
(Historia y evolución comentada del cuento argentino).
Buenos Aires: Editorial Plus Ultra, 1975. 334 pp.
Critical history of the Argentine short story as
well as anthology.

836. Ordaz, Luis, ed. Breve historia del teatro argentino.
Buenos Aires: Editorial Universitaria de Buenos
Aires, 1962-66. 8 vols.
Selections from more than 20 playwrights of the
19th and 20th centuries. Introductions to the theater
of each period.

837. Sarlo, Beatriz, ed. El cuento argentino contemporáneo.
Buenos Aires: Centro Editor de América Latina, 1976.
154 pp.
An anthology of selections by 12 major Argentine
writers: Borges, Cortázar, Ocampo, Moyano, and
Conti, among others.

838. Yahni, Roberto, ed. 70 años de narrativa argentina:
1900-1970. Madrid: Alianza Editorial, 1970. 212
pp.
Lugones, Güiraldes, Quiroga, Martínez Estrada,
Borges, Mallea, and Cortázar are among the 18 authors included. Contains a brief introduction and biobibliographic notes.

--Bolivia

839. Baptista Gumucio, Mariano, ed. Narradores bolivia-
      nos. Caracas: Monte Avila, 1969. 256 pp.
      Fourteen authors are included, most of whom
      started to publish around 1950.

840. Bedregal, Yolando, ed. Poesía de Bolivia: De la
      época precolombina al modernismo. 2d ed. Buenos
      Aires: Editorial Universitaria, 1969. 119 pp.
      General introduction. Most selections are from
      19th-century poets. Brief biographical notes.

841. Díaz Machicao, Porfirio, ed. Prosa y verso de Bo-
      livia. La Paz: Los Amigos del Libro, 1966-68.
      4 vols.
      Most of the writers are of the 20th century. In-
      cludes brief biobibliographic sketches for all authors
      represented.

842. Quirós, Juan, ed. Indice de la poesía boliviana con-
      temporánea. La Paz: Juventud, 1964. 440 pp.
      An extensive collection of Bolivian poets with con-
      cise biobibliographic and critical comments for each
      writer.

843. Soriano Badani, Armando, ed. El cuento boliviano.
      La Paz: Universidad Mayor de San Andrés, 1969.
      397 pp. Previous volume with same title published
      at Buenos Aires: Editorial Universitaria, 1964.
      160 pp.
      Each volume covers the years 1938 to 1967 and
      1900 to 1937 respectively. General introductions
      and brief biographical notes.

844. Viscarra Fabre, Guillermo, ed. Poetas nuevos de
      Bolivia. La Paz: Ministerio de Relaciones Exte-
      riores, 1941. 286 pp.
      Biographies and works of 25 poets.

--Central America

845. Ramírez, Sergio. Antología del cuento centroameri-
      cano. San José: EDUCA. 1973. 2 vols., 684,
      531 pp.
      Very complete selection from all six countries in-
      cluding those born in the early 1940s. Biobiblio-

graphical notes, chronological table, bibliography and chronological, national and thematic indices. A fifty-page introduction.

--Chile

846. Bunster, César; Julio Durán Cerda; Pedro Lastra; and Benjamín Rojas Piña, eds. Antología del cuento chileno. 2d ed. Santiago: Editorial Universitaria, Instituto de Literatura Chilena, 1965 (1963). 631 pp. Extensive anthology of 19th- and 20th-century Chilean short fiction. Biobibliographic data for each author.

847. Dölz Blackburn, Inés, comp. Antología crítica de la poesía tradicional chilena. México: Instituto Panamericano de Geografía e Historia, 1979. 240 pp. Includes traditional Chilean poetry from its beginnings to the 1970s. Besides many critical notes there is an extensive bibliography.

848. Durán Cerda, Julio, ed. Panorama del teatro chileno, 1842-1959. Santiago: Editorial del Pacífico, 1959. 371 pp. Contains introductory study to and bibliography of the Chilean theater.

849. Lafourcade, Enrique. Antología del cuento chileno. Barcelona: Ediciones Acervo, 1969. 3 vols. 1,260 pp. Ample selection but excessively brief biobibliographical notes at end of Vol. III. Thirty-page history of Chilean short story in Vol. I.

850. Montes, Hugo, and Julio Orlandi, eds. Historia y antología de la literatura chilena. 8th ed. Santiago: Editorial Zig-Zag, 1969 (1955). 573 pp. 1955 ed. published under title: Historia de la literatura chilena. Manual of Chilean literature from Valdivia's letters to Neruda. The second part, divided by generations, is devoted to fiction, the third to poetry, the fourth to criticism and the essay, and the fifth to theater.

851. Scarpa Roque, Esteban, and Hugo Montes, eds. Antología de la poesía chilena contemporánea. Madrid: Gredos, 1968. 372 pp.

Poetry since 1920 of 26 poets. Brief biobibliography for each author.

852. Silva Castro, Raúl, ed. Antología general de la poesía chilena. Santiago: Zig-Zag, 1959. 433 pp.
The best-known poems of all Chilean poets who were dead at the time of publication. Brief biobibliography for each poet.

853. Teatro chileno contemporáneo. Madrid: Aguilar, 1970. 498 pp.
Egon Wolff, Luis Alberto Heiremans, and Sergio Vodanovic are among the six dramatists represented.

854. Yáñez, María Flora, ed. Antología del cuento chileno moderno. 2d ed. Santiago: Editorial del Pacífico, 1965 (1958). 317 pp.
Chilean short fiction since 1938.

--Colombia

855. Arango, Daniel, ed. Las mejores poesías colombianas. Bogotá: Compañía Grancolombiana de Ediciones, 1959. 163 pp.
Twenty-seven poets from the time of the conquest to the middle of the 20th century. Rafael Pombo, José Asunción Silva, Guillermo Valencia, Eduardo Castillo, Porfirio Barba-Jacob, and Luis Carlos López are among the best represented. Andrés Holguín provides a brief introduction to Colombian literature.

856. Arbeláez, Fernando, ed. Panorama de la nueva poesía colombiana. Bogotá: Ministerio de Educación, Imprenta Nacional, 1964. 548 pp.
Chronological arrangement of poets. Lacks biobibliographic data.

857. Cobo Borda, Juan Gustavo, ed. Album de la nueva poesía colombiana. Caracas: Fundarte, 1981.
Anthology of 37 contemporary Colombian poets.

858. _____, ed. Obra en marcha 1: La nueva literatura colombiana. Bogotá: Instituto Colombiano de Literatura, 1975. 319 pp.
Thirty young writers (under age 40) are represented from all literary genres. Bibliographic notes on authors.

859. Collazos, Oscar, ed. Diez narradores colombianos.
      Barcelona: Bruguera, 1977. 186 pp.
      A useful collection, chronologically arranged, of
      mainly living authors. Includes a brief introduction
      by the editor and a biobibliographical sketch of each
      author.

860. Echeverría Mejía, Oscar, and Alfonso Bonella-Narr,
      eds. Veintiún años de poesía colombiana (1942-
      1963). Bogotá: Stella, 1964. 404 pp.
      Selections from 131 poets.

861. Holguín, Andrés, ed. Los mejores cuentos colombia-
      nos. Bogotá: Compañía Grancolombiana de Edi-
      ciones, 1959. 108 pp.
      Twelve short stories by as many writers from
      Jesús del Corral to Eduardo Caballero Calderón.
      No introduction or bibliography.

862. López Narváez, Carlos, ed. Poemas de Colombia.
      Medellín: Bedout, 1959. 623 pp.
      An extensive anthology sponsored by the Colom-
      bian Academy. Prologue and epilogue by Félix Res-
      trepo.

863. Luque Muñoz, Henry, ed. Narradores colombianos del
      siglo XIX. Bogotá: Instituto Colombiano de Cultura,
      1976. 643 pp.
      A large anthology of representative Colombian
      prose writers from the last century, most of whom
      are little known but worth knowing. Good, short
      prologue provides essential background information.
      Short bibliography.

864. Pacheco Quintero, Jorge, ed. Antología de la poesía
      en Colombia. Bogotá: Instituto Caro y Cuervo,
      1970. 2 vols.
      Poetry arranged chronologically. Short biographi-
      cal sketches and notes. Vol. 1 covers colonial peri-
      od and also "períodos renacentista y barroco"; Vol.
      2 covers neoclassicism and "romances tradicionales."

865. Pachón Padilla, Eduardo. Antología del cuento colom-
      biano. Bogotá: Plaza y Janés, 1980. 2 vols. 359
      and 334 pp.
      An expanded version of the author's 1959 and 1973-
      74 anthologies. The introductory comments on each
      author include critical judgments.

--Costa Rica

866. Bonilla, Abelardo, ed. Historia y antología de la li-
      teratura costarricense. San José: Trejes, 1957-61.
      2 vols.
      Extensive treatment from colonial era to the 1950s.
      Lacks bibliography.

867. Chase, Alfonso. Narrativa contemporánea de Costa
      Rica. San José: Ministerio de Cultura, 1975. 2
      vols. 467 and 521 pp.
      Generously large selections for each author from
      Max Jiménez (1900-1947) to Edgar R. Trigueros
      (1951). More than half of the anthology devoted to
      writers who began publishing in the 1960s. Intro-
      ductory essay of over 100 pages relating the devel-
      opment of prose fiction to national history.

868. Ferrero, Luis, ed. Ensayistas costarricenses. 2d
      ed. San José: Librería Antonio Lehmann, 1972
      (1971). 428 pp.
      History and anthology of the Costa Rican essay.
      Also contains a bibliography of individual essayists.

869. Menton, Seymour, ed. El cuento costarricense. Mé-
      xico: Ediciones de Andrea; Lawrence: University of
      Kansas Press, 1964. 184 pp.
      Only comprehensive presentation of the Costa Rican
      short story. Includes critical study, lengthy bibli-
      ography, and anthology of 24 short stories by 22 au-
      thors.

870. Sotela, Rogelio, ed. Escritores de Costa Rica. San
      José: Imprenta Lehmann, 1942. 885 pp.
      Brief selections of many authors from the colonial
      period to the 20th century.

--Cuba

871. Bueno, Salvador, ed. Antología del cuento en Cuba
      (1902-1952). La Habana: Ediciones de Cincuente-
      nario, Dirección de Cultura del Ministerio de Edu-
      cación, 1953. 339 pp.
      Short stories by 42 writers, with brief biographies.

872. _____, ed. and comp. Cuentos cubanos del siglo
      XX: Antología. La Habana: Editorial Arte y Li-
      teratura, 1975. 490 pp.

Recognized and less known authors included. Lino
Novás Calvo and Cabrera Infante are not included.

873. Caballero Bonald, José Manuel, ed. Narrativa cubana
de la revolución. Madrid: 3d ed. Alianza Editorial,
1971 (1968). 258 pp.
Twenty-four representative contemporary writers
from Carpentier to Arenas. Biobibliographic data
on each author.

874. Desnoes, Edmundo. Los dispositivos en la flor: Cuba,
literatura desde la revolución. Hanover, N. H.: Ediciones del Norte, 1981. 557 pp.
The most extensive anthology of Cuban literature
since 1959. Includes short stories, chapters from
novels, poetry, and selections from the speeches and
writings of Fidel Castro, Che Guevara, Celia Sánchez, and Haydée Santamaría. Selections from de-
fectors also included: Cabrera Infante, Casey, Be-
nítez Rojo, Padilla, etc.

875. Fornet, Ambrosio, ed. Antología del cuento cubano
contemporáneo. 4th ed. México: Ediciones Era,
1979 (1967). 241 pp.
Jesus Castellanos, Cabrera Infante, and Humberto
Arenal are among the authors represented. Introduction and comments on each author are included.

876. García Vega, Lorenzo, ed. Antología de la novela cubana. La Habana: Ministerio de Educación, 1960.
508 pp.
Selections of 10 to 50 pages from 22 Cuban novelists, beginning with Cirilo Villaverde and extending
through Alejo Carpentier to four younger authors,
for example, Lezama Lima. Biographical data and
some critical comments.

877. Lezama Lima, José, ed. Antología de la poesía cubana. La Habana: Consejo Nacional de Cultura,
1965. 3 vols.
Copious anthology of Cuban poetry from its beginnings to the late 19th century. Introduction, commentaries, and bibliographies.

878. Martíde Cid, Dolores, ed. Teatro cubano contemporáneo. 2d ed. Madrid: Aguilar, 1962. 448 pp.
Six plays. Also contains an essay on the Cuban
theater before Castro by José Cid Pérez.

--Dominican Republic

879. Alcántara Almanzar, José, ed. <u>Antología de la litera-</u>
      <u>tura dominicana</u>. Santo Domingo: Editorial Cultural
      Dominicana, 1972. 439 pp.
      Selections from poetry and prose.

880. Cartegena, Aída, ed. <u>Narradores dominicanos</u>. Cara-
      cas: Monte Avila, 1969. 153 pp.
      Includes 11 authors, of whom nine belong to the
      post-Trujillo era.

881. Fernández Spencer, Antonio, ed. <u>Nueva poesía domini-</u>
      <u>cana</u>. Madrid: Cultura Hispánica, 1953. 344 pp.
      Large number of compositions by nine poets who
      represent the period 1916-47.

--Ecuador

882. Calderón Chico, Carlos, ed. <u>Nuevos cuentistas del</u>
      <u>Ecuador</u>. Prólogo de Hugo Salazar Tamariz. Gua-
      yaquil: Casa de la Cultura Ecuatoriana, 1975. 133
      pp.
      Fourteen writers included with biobibliographic
      notes.

883. Carrión, Benjamín, ed. <u>El nuevo relato ecuatoriano</u>.
      2d ed. Quito: Casa de la Cultura Ecuatoriana, 1958
      (1950-51). 1,124 pp.
      Extensive collection of Ecuadorian prose fiction
      with a long but interesting personal criticism by the
      editor which includes comparisons with other notable
      American and European literary figures.

884. Medina Cifuentes, Enrique, ed. <u>Poetas del Ecuador</u>.
      Quito: Ediciones Medina, 1966. 197 pp.
      One hundred poets are represented in alphabetical
      order, with no information given on them.

885. Pesantez Rodas, Rodrigo, ed. <u>La nueva literatura</u>
      <u>ecuatoriana</u>. Vol. 1, <u>Poesía</u>. Guayaquil: Univer-
      sidad de Guayaquil, 1966. 219 pp.
      Contemporary poets of Ecuador. Apparently first
      of a series of anthologies which will cover all gen-
      res. Brief biographies of each poet.

886. Rodríguez Castelo, Hernán. <u>Cuento ecuatoriano con-</u>

temporáneo. Guayaquil-Quito, "Ariel," n.d. [c. 1970].
2 vols., 156 and 163 pp.
Selections from authors born between 1920 and
1950. Relatively long biobibliographical notes and a
ten-page introductory survey.

--El Salvador

887. Barba Salinas, Manuel, ed. Antología del cuento sal-
vadoreño (1880-1955). 2d ed. San Salvador: Ministerio de Educación, 1976 (1959). 383 pp.
Twenty-eight authors are represented, with brief
biographical notes on each.

888. Cea, José Roberto, ed. Antología general de la poesía
salvadoreña. San Salvador: Editorial Universitaria,
1971. 482 pp.
Chronological arrangement, beginning with Francisco Gavidia. Concise general introduction and basic biobibliographies.

--Guatemala

889. Echeverría, B., and R. Amílcar, eds. Antología de
la literatura guatemalteca: Prosa y verso, leyenda,
tradición, novela, cuento, crónica, ensayo, picaresca,
poesía. Guatemala: Editorial Savia, 1960. 759 pp.
A broad spectrum of Guatemalan literature.

890. Lamb, Ruth, ed. Antología del cuento guatemalteco.
México: Ediciones de Andrea, 1959. 142 pp.
Contains a variety of stories and bibliography.

891. Solórzano, Carlos, ed. Teatro guatemalteco contemporáneo. Madrid: Aguilar, 1978 (1964). 327 pp.
Plays by Arévalo, Asturias, Marsicovêtere, Galich,
and Solórzano.

--Honduras

892. Acosta, Oscar, ed. Poesía hondureña de hoy. Tegu-
cigalpa: Nuevo Continente, 1971. 271 pp.
Includes the traditional and social poetry of 20
Honduran poets.

893. _____, and Roberto Sosa, eds. Antología del cuento
hondureño. Tegucigalpa: Universidad Nacional Autó-

noma de Honduras, Departamento de Extensión Universitaria, 1968. 242 pp.
First anthology of the Honduran short story, which includes 39 stories by 27 authors from Juan Ramón Molina to César Escoto (b. 1944).

894. Durón, R. E., ed. Honduras literaria: Colección de escritos en prosa y verso, escritores en verso precedidos de apuntes biográficos. Tegucigalpa: Ministerio de Educación Pública, 1957-1958. 2 vols.

895. Luna Mejía, Manuel, ed. Indice general de la poesía hondureña. Prólogo de Eliseo Pérez Cadalso. México: Editora Latinoamericana, 1961. 1,126 pp.
A comprehensive collection of selected poems by 155 Honduran poets from the early 19th century to 1950.

--Mexico

896. Abreu Gómez, E., J. Zavala; C. López Trujillo; and A. Henestrosa, eds. Cuatro siglos de literatura mexicana. México: Leyenda, 1946. 1,060 pp.
Broad and varied in scope, this anthology contains selections from poetry, theater, novel, and short fiction.

897. Castro Leal, Antonio, ed. Las cien mejores poesías líricas mexicanas. 7th ed. México: Porrúa, 1971 (1914). xxv, 307 pp.
A basic anthology by a good critic.

898. _____. La novela de la revolución mexicana. 4th ed. Madrid-México: Aguilar, 1971-72 (1963). 2 vols.
Contains a general introduction, a historical chronology, lists of characters and places, as well as vocabulary and bibliography for a good representation of the novel of the Mexican Revolution.

899. _____. La novela del México colonial (1517-1821). 4th ed. México: Aguilar, 1972-73 (1964). 2 vols.
Contains an introductory study. Bibliographies and biographies of novelists are also included.

900. Debicki, Andrew P. Antología de la poesía mexicana moderna. London: Tamesis Books, 1977. 305 pp.

Many selections with notes on Mexicanisms. From Modernism through the 1960s.

901. Glantz, Margo. Onda y escritura en México: Jovenes de 20 a 33. México: Siglo XXI, 1971. 473 pp.
Excellent introduction dividing the authors into two camps: the very Mexican "onda" of José Agustín and Gustavo Saínz and the more cosmopolitan "escritura" exemplified by the older Salvador Elizondo.

902. Leal, Luis, ed. Antología del cuento mexicano. México: Ediciones de Andrea, 1957. 162 pp.
Mexican short stories from the Popol Vuh to Revueltas, Arreola, and Rulfo.

903. Mancisidor, José. Cuentos mexicanos del siglo XIX. México: Editorial Nueva España, 1947. 750 pp.
Excellent selection.

904. _____. Cuentos mexicanos de autores contemporáneos. México: Editorial Nueva España, 1946. 760 pp.
Excellent selection of the pre-Rulfo to Arreola period.

905. Martínez, José Luis, ed. El ensayo mexicano moderno. 2d ed. México: Fondo de Cultura Económica, 1971 (1958). 2 vols. English version, The Modern Mexican Essay, translated by H. W. Hilborn (Toronto: University of Toronto Press, 1965). 524 pp.
General introduction to the essay and biobibliographies of the 56 essayists represented. The writers range from the 19th century to 1958.

906. Millán, María del Carmen, ed. Poesía romántica mexicana. México: Libro Mexicano Editores, 1957. 145 pp.
Contains an introductory study and compositions of 21 poets. Also has bibliographies.

907. Monterde, Francisco; Antonio Magaña Esquivel; and Celestino Gorostiza, eds. Teatro mexicano del siglo XX. México: Fondo de Cultura Económica, 1956-70. Vols. 1-3, 1956; vols. 4-5, 1970.
Biographies and works of many dramatists up to the 1960s.

908. Paz, Octavio, et al., eds. Poesía en movimiento:
     México: 1915-1966. Prologue by Octavio Paz. 14th
     ed. México: Siglo XXI Editores, 1979 (1966). xv,
     476 pp.
          Twentieth-century Mexican poetry represented with
     no apparent plan of organization.

909. Rojas Garcidueñas, José, ed. Autos y coloquios del
     siglo XVI. México: Universidad Nacional Autónoma
     de México, 1972 (1939). 172 pp.
          Introduction and four plays.

910. Sainz, Gustavo. Jaula de palabras. México: Editorial
     Grijalbo, 1980. 479 pp.
          Fifty-two stories written in the late 1970s by au-
     thors born between 1903 and 1957. Brief but percep-
     tive introduction, photographs and a biobibliographical
     paragraph for each writer.

     --Nicaragua

911. Antología del cuento nicaragüense. Managua: Ediciones
     del Club del Libro Nicaragüense, 1957. 278 pp.
          Sixteen writers of the 20th century are represented,
     each by three short stories. Short biobibliographic
     introductions to each writer. Also includes a ten-
     page glossary of nicaraguanismos.

912. Cardenal, Ernesto, ed. Poesía nicaragüense. Managua:
     Ed. Nueva Nicaragua, 1982. 605 pp.
          An extensive collection of poetry by a large num-
     ber of poets.

913. Gutiérrez, Ernesto, and José Reyes Monterrey, eds.
     Poesía nicaragüense postdariana. León: Universidad
     Nacional Autónoma de Nicaragua, 1967. 250 pp.
          Contains compositions of 30 poets arranged more
     or less by generation.

914. Ramírez, Sergio, ed. El cuento nicaragüense: An-
     tología. 2d ed. Managua: Ed. Nueva Nicaragua,
     1982 (1976). 302 pp. First ed. published by El
     Pez y la Serpiente.
          There were 34 short stories by 16 authors, from
     Rubén Darío on, included in the first edition, which
     has been enlarged.

915. Sánchez, María Teresa, ed. Poesía nicaragüense:
      Antología. Managua: Nuevos Horizontes, 1948.
      320 pp.
      About 180 poets, born as far back as 1779, are
      represented, each with one composition in most
      cases.

916. White, Stephen F., ed. Poets of Nicaragua: A Bi-
      lingual Anthology, 1918-1979. Greensboro, N.C.:
      Unicorn Press, 1982. viii, 209 pp.
      Thirteen poets are included, with translations by
      White.

      --Panamá

917. Jaramillo Levi, Enrique, ed. Antología crítica de la
      joven narrativa panameña. México: Federación Edi-
      torial Mexicana, 1971. 285 pp.
      Includes 45 short stories of 11 authors, with com-
      ments on most of the stories.

918. Miró, Rodrigo, ed. Cien años de poesía en Panamá
      (1852-1952). 2d ed. Panamá: Librería Advance,
      1966 (1953). xx, 351 pp.
      Panorama of the history of poetry in Panama from
      1852 to 1952. A brief introduction outlines a view
      of the period concerned and defines the various move-
      ments into which the selections are grouped: roman-
      tics, modernistas, first and second generations of the
      Republic, the "new poetry," and the latest arrivals.
      Biobibliographic data.

919. _____. El cuento en Panamá. Panamá: Imprenta
      de la Academia, 1950. 208 pp.
      Contains a general introduction by the editor and
      short stories of 22 authors since the 17th century,
      beginning with Gonzalo Fernández de Oviedo. Bio-
      bibliographic data on each author and general bibli-
      ography of the short story and the novel in Panama.

920. Sánchez, Agustín del, ed. Nueva poesía panameña.
      Madrid: Cultura Hispánica, 1954. 430 pp.
      Introductory study and biobibliographic data of 36
      poets represented.

      --Paraguay

921. Pérez-Maricevich, Francisco, ed. Breve antología del

cuento paraguayo. Asunción: Ediciones Comuneros,
1969. 200 pp.
    Of the seven authors, Roa Bastos is represented
by four stories and Gabriel Casaccia and Josefina Plá
by two each. Contains a ten-page introduction.

922. Plá, Josefina. Antología de la poesía paraguaya. Ma-
     drid: Imprenta Nacional del Estado, 1966. 45 pp.
     A brief sampling by a creative writer and prolific
     critic.

923. Vallejos, Roque, ed. Antología crítica de la poesía
     paraguaya contemporánea. Asunción: Editorial Don
     Bosco, 1968. 195 pp.
     Selections and presentation of outstanding Para-
     guayan poets from 1940 on. Contains bibliography.

--Peru

924. Escobar, Alberto, ed. Antología de la poesía peruana.
     Lima: Ediciones Peisa, 1973? (1965). 2 vols.
     Contains history of Peruvian poetry, biobiblio-
     graphic data, and stylistic study. Vol. 1 1911-60.
     Vol. 2 1960-73.

925. _____. El cuento peruano (1825-1925). Buenos
     Aires: Editorial Universitaria, 1964. 120 pp.
     Twelve writers are represented. Brief general
     introduction and biographical note for each writer
     included.

926. _____. La narración en el Perú: Estudio preliminar,
     antología. 2d ed. Lima: Mejía Baca, 1960 (1956).
     xxxvi, 512 pp.
     Informative, historically arranged introduction.
     Good selection of Peruvian stories showing certain
     constants that lend a continuity to the Peruvian nar-
     rative.

927. Hesse Murga, José, ed. Teatro peruano contempo-
     ráneo. 2d ed. Madrid: Aguilar, 1963 (1959). 409
     pp.
     Five dramatists are represented: Percy Gibson
     Parra, Juan Ríos, Bernardo Roca Rey, Sebastián
     Salazar Bondy, and Enrique Solari Swayne.

928. Oquendo, Abelardo, ed. Narrativa peruana, 1950-1970.
     Madrid: Alianza Editorial, 1973. 308 pp.

Among the 14 novelists represented are such writers as Vargas Llosa, C. F. Zavaleta, Alfredo Bryce Echenique, Julio Ortega, and Luis Loayza. A 38-page introductory section contains the responses of each author to seven questions on the current Peruvian narrative and aspects of the author's literary life.

929. Oviedo, José Miguel, ed. Estos 13: ... Poemas, documentos. Lima: Mosca Azul Editores, 1973. 189 pp.
Contains poems of the polemical and even aggressive poets who began to write toward the end of the 1960s.

930. _____, ed. Narradores peruanos. 2d ed. Caracas: Monte Avila, 1976 (1968). 239 pp.
Twentieth-century Peruvian writers of fiction are represented, mostly by one story except for the four most "important" authors (Alegría, Arguedas, Ribeyro, and Vargas Llosa), who are represented by two stories each. Oviedo provides an introduction to contemporary Peruvian short fiction.

--Puerto Rico

931. Arce de Vázquez, Margot; Laura Gallego; and Luis de Arrigoitia, eds. Lecturas puertorriqueñas: Poesía. Sharon, Conn.: Troutman Press, 1968. 445 pp.
Includes poets from Manuel Alonso to the 1960s. Contains critical annotations and bibliography.

932. Marqués, René, ed. Cuentos puertorriqueños de hoy. 6th ed. Río Piedras, P.R.: Editorial Cultural, 1977 (1959). 287 pp.
Short-story writers who belong to the generation of 1940. Includes notes in which each author explains his concept of his story included in the anthology.

933. Martínez Masdeu, Edgar; and Esther M. Melón, eds. Literatura puertorriqueña: Antología general. Río Piedras: Edil, 1971. 2 vols.
Volume 1 covers the 19th century, and volume 2 the 20th. Poets, essayists, novelists, playwrights, and short-story writers are included. Biographical sketches are provided for each author.

934. Meléndez, Concha, ed. El arte del cuento en Puerto
      Rico. 4th ed. San Juan, P. R.: Editorial Cordi-
      llera, 1975 (1961). 446 pp.
      Introduction to the Puerto Rican short story and
      anthology from the generation of the 1930s to the
      present.

935. Teatro puertorriqueño. San Juan: Instituto de Cultura
      Puertorriqueña, 1959-60. 2 vols.
      Plays by M. Méndez Ballester, E. S. Belaval, F.
      Arriví, R. Marqués, and others.

936. Valbuena Briones, Angel, and L. Hernández Aquino,
      eds. Nueva poesía de Puerto Rico. Madrid: Cul-
      tura Hispánica, 1952. 388 pp.
      Introduction, biographies, and works of 34 poets.

      --Uruguay

937. Bordoli, Domingo L., ed. Antología de la poesía uru-
      guaya contemporánea. Montevideo: Universidad de
      la República, 1966. 2 vols.
      An extensive representation of Uruguayan poetry.

938. Casal, Julio, ed. Exposición de la poesía uruguaya:
      Desde su origen hasta 1940. Montevideo: Claridad,
      1940. 767 pp.
      An all-inclusive omnibus. Contains critical com-
      ments and notes.

939. Cotelo, Rubén, ed. Narradores uruguayos. Caracas:
      Monte Avila, 1969. 289 pp.
      Short stories written since 1939 by 11 writers
      from the 20th century.

940. Silva Valdés, Fernán, ed. Teatro uruguayo contempo-
      ráneo. 2d ed. Madrid: Aguilar, 1966 (1960). 556
      pp.
      Plays by six dramatists, including Florencio Sán-
      chez and Vicente Martínez Cuitiño.

941. Visca, Arturo, ed. Antología del cuento uruguayo.
      Montevideo: Banda Oriental, 1968. 6 vols.
      From the end of the 19th century to the 1960s.

942. _____, ed. Nueva antología del cuento uruguayo.
      Montevideo: Ediciones de la Banda Oriental, 1976.
      411 pp.

Includes short stories by 28 authors, from the last
decade of the 19th century to the 1960s. Includes a
brief historical account of the short narrative in Uruguay.

--Venezuela

943.   Castellanos, Rafael Ramón, ed. Cuentos venezolanos:
       Antología. Caracas: Publicaciones Españolas, 1975.
       2 vols.
       From Modernismo to present. Brief bibliographic
       note for each author.

944.   Escalona-Escalona, José Antonio, ed. Antología gene-
       ral de la poesía venezolana. Madrid: Edime, 1966.
       1,051 pp.
       Contains prologue and notes by the compiler in ad-
       dition to an extensive anthology.

945.   Fabbiani Ruiz, José, ed. Antología personal del cuento
       venezolano, 1933-68. Caracas: Ediciones de la Fa-
       cultad de Humanidades y Educación, Instituto de In-
       vestigaciones Literarias, Universidad Central de Vene-
       zuela, 1977. 489 pp.
       A "personal anthology" of 15 authors each repre-
       sented by three short stories. Short biobibliographi-
       cal sketches.

946.   Medina, José Ramón, ed. Antología venezolana (prosa).
       Madrid: Gredos, 1962. 331 pp.
       Twenty-eight writers are covered, including Ró-
       mulo Gallegos, Teresa de la Parra, Picón Salas, and
       Uslar Pietri. Short introduction.

947.   _____. Antología venezolana (verso). Madrid:
       Gredos, 1962. 336 pp.
       Fifty-seven poets represented from the period
       1918-50. Contains a short introduction.

948-   Meneses, Guillermo, ed. Antología del cuento vene-
9.   zolano. Caracas: Editorial del Ministerio de Edu-
       cación, 1955. 420 pp.
       A personal selection from Emilio Coll to Oswaldo
       Trejo (b. 1928). Each story is preceded by a com-
       ment of at least 200 words.

950.   Picón Salas, Mariano, ed. Dos siglos de prosa vene-
       zolana. Madrid: Edime, 1965. xii, 125 pp.

Represents the various prose genres from the 18th
century to the present. Useful preface.

951. Prisco, Rafael di, ed. Narrativa venezolana contemporánea. Madrid: Alianza Editorial, 1971. 276 pp.
Short stories and fragments of novels in addition
to biobibliographies of authors included.

952. Suárez Radillo, Carlos Miguel, ed. 13 autores del
nuevo teatro venezolano. Caracas: Monte Avila,
1971. 535 pp.
Covers the newer theater in Venezuela. Bibliographies of the dramatists' works and a short bibliography of the contemporary theater.

8. CHICANO BIBLIOGRAPHY AND LITERATURE

BIBLIOGRAPHIES

953. Cabello-Argandoña, Roberto, et al. The Chicana: A
Comprehensive Bibliographical Study. Los Angeles:
Chicano Studies Center at UCLA, 1976. 303 pp.
Thorough bibliographic compilation on the Chicana
from a wide range of perspectives. Contains useful
indexes.

954. Committee for the Development of Subject Access to
Chicano Literature. A Cumulative Index to Selected
Periodicals Published Between 1967 and 1978. Boston: G. K. Hall, 1981. 700 pp.
Provides access to 4,900 articles. Includes book
reviews, conference reports, creative works, accounts of current events, and interviews taken from
18 Chicano publications. Contains "The Chicano Thesaurus for Indexing Chicano Materials." Primary
arrangement by subject. Author-title index.

955. Eger, Ernestina N. A Bibliography of Criticism of
Contemporary Chicano Literature. Berkeley: Chicano Studies Library, University of California, 1981.
xxl, 295.
Comprises about 2,200 unannotated entries on creative genres: novel, short story, poetry, theater,
and autobiography. Emphasis on post-1966 works.
Classified in an MLA-type taxonomy, this bibliography seeks to be exhaustive rather than selective.

956. Martínez, Julio A., ed. and comp. Chicano Scholars
and Writers: A Biobibliographical Directory. Metuchen, N.J.: Scarecrow Press, 1979. 579 pp.
Biobibliographical data on more than 500 living

Chicano scholars and writers and non-Chicanos who
have written on Chicanos or other Hispanics in the
U.S. Includes index of authors arranged by subject
specialization.

957.   Robinson, Barbara J., and J. Cordell Robinson. The
       Mexican American. Greenwich, Conn.: JAI Press,
       1980. 287 pp.
       Includes 668 annotated items of published and un-
       published works. Organized in 17 chapters in two
       major sections: general works and subject bibliogra-
       phies. Indexes of authors, titles, and subjects.

958.   Tatum, Charles M. A Selected and Annotated Bibliog-
       raphy of Chicano Studies. 2d ed. Lincoln, Neb.:
       Society of Spanish and Spanish American Studies,
       1979 (1976). 121 pp.
       Contains 526 critically annotated items covering
       bibliographies, background and general interest,
       readers and anthologies, the Chicana, periodicals,
       and language and linguistics. Includes an index.
       One of the first bibliographies devoted almost com-
       pletely to the humanities.

959.   Teschner, Richard V.; Garland D. Bills; and Jerry C.
       Craddock. Spanish and English of United States His-
       panos: A Critical Annotated Linguistic Bibliography.
       Arlington, Va.: Center for Applied Linguistics, 1975.
       xxii, 352 pp.
       Includes 675 extensively annotated (many critically)
       entries. Exhaustive bibliography of studies on the
       "speech and language behavior of U.S. resident/citi-
       zens of Hispanic background, chiefly Chicanos (Mexican-
       Americans) and mainland Puerto Ricans but also Cu-
       bans, Sephardic Jews, peninsulares (Spaniards) and
       isleños (Canary Islanders in Louisiana)."

960.   Woods, Richard D. Reference Materials on Mexican
       Americans. Metuchen, N. J.: Scarecrow Press,
       1976. 190 pp.
       Contains 387 titles that are amply annotated. In-
       cludes works that are entirely or partially dedicated
       to Mexican Americans. Indexes for authors, titles,
       and subjects.

961.   _____, and Ann Hartness Graham. "Hispanic Amer-
       ican Periodicals for Libraries." The Serials Librar-
       ian 4 (Fall 1979), 85-98.

An annotated listing of 49 periodicals current as
of October 1978.

ANTHOLOGIES, LITERARY CRITICISM, LANGUAGE

962. Castañeda Shular, Antonia; Tomás Ybarra-Frausto; and
Joseph Sommers, eds. Literatura Chicana: Texto
y contexto/Chicano Literature. Englewood Cliffs,
N. J.: Prentice-Hall, 1972. xxvii, 368 pp.
Bilingual anthology that includes selections from
Mexican and other Latin American works as well as
Chicano literature. Major themes treated are social
protest, Chicano culture, and the migratory experi-
ence.

963. Galvan, Roberto A., and Richard V. Teschner. El
diccionario del español Chicano/The Dictionary of
Chicano Spanish. Revised ed. Silver Spring, Md.:
Institute of Modern Languages, 1977 (1975). xi, 144
pp.
Contains around 8,000 lexical items from Florida
to California taken mostly from spoken Spanish. Appendixes on proverbs, verb conjugations, and bibliography on Chicano vocabulary.

964. Harth, Dorothy E., and Lewis M. Baldwin, eds. Voices
of Azatlán: Chicano Literature of Today. New York:
New American Library, 1974. 246 pp.
Some of the best Chicano writers are represented.
Contains bibliography and glossary.

965. Kanellos, Nicolás, ed. A Decade of Hispanic Literature:
An Anniversary Anthology. Houston, Texas: Revista
Chicano-Riqueña, 1982. 308 pp.
An anthology of writings by the major Hispanic
writers of the United States. It contains prize-
winning stories, poems, and essays by such writers
as Miguel Algarín, Rudy Anaya, Andrés Burger,
Abelardo Delgado, Sergio Elizondo, Rolando Hino-
josa, Miguel Piñero, Estela Portillo, Tomás Rivera,
and Evangelina Vigil.

966. Keller, Gary D., and Francisco Jiménez, eds. Hispanics in the United States: An Anthology of Creative Literature. Ypsilanti, Mich.: Bilingual Review/
Press, 1980. x, 165 pp.
The texts deal with Hispanic life in the United

States (including Puerto Rico).   About 80 percent of
the text is in English.

967.   Lomelí, Francisco A. , and Donaldo W. Uriosto.   Chi-
       cano Perspectives in Literature: A Critical and An-
       notated Bibliography.   Albuquerque, N. M. :   Pajarito
       Publications, 1976.   120 pp.
          Extensive comments on literary works.   Contains
       sections on poetry, novel, short fiction, theater, an-
       thology, literary criticism, oral tradition in print,
       journal, and "literatura Chicanesca." Useful glos-
       sary and index.

968.   Ortego, Philip D. , ed.   We Are Chicanos: An An-
       thology of Mexican-American Literature.   New York:
       Washington Square Press, 1973.   xxi, 330 pp.
          Contains a wide range of selections.   The editor
       also contributes perceptive observations about Chi-
       cano literature.   Contains a glossary and bibliogra-
       phy.

969.   Romano-V. , Octavio I. , and Herminio Ríos C. , eds.
       El Espejo/The Mirror: Selected Chicano Literature.
       Rev. ed.   Berkeley, Calif. :   Quinto Sol, 1972 (1969).
       284 pp.
          All literary genres are represented in this bi-
       lingual edition.   The revised version is practically
       a new book.   Some of the best Chicano authors are
       represented in the more than 20 selections.

970.   Sommers, Joseph, and Tomás Ybarra-Frausto, eds.
       Modern Chicano Writers.   Englewood Cliffs, N. J. :
       Prentice-Hall, 1979.   xv, 190 pp.
          Contains some excellent models of criticism on
       Chicano literature, language, and culture.   Special-
       ists consider this the best work yet published.

971.   Tatum, Charles.   Chicano Literature: A Critical His-
       tory.   Boston: Twayne, 1982 (1983).
          Provides a synthesis of the history of the Chicano
       people in Chapter 1; traces the evolution of Chicano
       literature from its origins in the 16th century to
       about 1960 in Chapter 2; and then devotes Chapters
       3 to 6 to Chicano theater, short story, novel, and
       poetry.   The "selected bibliography" includes studies
       of the Chicanos and their culture and critical studies
       of their literature.

972. Villanueva, Tino, comp. <u>Chicanos: Antología histórica y literaria</u>. México: Fondo de Cultura Económica, 1980. 531 pp.

Contains new historical selections and reprinted critical-historical essays. Very good poetry section, but prose selections were previously available.

9. BOOKS ON METRICS

973. Baehr, Rudolf. Manual de versificación. 2d printing. Madrid: Gredos, 1981 (1973). 444 pp. College manual on regular and irregular versification. It shows the origin and evolution of strophic forms.

974. Balaguer, Joaquín. Apuntes para una historia prosódica de la métrica castellana. Madrid: Consejo Superior de Investigaciones Científicas, 1954. 269 pp. Rpt., Santo Domingo: República Dominicana, 1974. Studies on the poetry of Juan de Mena and other important aspects of Spanish versification.

975. Balbín, Rafael de. Sistema de rítmica castellana. 3d ed. Madrid: Gredos, 1975 (1963). 420 pp. Rather complex study but valuable for its new approaches to metrics.

976. Carballo Picazo, Alfredo. Métrica española. Madrid: Instituto de Estudios Madrileños, 1956. 161 pp. A clear exposition of Spanish metrics. It also contains an extensive bibliography with some annotations.

977. Clarke, Dorothy C. A Chronological Sketch of Castilian Versification Together with a List of Its Metric Terms. Berkeley and Los Angeles: University of California Press, 1952. 104 pp. Based primarily on versification of lyric and epic poetry. Lengthy bibliography which serves as a supplement to the author's Una bibliografía de versificación española (University of California Publications in Modern Philology, vol. 20, no. 2 [1937]).

166

978. _____. Morphology of Fifteenth-Century Castilian
Verse. Pittsburgh, Pa.: Duquesne University Press,
1964. 233 pp.
Based on the works of numerous 15th-century poets. The author studies arte mayor, minor meters,
and the emergence of syllable count in octosyllabic
verse.

979. Díez-Echarri, Emiliano. Teorías métricas del Siglo
de Oro. Madrid: Consejo Superior de Investigaciones Científicas, 1970. 355 pp. Rpt. of 1949 ed.
Passages on metrical theory of the Golden Age ac-
companied by the author's comments and evaluations.

980. Henríquez Ureña, Pedro. Estudios de versificación española. Buenos Aires: Universidad de Buenos Aires,
1961. 399 pp.
Collection of studies mainly on early Spanish poetry. Also treats Mexican poetry of the Independence
period, and Rubén Darío.

981. _____. La versificación española irregular. 2d ed.
Madrid: Centro de Estudios Históricos, 1933 (1920).
viii, 369 pp.
A study of the irregular Spanish verse from the
medieval period to 1920. Very informative work for
any student of poetic form. Indexes of themes and
authors.

982. López Estrada, Francisco. Métrica española del siglo
XX. Madrid: Gredos, 1974. 225 pp. Rpt. of 1969
ed.
Student manual that stresses 20th-century metrics
but also links it to previous poetry. Detailed study
of Dámaso Alonso's "A un río le llamaban Carlos."
Subject and author indexes.

983. Navarro Tomás, Tomás. Arte del verso. 7th ed.
México: Colección Málaga, 1977 (1959). 187 pp.
Very helpful outline of meters, stanzas, and ir-
regular forms.

984. _____. Métrica española; reseña histórica y des-
criptiva. 5th ed. Madrid and Barcelona: Ed.
Guadarrama-Labor, 1978 (1956). 581 pp.
Fundamental work which studies the poetic forms

of each epoch, showing innovations and influences by
numerous references to poets and their works.

985. Quilis, Antonio. Métrica española. 4th ed. Madrid:
      Alcalá, 1978 (1969). 197 pp.
      A succinct, useful handbook for students. Many
      examples along with sample analyses.

986. Riquer, Martín de. Resumen de versificación española.
      Barcelona: Seix Barral, 1950. 86 pp.
      Gives essential information on metrics.

987. Corvalán, Graciela N. V. Latin American Women
Writers in English Translation: A Bibliography.
(Latin American Bibliography Series, 9.) Los Angeles: Latin American Studies Center, 1980. iv,
109 pp.
Covers 282 women writers whose works have been
translated into English or concerning whom there ex-
ists critical and biographical studies in English.

988. Engber, Marjorie, comp. Caribbean Fiction and Poetry. New York: Center for Inter-American Relations, 1970. 86 pp.
Includes anthologies, poetry, short stories, and
novels published in the United States and Great Britain between 1900 and 1970. No annotations.

989. Freudenthal, Juan R., and Patricia M. Freudenthal.
Index to Anthologies of Latin-American Literature in
English Translation. Boston: G. K. Hall, 1977.
199 pp.
Information about translations of works by over
1,100 Latin American writers (born since 1850), pub-
lished in over 100 English-language anthologies in
North and South America and England.

990. Hulet, Claude L. Latin American Poetry in English
Translation: A Bibliography. Washington, D. C.:
Pan American Union, 1964. xiii, 192 pp.
From the pre-Columbian period to 1963.

991. _____. Latin American Prose in English Translation: A Bibliography. Washington, D. C.: Pan
American Union, 1964. 191 pp.
Lists translations of prose from the 16th century
to the 1960s.

992. Index translationum. Paris: UNESCO, 1949- .
      Annual listing of translated books. More than 70
      countries are included. Author index includes indexes
      of translators and publishers.

993. Levine, Susan G. , comp. Latin America: Fiction and
      Poetry in Translation. New York: Center for Inter-
      American Relations, 1970. 72 pp.
      List of anthologies (authors given) and individual
      works. No annotations.

994. Mitchell, Eleanor. Spanish and Portuguese Translations
      of United States Books (1955-1962). Washington, D.C.:
      Hispanic Foundation, Library of Congress, 1963. 506
      pp.
      Works of fewer than 100 pages are included only
      if they are plays, books of poetry, or speeches. Ar-
      ticles are included only if they have appeared in
      books.

995. O'Brien, Robert. Spanish Plays in English Translation.
      New York: Las Americas, 1963. 82 pp.
      Brief descriptions of each author and play plus in-
      formation useful to potential producers.

996. Parks, George B. , and Ruth Z. Temple, eds. The
      Literatures of the World in English Translation: A
      Bibliography. New York: Frederick Ungar Publish-
      ing Co. , 1970. Vol. 3, The Romance Literatures.
      Remigio U. Pane prepared the bibliography for
      Spanish literature in translation (pp. 237-328), which
      includes books on background, literary studies, col-
      lections, and individual authors by period (medieval
      period, Renaissance, Golden Age, 18th, 19th, and
      20th centuries). Willis Knapp Jones prepared the
      bibliography for Spanish American literature (pp.
      329-453), which includes background, literary stud-
      ies, collections, colonial Spanish American litera-
      ture, and individual authors by countries.

997. Randall, Dale B. J. The Golden Tapestry: A Criti-
      cal Survey of Non-Chivalric Spanish Fiction in Eng-
      lish Translation, 1543-1657. Durham, N.C.: Duke
      University Press, 1963. vii, 262 pp.
      A well-organized, useful compilation.

998. Rudder, Robert S. The Literature of Spain in English

Translation. New York: Frederick Ungar Publishing Co., 1975. 637 pp.
    Works translated are arranged by period from the
    Medieval to the 20th century. Carefully cross-
    referenced and indexed.

999. Shaw, Bradley A. Latin American Literature in Eng-
      lish Translation: An Annotated Bibliography. New
      York: New York University Press, 1976. x, 144
      pp. Supplement: "Latin American Literature in Eng-
      lish 1975-1978," supplement to Review (Center for
      Inter-American Studies Relations), 24 (1979), 23 pp.
          Contains 624 annotated entries through 1974 with
      an additional 111 annotated entries in the supplement.
      Includes only book publications arranged by genre and
      then by country.

11. LINGUISTICS

BIBLIOGRAPHIES

Besides the bibliographies listed below, consult the linguistics journals listed in chapter 12. Especially useful are the bibliographies in the Modern Language Association International Bibliography, the Nueva revista de filología hispánica, the Revista de filología hispánica (1939-46), the Revista hispánica moderna (to vol. 34, 1966), the Revista de filología española, the Romanische Bibliographie/Bibliographie romane/Romance Bibliography, the Bibliographie linguistique/Linguistic Bibliography (see below), and The Year's Work in Modern Language Studies.

1000. Alvar, Manuel. Dialectología española. (Cuadernos Bibliográficos no. 7.) Madrid: Consejo Superior de Investigaciones Científicas, 1962. 96 pp.
    Contains the following sections: general, vulgar, and regional Spanish; mozárabe; Spanish dialects (leonés, extremeño, riojano, aragonés murciano, andaluz, canario); Spanish of America; papiamento; Philippine Spanish; and Judeo-Spanish.

1001. Arellano, Jorge Eduardo. "El español en Nicaragua: Bibliografía fundamental (1837-1977)." Extracted from Boletín Nicaraguense de Bibliografía y Documentación, No. 19 (September-October, 1977), 92-124, with an Appendix of 10 additional entries. Managua, January 1978. 40 pp.
    Annotated bibliography of 70 articles and books on the Spanish of Nicaragua.

1002. Avellaneda, María R. "Contribución a una bibliografía de dialectología española y especialmente hispanoamericana." Boletín de la Real Academia Española 46 (1966): 335-69, 525-55; 47 (1967): 125-56, 311-42.
Arranged by author's last name. Good for early works (before 1960).

1003. Bach, Kathryn, and Glanville Price. Romance Linguistics and the Romance Languages: A Bibliography of Bibliographies. London: Grant and Cutler, 1977. 194 pp.
Annotated listing of books, articles, theses and festschriften on Romance linguistics. Catalan, Spanish and Spanish American are covered on pages 73 to 97.

1004. Bibliographie linguistique/Linguistic Bibliography. Utrecht and Brussels: Spectrum, 1939- . Published annually.
Published under the auspices of the Permanent International Committee of Linguists. Includes Iberian and American Spanish in its coverage of all regions of the world.

1005. Bibliographie linguistique des années 1939-1947/Linguistic Bibliography for the Years 1939-1947. Utrecht and Brussels: Spectrum, 1949-50. 2 vols.
Supported by UNESCO to fill gap caused by Second World War. Author index at end of volume 2.

1006. Biblioteca de dialectología hispanoamericana. Buenos Aires: Instituto de Filología, Universidad de Buenos Aires, 1930-49. 7 vols.
Contains a number of worthwhile bibliographies.

1007. Carrión Ordóñez, Enrique, and Tilbert Diego Stegmann. Bibliografía del español en el Perú. Tübingen: Max Niemeyer Verlag, 1973. 274 pp.
Includes 630 entries containing works consulted, general studies, and specific lexical studies on Peruvian Spanish. Indexes of works studied, authors, titles, journals and newspapers, subjects, etc.

1007a. Davis, Jack Emory. The Spanish of Argentina and Uruguay: An Annotated Bibliography for 1940-1978. West Berlin: Mouton Publishers, 1982. 360 pp.

A comprehensive, critical, annotated bibliography
of books, articles, etc., dealing with the Spanish
language in these two countries. Covers over 1,200
items published in Latin America, the United States
and Canada, and Europe.

1008.   Gazdar, Gerald; Ewan Klein; and Geoffrey K. Pullum.
        A Bibliography of Contemporary Linguistic Research.
        New York: Garland, 1978. xix, 425 pp.
        Over 5,000 items on the "core areas of syntac-
        tic, semantic, phonological, and pragmatic theory."
        Coverage is primarily for the years 1970-77. Con-
        tains indexes for languages and for subjects.

1009.   McKay, John C. A Guide to Romance Reference
        Grammars: The Modern Standard Languages. (Am-
        sterdam Studies in the Theory and History of Lin-
        guistic Science, V: Library and Information Sources
        in Linguistics, 6.) Amsterdam: Benjamins, 1979.
        xviii, 126 pp.
        Surveys 20th-century reference grammars includ-
        ing Spanish, Catalan, and Portuguese. Intended for
        non-specialists. Contains an introductory overview
        of linguistic schools and theories. Each chapter,
        except Catalan, has two sections: one on grammar
        in general and another on syntax. Includes a bib-
        liography and author/title index.

1010.   Malkiel, Yakov. Linguistics and Philology in Spanish
        America: A Survey (1925-1970). The Hague and
        Paris: Mouton, 1972. 179 pp.
        Useful selective review of scholarly activity in
        the field of American Spanish.

1011.   Nichols, Madaline Wallis. A Bibliographical Guide to
        Materials on American Spanish. Cambridge, Mass.:
        Harvard University Press, 1941. 114 pp.
        Annotated bibliography classified by country and
        subject. Still very useful. The following attempts
        have been made to supplement Nichols on a country-
        by-country or area-by-area basis: Hensley C. Wood-
        bridge, "The Spanish of the American Southwest and
        Louisiana: A Bibliographical Survey for 1940-53,"
        Orbis 3 (1954): 236-44; Woodbridge, "Central Amer-
        ican Spanish, A Bibliography (1940-53)," Inter-
        American Review of Bibliography 6 (1956): 103-15;
        Woodbridge, "An Annotated Bibliography of Publica-

tions Concerning the Spanish of Bolivia, Cuba, Ecuador, Paraguay, and Peru for the Years 1940-57," Kentucky Foreign Language Quarterly 7 (1960): 37-54; Jack Emory Davis, "The Spanish of Argentina and Uruguay: An Annotated Bibliography for 1940-65," Orbis 15 (1966): 160-89, 442-88; ibid. 17 (1968): 232-77, 539-73; ibid. 19 (1970): 205-32; ibid. 20 (1971): 236-69; Davis, "The Spanish of Mexico: An Annotated Bibliography for 1940-69," Hispania 54 (1971): 624-56; Michael Fody III, "The Spanish of the American Southwest and Louisiana: A Bibliographical Survey for 1954-69," Orbis 19 (1970): 529-40.

1012.   Nuessel, Frank H., Jr. "An Annotated, Critical Bibliography of Generative-Based Grammatical Analyses of Spanish: Phonology and Morphology." The Bilingual Review/La Revista Bilingüe 5, 3 (1978), 207-37.
Covers 116 items for years 1960-76. Extensive annotations. Includes theses and dissertations.

1013.   _____. "An Annotated, Critical Bibliography of Generative-Based Grammatical Analyses of Spanish: Syntax and Semantics." The Bilingual Review/La Revista Bilingüe 6, 1 (1979), 39-80.
Covers 197 items for years 1963-76. Extensive annotations. Includes theses and dissertations.

1014.   Parodi, Claudia. La investigación lingüística en México (1970-1980). México: Universidad Nacional Autónoma de Mexico, 1981. 205 pp.
Contains a long introductory essay (pp. 15-77) in addition to an unannotated bibliography. Useful indexes of authors, languages, and subjects.

1015.   Pluto, Joseph A. "Contribución a una bibliografía anotada de los estudios sobre el español de Colombia (1965-1975)." Thesaurus, 35, 2 (Mayo-Agosto 1980), 289-358.
Annotated bibliography that covers books, articles, doctoral dissertations, and book reviews written after 1964 for the years mentioned in the title. Contains one index of authors and another of themes, words, expressions, persons, and places. Supplements José Joaquín Montes Giraldo's "Contribución a una bibliografía de los estudios sobre el español

de Colombia" (Thesaurus, 20 [1965], 425-65), an
unannotated bibliography whose cutoff year is 1964.

1016. Quilis, Antonio.   Fonética y fonología del español.
(Cuadernos Bibliográficos no. 10.)   Madrid: Consejo Superior de Investigaciones Científicas, 1963.
104 pp.
Useful basic bibliography which also contains a
section on American Spanish.

1017. Rice, Frank, and Allene Guss.   Information Sources
in Linguistics.   Washington, D.C.:   Center for Applied Linguistics, 1965.   viii, 42 pp.
Attempts coverage of all major traditional fields
of linguistics.

1018. Rohlfs, Gerhard.   Manual de filología hispánica: Guía
bibliográfica, crítica y metódica.   Translated by
Carlos Patiño Rosselli.   Bogotá: Instituto Caro y
Cuervo, 1957.   337 pp.
Studies dealing with language of the Iberian pen-
insula from prehistorical times.   Includes Spanish
America and Brazil.

1019. Serís, Homero.   Bibliografía de la lingüística española.
Bogotá: Instituto Caro y Cuervo, 1964.   lix, 981
pp.
An extensive, fundamental bibliography that covers
the following: general linguistics, Romance linguistics, Spanish linguistics, peninsular languages,
Hispanic dialects (including Judeo-Spanish), American Spanish (including indigenous languages and the
Spanish of the Philippines and Africa), and the teaching of Spanish.   A number of the items are annotated, and many references to book reviews are
given.   Lengthy index and detailed table of contents.

1020. Solé, Carlos A.   Bibliografía sobre el español en
América, 1920-1967.   Washington, D.C.:   George-
town University Press, 1970.   175 pp.
Contains more than 1,450 items, many of which
are annotated.   Extremely detailed classified arrangement.   Includes general and other linguistic
studies and bibliographies as well as bibliographies
and linguistic studies relating to all Spanish-speaking
countries in America, including the United States.

1021. Stevenson, John. "Morfosintaxis del moderno español
       peninsular: Ensayo bibliográfico de estudios de-
       scriptivos (1950-1975)." Español Actual 31 (1976),
       1-32.
            There are 977 entries contained in this enumera-
       tive bibliography which is divided into the traditional
       parts of speech.

1022. Woodbridge, Hensley C., and Paul Olson. "A Tenta-
       tive Bibliography of Hispanic Linguistics." Mimeo-
       graphed. Urbana: University of Illinois, Depart-
       ment of Spanish, Portuguese, and Italian, 1952.
       xxii, 203 pp.
            Classified selective bibliography based on works
       cited by Yakov Malkiel in his footnotes. The 1879
       entries cover six main divisions: Vulgar and medi-
       eval Latin, comparative Romance linguistics, sub-
       strata, Catalan, Spanish, and Portuguese. Con-
       tains author index and word index.

1023. Zubatsky, David S. "Hispanic Linguistic Studies in
       Festschriften: An Annotated Bibliography (1957-75)."
       Hispania 60 (1977), 656-717. Updates linguistic
       sections of Herbert H. Golden and Seymour O.
       Simches' Modern Iberian Language and Literature:
       A Bibliography of Homage Studies (Cambridge: Har-
       vard University Press, 1958).
            Covers Basque, Catalan, Spanish Peninsular and
       Spanish American. Includes some items missed by
       Golden and Simches.

                        GENERAL WORKS

1024. Alonso, Amado. Estudios lingüísticos: Temas es-
       pañoles. 3d ed. Madrid: Gredos, 1974 (1951).
       286 pp.
            A collection of essays that includes linguistic
       geography, phonemics, and stylistics.

1025. _____. Estudios lingüísticos: Temas hispanoameri-
       canos. 3d ed. Madrid: Gredos, 1976 (1953). 358
       pp.
            Includes such studies on the language of Spanish
       America as the linguistic basis of American Spanish
       and the origin of the seseo.

1026.   Canfield, D. Lincoln, and J. Cary Davis. An Intro-
        duction to Romance Linguistics. Carbondale and Ed-
        wardsville, Ill.: Southern Illinois University Press,
        1975. xxviii, 203 pp.
            An updated textbook on comparative Romance Lin-
        guistics which contains texts and problems for prac-
        tical application of linguistic principles explicated in
        the text.

1027.   Catalán, Diego. Lingüística ibero-románica: Crítica
        retrospectiva. Madrid: Gredos, 1974. 365 pp.
        Preliminary version in Linguistics in Western Eu-
        rope: Current Trends in Linguistics, Vol. 9 (The
        Hague and Paris, 1972), 927-1106.
            Thorough review of schools, trends, achieve-
        ments and failures in Peninsular linguistics since
        1870. Also evaluates contributions of major in-
        dividual scholars.

1028.   Cerdá Massó, Ramón. Lingüística hoy. 4th ed. Bar-
        celona: Teide, 1977 (1969). 158 pp.
            A clear, general introduction to contemporary
        linguistics.

1029.   Criado de Val, Manuel. Fisonomía del idioma es-
        pañol: Sus características comparadas con las de
        francés, italiano, portugués, inglés y alemán. Ma-
        drid: Saeta, 1972. 328 pp. Expanded version of
        ed. published by Aguilar, 3d ed., 1962.
            Concise work. Maps showing bilingual and dia-
        lectal zones. Also contains material on American
        Spanish.

1030.   Current Trends in Linguistics. Edited by Thomas A.
        Sebeok. Vol. 4, Ibero-American and Caribbean
        Linguistics, edited by Robert Lado, Norman A. Mc-
        Quown, Sol Saporta, and Yolanda Lastra. The
        Hague: Mouton, 1968. 659 pp.
            Part 1 deals with general and Ibero-American
        linguistics and has articles on phonology, lexicogra-
        phy, dialectology, and philology. Part 2 deals with
        the linguistics of non-Iberoamerican languages.
        Part 3 deals with such topics as bilingualism, lan-
        guage teaching in America, and applied linguistic
        research. Part 4 deals with the organization of
        linguistic activities and the present state of lin-
        guistics. This important work has articles by

such well-known scholars as Yakov Malkiel, Juan
M. Lope Blanch, and Robert A. Hall, Jr., in addition to the editors listed above.

1031. Elcock, W. D. The Romance Languages. Rev. ed.
London: Faber & Faber, 1975 (1960). 589 pp.
Good treatment of Spanish. Valuable for a broad
view of the Romance linguistic world, it concentrates on the earlier stages of the languages.

1032. Enciclopedia lingüística hispánica. Directed by M.
Alvar, et al. Madrid: Consejo Superior de Investigaciones Científicas, 1960-62. Vol. 1 and
supplements to vol. 1, 656 pp. Vol. 2 (1967),
460 pp.
A scholarly treatment of the Spanish language.
Chapters by specialists with bibliographic footnotes.

1033. Polo, José. Lingüística, investigación y enseñanza
(Notas y bibliografía). Madrid: Oficina de Educación Ibero-americana, 1972. 181 pp.
Chapter 2 (pp. 21-92) is an unannotated bibliography of general and specific works on linguistics for
college students. It also contains material on the
teaching of Spanish for Spanish- and English-speaking
students.

1034. Posner, Rebecca. The Romance Languages: A Linguistic Introduction. Rpt., Gloucester, Mass.: P.
Smith, 1970 (1966). 336 pp.
A comparative introduction to the major modern
Romance languages (French, Italian, Spanish, Portuguese, and Rumanian). Analyzes the historical development, internal structure, and present-day variants and dialects of each language.

1035. Vidos, B. E. Manual de lingüística románica. 2d
ed. Madrid: Aguilar, 1973 (1963). xxiv, 416 pp.
Translation of Handbook tot de Romaanse Taalkunde
(1956).
A good general introduction. Covers such topics
as the origin of Romance linguistics, Romance linguistics as a historical science, the comparative
historical method, and 20th-century Romance linguistics. Diagrams and bibliography.

DEVELOPMENT OF THE SPANISH LANGUAGE

1036.   Baldinger, Kurt.   La formación de los dominios lin-
         güísticos en la península ibérica.   Translated by
         Emilio Lledó and Monserrat Macau.   2d ed.   Ma-
         drid: Gredos, 1972 (1958).   496 pp.
         A thorough historical and comparative linguistic
         study.   From Romanization through the Reconquest.
         Extensive bibliography and maps.

1037.   Bolaño e Isla, Amancio.   Manual de la historia de la
         lengua española.   3d ed.   México: Porrúa, 1971
         (1959).   221 pp.
         A clear, well-organized introduction to the his-
         tory of the Spanish language.

1038.   Entwistle, William J.   The Spanish Language.   Rpt.,
         London: Gordon, 1975 (1936).   367 pp.   Spanish
         version, by Francisco Villar, Las lenguas de Es-
         paña (Madrid: Ediciones Istmo, 1972).   420 pp.
         Traces the Spanish language from pre-Roman
         times to today.   Spanish American included, as
         well as Portuguese, Catalan, and Basque.

1039.   García de Diego, Vicente.   Gramática histórica es-
         pañola.   3d ed.   Madrid: Gredos, 1970 (1951).
         624 pp.
         History and origin of Spanish words with respect
         to phonetics, morphology, and syntax.

1040.   Lapesa, Rafael.   Historia de la lengua española.   9th
         ed.   Madrid: Editorial Gredos, S.A., 1980 (1942).
         690 pp.
         Standard work on language from pre-Roman times
         to the present.   Includes such topics as the Latin
         language in Spain, Arabic influence, archaic Spanish,
         modern Spanish, Judeo-Spanish.   The present edi-
         tion contains many added references to research
         through the 1970s.

1041.   Lenz, Rodolfo.   La oración y sus partes.   4th ed.
         Santiago de Chile: Nascimiento, 1944.   572 pp.
         Studies the Spanish language in its relation to
         linguistic psychology.

1042.   Menéndez Pidal, Ramón.   Orígenes del español: Es-
         tado lingüístico de la península ibérica hasta el siglo

XI. 8th ed. Madrid: Espasa-Calpe, 1972 (1926).
xv, 592 pp. El idioma español en sus primeros
tiempos (Madrid: Espasa-Calpe, 1973) is a synthe-
sis of this work in 160 pp.
The monumental work of Spanish historical linguistics covering the 9th through 11th centuries.

1043. Spaulding, Robert K. How Spanish Grew. 2d ed.
Berkeley and Los Angeles: University of California
Press, 1968 (1943). 259 pp.
A clearly presented, standard treatment of the
development of the Spanish language.

DIALECTOLOGY

Only general works on Spanish and Spanish
American dialectology are included in this section. Consult beginning of this chapter for bibliographies of Hispanic dialectology.

1044. Alvar, Manuel. Textos hispánicos dialectales: Antología histórica. Madrid: Consejo Superior de
Investigaciones Científicas, 1960. 2 vols. Supplement to Revista de filología española, vol. 73.
Also contains texts from American Spanish in
volume 2.

1045. García de Diego, Vicente. Manual de dialectología
española. 3d ed. Madrid: Instituto de Cultura
Hispánica, 1978 (1946). 390 pp.
A standard reference guide to the dialects of
Spain and Spanish America. Also includes Judeo-
Spanish.

1046. Lope Blanch, Juan M. El español de América. Madrid: Alcalá, 1968. 150 pp.
This basic book for Spanish American dialectology
contains general studies on all of Spanish America,
methodology and geographic linguistics, substratum,
and studies on individual nations.

1047. Pop, Sever. La dialectologie: Aperçu historique et
méthodes d'enquêtes linguistiques. Louvain: University of Louvain and UNESCO, 1950. 2 vols.
Deals with Romance dialectology in volume 1,

and specifically with Spanish on pages 337 to 434.
Extensive bibliography.

1048.   Wagner, Max Leopold.   Lingua e dialetti dell-America
         Spagnola.   Florence: Le Lingue Estere, 1949.   190
         pp.
             Offers a clear and substantial compendium of the
         main aspects of American Spanish, with particular
         reference to popular speech.

1049.   Zamora Vicente, Alonso.   Dialectología española.   3d
         ed.   Madrid: Gredos, 1979 (1960).   588 pp.
             A basic reference work on dialects in Spain, with
         a final chapter on American Spanish.   Contains a
         lengthy bibliographic guide.

                   PHONOLOGY AND PHONETICS

1050.   Alarcos Llorach, Emilio.   Fonología española.   4th
         ed., 5th printing.   Madrid: Gredos, 1981 (1954).
         290 pp.
             Contains examples, charts, and much biblio-
         graphic data.   A good work, but probably not
         suited for the beginner.   Prague school approach
         to the analysis of the phonological structure of
         Spanish.

1051.   Alonso, Amado.   De la pronunciación medieval a la
         moderna en español.   2d ed.   Madrid: Gredos,
         1969 (1955).   3 vols.
             Important series prepared for publication by Ra-
         fael Lapesa.   A fundamental work that traces the
         history of Spanish pronunciation.

1052.   Canfield, D. Lincoln.   Spanish Pronunciation in the
         Americas.   Chicago: University of Chicago Press,
         1981.   118 pp.   Thorough revision of La pronun-
         ciación del español en América: Ensayo historico-
         descriptivo.   Bogotá: Instituto Caro y Cuervo,
         1962.   103 pp.
             Covers each Spanish-speaking country individually
         and also compares the pronunciation among countries
         when appropriate.   Each chapter has a chronological
         bibliography and there is a current general bibliog-
         raphy.

1053. Cressey, William W. Spanish Phonology and Mor-
       phology: A Generative View. Washington, D. C. :
       Georgetown University Press, 1978. xv, 169 pp.
       This study focuses on the following rules types
       within a generative transformational framework:
       Detail rules, low-level allophonic rules; word-level
       phonology rules, everywhere rules, inflectional mor-
       phology rules, and abstract rules.

1054. Dalbor, John B. Spanish Pronunciation: Theory and
       Practice. 2d ed. New York: Holt, Rinehart and
       Winston, 1980 (1969). xi, 334 pp.
       Thorough and careful revision is the hallmark of
       this important textbook on Spanish phonetics. In-
       cludes a lengthy bibliography.

1055. Gili Gaya, Samuel. Elementos de fonética general.
       5th ed. Madrid: Gredos, 1975 (1950). 198 pp.
       A basic introduction to Spanish phonetics. Bib-
       liography.

1056. Harris, James W. Spanish Phonology. Cambridge,
       Mass. : MIT Press, 1969. 218 pp.
       An important contribution in that it represents
       an attempt to apply Chomsky and Halle's Sound Pat-
       tern of English (New York: Harper & Row, 1968),
       a transformational approach, to the description of
       Spanish phonological universals.

1057. Hooper, Joan (Bybee). An Introduction to Natural
       Generative Phonology. New York: Academic
       Press, 1976. xviii, 254 pp.
       The emerging phonological theory of Natural
       Generative Phonology, which focuses on morpho-
       phonological alternations, is applied to Spanish
       data.

1058. Macpherson, I. R. Spanish Phonology: Descriptive
       and Historical. Manchester: Manchester University
       Press, 1975. 181 pp.
       A clear, well-organized introduction to phonetics
       and phonology. Exercises and bibliography.

1059. Navarro Tomás, Tomás. Fonología española. New
       York: Las Americas, 1966 (1946). 217 pp. Eng-
       lish translation, Studies in Spanish Phonology (Coral

Gables, Fla.: University of Miami Press, 1968).
160 pp.
Basic study on the development of Spanish phonology from the Cid to Miró.

1060.   _____. Manual de entonación española. 4th ed.
Madrid: Guadarrama, 1974 (1944). 228 pp.
A basic study of Spanish intonation which also
takes Spanish American speech into account.

1061.   _____. Manual de pronunciación español. 20th
ed. Madrid: Revista de Filología Española, 1980
(1918). 326 pp.
A standard work on Spanish pronunciation. Only
deals with Castilian Spanish. Great wealth of ar-
ticulatory phonetic data and many sketches and diagrams.

1062. Otero, Carlos-Peregrín. Evolución y revolución en
romance: Mínima introducción a la fonología. 2d
ed. Barcelona: Seix Barral, 1980. 322 pp.
Uses the contributions of Chomsky and J. W.
Harris in his study of diachronic Romance phonology, with emphasis on gallego-portugués and Spanish. Extensive bibliography and useful indexes,
maps, and an appendix which contains phonological
processes.

1063. Quilis, Antonio, and Joseph A. Fernández. Curso de
fonética y fonología españolas. 9th ed., revised
and enlarged. Madrid: Consejo Superior de Investigaciones Científicas, 1979 (1964). xxxiii, 224
pp.
Sound, cogent treatment of theory and practice
for English-speaking students. Contains many diagrams and sketches.

1064. Resnick, Melvyn C. Phonological Variants and Dialects Identification in Latin American Spanish. The
Hague: Mouton, 1975. 484 pp. Reprinted 1980.
An outstanding computer-assisted compilation of
previously published dialect studies which focuses on
allophonic variation of the segmental phonemes of
Spanish as a way of identifying specific dialect zones
and areas.

1065. Stockwell, Robert P., and J. Donald Bowen. The

Sounds of English and Spanish. Chicago: University of Chicago Press, 1965. 168 pp.
Structural and contrastive approach to phonology incorporating audiolingual advances in language teaching.

GRAMMARS, MORPHOLOGY, AND SYNTAX

1066.   Alarcos Llorach, Emilio. Gramática estructural. 2d ed. Madrid: Gredos, 1977 (1951). 129 pp.
Structural grammar according to the School of Copenhagen, with special attention to the Spanish language.

1067.   Alcina Franch, Juan, and José Manuel Blecua. Gramática española. Barcelona: Ariel, 1976. 1,244 pp.
Follows a tripartite division: phonetics-phonology, morphology, syntax. Extensive introduction by Blecua on historical development of linguistics from antiquity to transformational grammar.

1068.   Alonso, Amado, and Pedro Henríquez Ureña. Gramática castellana. 28th ed. Buenos Aires: Losada, 1977 (1939). 2 vols.
Fundamental work. A thorough introduction to Spanish grammar with ample use of literary texts.

1069.   Bello, Andrés. Gramática de lengua castellana. México: Ediplera; Madrid: Edaf, 1980 (1847). 415 pp.
Notes by Rufino J. Cuervo in 2d pt.
Still a basic reference work for Spanish grammar.

1070.   Bosque, Ignacio. Problemas de morfosintaxis. Madrid: Editorial de la Universidad Complutense, n. d., 1980. 135 pp.
Designed as a problem set for advanced students, this workbook offers insights into many difficult areas of Spanish syntax and semantics. It focuses on transformational resolutions of these issues.

1071.   Contreras, Heles. A Theory of Word Order with Special Reference to Spanish. (North-Holland Linguistics Series, Volume 29.) Amsterdam: North-Holland Press, 1976. xii, 152. Spanish edition:

El orden de palabras en español. Madrid: Ediciones Cátedra, 1978. 163 pp.
The Prague school notions of theme (given information) and rheme (new information) are applied to
problems of Spanish word order.

1072. Criado de Val, Manuel. Síntesis de morfología española. 2d ed. Madrid: Consejo Superior de Investigaciones Científicas, 1961 (1952). 186 pp.
A fine introductory study intended primarily for
non-native students of Spanish.

1073. D'Introno, Francesco. Sintaxis transformacional del
español. Madrid: Ediciones Cátedra, S. A., 1979.
307 pp.
An excellent up-to-date analysis of Spanish syntax in a transformational framework.

1074. Gili Gaya, Samuel. Curso superior de sintaxis española. 13th ed. Barcelona: Bibliograf, 1981
(1943). 347 pp.
A well-organized and clear exposition of Spanish
syntax intended for students.

1075. Hadlich, Roger L. A Transformational Grammar of
Spanish. Englewood Cliffs, N. J.: Prentice-Hall,
1971. ix, 253 pp. Spanish version: Gramática
transformativa del español (Madrid: Gredos, 1975).
464 pp.
A complete transformational grammar of Spanish,
based largely on Chomsky's Aspects of the Theory
of Syntax.

1076. Kany, Charles E. American-Spanish Syntax. 2d ed.
Chicago: University of Chicago Press, 1975 (1945).
xiii, 467 pp. Spanish version, Sintaxis hispano-
americana (Madrid: Gredos, 1969). 550 pp.
Treats the most important tendencies of American-
Spanish syntax, with emphasis on popular expression.

1077. López García-Molins, Angel. Elementos de semántica
dinámica: Semántica española. Zaragoza, Spain:
Libros Pórtico, 1977. 262 pp.
Combines Ullmann tradition of semantics with
generative syntax.

1078. Lorenzo, Emilio. El español de hoy, lengua en ebu-
llición. 3d ed. Madrid: Gredos, 1980. 284 pp.

Eight studies on morphology, syntax, and phonology of present-day Spanish, with emphasis on
the verb.

1079. Mateos M., Agustín. Etimologías latinas del español.
14th ed. México: Editorial Esfinge, S. A., 1974.
274 pp.
This historical grammar of Spanish focuses on
the Latin origins of Spanish. Phonological, mor-
phological, syntactic and lexical aspects are high-
lighted. Other linguistic influences (pre-Latin languages, Germanic, Arabic, and French) are noted.

1080. Menéndez Pidal, Ramón. Manual de gramática histórica española. 15th ed. Madrid: Espasa-Calpe,
1977 (1904). vii, 367 pp.
A fundamental work.

1081. Ramsey, Marathon M., and Robert K. Spaulding. A
Textbook of Modern Spanish. 2d ed. New York:
Holt, Rinehart & Winston, 1956 (1894). xix, 692,
xvii pp.
A classic work revised by Spaulding. Valuable
reference.

1082. Real Academia Española. Esbozo de una nueva gramática de la lengua española. Madrid: Espasa-
Calpe, 1979 (1931). 592 pp.
A standard reference which comprehensively covers Spanish grammar. This edition has a totally
new section on phonology, a revised section on morphology, and an updated section on syntax. American as well as peninsular Spanish is covered.

1083. Solé, Yolanda, and Carlos A. Solé. Modern Spanish
Syntax: A Study in Contrasts. Lexington, Mass.:
D. C. Heath, 1977. 405 pp.
A comprehensive coverage of Spanish syntax
which focuses primarily on the contrasts existing
within Spanish, and secondarily on the contrasts
that exist in relation to English.

1084. Spaulding, Robert K. Syntax of the Spanish Verb. 2d
ed. Liverpool: University Press, 1967 (1952). xx,
136 pp.
Concise explanation of the principal uses of the
Spanish verb as found in modern writings.

1085. Stevenson, C. H. The Spanish Language Today. Lon-
       don: Hutchinson University Library, 1970. 146 pp.
       Concise survey of the Spanish language, and not
       a study of grammar. Deals with the phonetic sys-
       tem, verbs, definite and indefinite articles, word
       order, word formation, and other topics. Basic
       bibliography included.

1086. Stockwell, Robert P.; J. D. Bowen; and J. W. Mar-
       tin. Grammatical Structures of English and Spanish.
       Chicago: University of Chicago Press, 1965. xi,
       328 pp.
       A contrastive approach to morphology and syntax
       with much information on methodology of teaching
       Spanish.

                          DICTIONARIES

Bibliographies

1087. Bibliographie der Wörterbucher/Bibliography of Dic-
       tionaries, 1945-1961. Warsaw: Wydawnictwa
       Naukowo-Techniczne, 1965-70. 5 vols.

1088. Fabbri, Maurizio. A Bibliography of Hispanic Dic-
       tionaries. Catalan, Galician, Spanish in Latin
       America and the Philippines. Appendix: A Bib-
       liography of Basque Dictionaries. Imola (Galeati):
       Biblioteca di "Spicilegio Moderno, " 1979. xiv, 381
       pp.
       Unannotated list of more than 3,500 dictionaries,
       vocabularies and glossaries with full bibliographic
       details. Covers dictionaries of Spanish in its var-
       ious European and non-European regional forms.
       Analytical indexes by author, language, and sub-
       ject.

1089. Marton, T. W. Foreign Language and English Dic-
       tionaries in the Physical Sciences and Engineering.
       U.S. National Bureau of Standards. Washington,
       D.C.: Government Printing Office, 1964. 189 pp.
       Covers more than 2,800 items published from
       1951 to 1962. Most items are English-based.

1090. Saur, K. O. Technik und Wirtschaft in fremden Spra-

chen: Internationale Bibliographie der Fachwörter-
buch. 3d ed. Munich: Verlag Dokumentation,
1966. cxlvi, 304 pp.
Fullest list of current language dictionaries; contains 3,632 items in 12 sections. Supplement (1967)
has 967 entries. No annotations.

1091. Walford, A. J., ed. A Guide to Foreign Language
Grammars and Dictionaries. 2d ed. London: Library Association, 1967 (1964). 240 pp.
Annotated entries--complete bibliography, critical analyses, and contents. Pages 67-88 devoted
to Spanish.

1092. Zaunmuller, Wolfram. Bibliographisches Handbuch
der Sprachwörterbucher; ein Internationales Ver-
zeichnis von 5600 Wörterbuchern der Jahre 1460-
1958 für mehr als 500 Sprachen und Dialekte.
Stuttgart: A. Hiersemann, 1958. 496 columns.
A number of Spanish dictionaries are included.

General (including historical, etymological, and grammatical)

1093. Alemany y Bolufer, José. Nuevo diccionario de la
lengua española. Barcelona: Sopena, 1964 (1957).
1,130 pp.
Gives both peninsular and American usages.

1094. Alonso Pedraz, Martín. Enciclopedia del idioma:
Diccionario histórico y moderno de la lengua española (siglos XII al XX) etimológico, tecnológico,
regional e hispanoamericano. Madrid: Aguilar,
1968. 3 vols.
Explains meaning and evolution of 30,000 Spanish
and Spanish American words based on the authority
of more than 1,500 authors from the Middle Ages
to the present.

1095. Cejador y Frauca, Julio. Vocabulario medieval castellano. Rpt., New York: G. Olms, 1971 (1929).
xii, 414 pp.
Alphabetical listing of words no longer used or
those with different meanings. Examples given from
medieval texts.

1096. Corominas, Joan. Breve diccionario etimológico de

la lengua castellana.   3d ed.   Madrid: Gredos,
1980 (1961).   628 pp.
Abbreviated, revised edition of Corominas's extensive work (see entry below).

1097. _____, with José A. Pascual.   Diccionario crítico
etimológico castellano e hispánico.   New, expanded
ed.   Madrid: Gredos, 1980-81 (1954-57).   4 vols.
2 additional vols. scheduled for publication.
Each entry begins with generally accepted etymology and then offers more speculative etymology.
Gives passages to demonstrate use of word in written works, bibliographic data, and complete lexico-
graphical data.   An indispensable reference.

1098. Covarrubias, Sebastián de.   Tesoro de la lengua castellana o española.   Rpt., Madrid: Turner, 1977
(1611).   1,093 pp.
Famous dictionary of the 17th century.   Very
useful.

1099. Criado de Val, Manuel.   Diccionario del español equí-
voco.   Madrid: SGEL, 1981.   124 pp.
Words chosen from the Libro de buen amor, La
lozana andaluza, as well as from 20th-century vocabulary with possibilities of mistaken meaning.

1100. Duden español: Diccionario por la imagen.   London:
Harrap, 1963.   672, 111, 128 pp.
One of the well-known Duden dictionaries.   First
part consists of illustrations grouped by subjects.
On page opposite each illustration are listed the
Spanish terms.

1101. Fontecha, Carlos.   Glosario de voces comentadas en
ediciones de textos clásicos.   Madrid: Consejo Superior de Investigaciones Científicas, 1941.   viii,
409 pp.
Compilation of definitions taken from numerous
critical editions.   Of great value for reading literature of past centuries.

1102. Gili Gaya, Samuel.   Tesoro lexicográfico (1492-1726).
Madrid: Consejo Superior de Investigaciones Científicas, 1947-57.   4 fascicles (A-E).
This valuable contribution is a compilation of lex-
icographical works from Nebrija's grammar to the
first dictionary of the Royal Academy.

1103. Márquez Villegas, Luis. Vocabulario del español
       hablado. Madrid: Sociedad Española de Librería,
       1975. 129 pp.
       Basic vocabulary of frequently used colloquial
       words. Includes classification by frequency of use,
       grammatical distribution and a complete list of
       words in alphabetical order.

1104. Martínez Amador, Emilio. Diccionario gramatical.
       Barcelona: Sopena, 1961. 1,498 pp.
       Explanations of grammatical and rhetorical terms,
       orthography, and abbreviations.

1105. Moliner, María. Diccionario de uso del español. Ma-
       drid: Gredos, 1979 (1966-67). 2 vols.
       Serves as a dictionary of synonyms, and of ac-
       cepted grammatical usage. Resolves doubts about
       expressions and constructions.

1106. Oelschlager, Victor R. B. A Medieval Spanish Word
       List. Rpt., Madison: University of Wisconsin
       Press, 1976 (1940). x, 230 pp.
       Very useful list, based on published texts from
       the 10th century to Berceo. Author attempts to date
       first appearance of words.

1107. Pequeño Larousse ilustrado. Paris: Larousse, 1980
       (1912). viii, 1,663 pp. Many editions.
       Good dictionary plus an encyclopedia section (his-
       tory, geography, and biography) of almost 600 pages.
       Many illustrations.

1108. Real Academia Española. Diccionario de la lengua
       castellana. Facsimile ed. Madrid: Gredos, 1979.
       3 vols. (1726-39, 6 vols.).
       This masterpiece, usually called Diccionario de
       autoridades, was the Spanish Royal Academy's first
       dictionary and is still a rich source for contempo-
       rary researchers.

1109. _____. Diccionario de la lengua española. Ma-
       drid: Real Academia Española/Espasa-Calpe, 1981
       (1726-39). xxix, 1,426 pp. Over 20 editions.
       The standard authority on current usage published
       by the Spanish Royal Academy.

1110. _____. Diccionario histórico de la lengua española.
       Madrid: Real Academia Española, 1960- .

Compilation of the different usages of each word through the centuries.

1111.   . Diccionario manual e ilustrado de la lengua española. 2d ed. Madrid: Espasa-Calpe, 1979 (1950), xi, 1,572 pp.
Based on the sixteenth and seventeenth editions of the Diccionario de la Academia, and at the same time a supplement because it lists new words, including Spanish American words, which have not received the official approval of the academy.

1112. Seco, Manuel. Diccionario de dudas y dificultades de la lengua española. 8th ed. Madrid: Aguilar, 1980 (1956). xx, 533 pp.
Aid in solving grammatical and lexical difficulties. Bibliography. Information on orthography and prosody.

1113. Vox: Diccionario general ilustrado de la lengua española. Prologue by R. Menéndez Pidal. Revised by S. Gili Gaya. 4th ed. Barcelona: Bibliograf, 1980 (1945). xl, 1,711 pp.
Authoritative, comprehensive, up to date. Gives etymology and synonyms and includes Central and South American words.

Anglicisms

1114. Alfaro, Ricardo J. Diccionario de anglicismos. 2d expanded ed. Madrid: Gredos, 1970 (1964). 520 pp.
Carefully examined compilation of anglicismos with many examples of their use. Contains index of words and an eight-page supplement.

1115. Teschner, Richard V. "A Critical, Annotated Bibliography of Anglicisms in Spanish." Hispania 57 (1974), 631-78.
Includes words from 1850 to 1973 that deal with Anglicisms in Spanish. Very comprehensive.

American Spanish

1116. Kany, Charles E. American-Spanish Euphemisms.

Berkeley and Los Angeles: University of California
Press, 1960.   xiii, 249 pp.
An important contribution, together with its com-
panion volume (see entry below) to lexicology and
semantics in Spanish America.

1117.   .   American-Spanish Semantics.   Berkeley
and Los Angeles: University of California Press,
1960.   viii, 352 pp.   Spanish translation, Semántica
hispanoamericana (Madrid: Aguilar, 1969 [1962],
xvi, 298 pp.)
First comprehensive volume on the subject.   Special emphasis on popular speech.   Explains how American Spanish differs from the Spanish norm.   Bibliography of about 300 titles and 27-page word index.

1118.   Lerner, Isaías.   Arcaísmos léxicos del español de
América.   Madrid: Insula, 1974.   274 pp.
Includes some 500 words.   The author used over
250 dictionaries and other works of reference.   Extensive bibliography of over 30 pages.

1119.   Malaret, Augusto.   Diccionario de americanismos (con
un índice científico de fauna y flora).   3d ed.   Buenos Aires: Emecé, 1946 (1925).   835 pp.
Lists Spanish words which have different meanings in America.   Considered by some to be the
most important and complete work on the Spanish
of America.

1120.   Morínigo, Marcos A.   Diccionario manual de americanismos.   Buenos Aires: Muchnik, 1966.   738 pp.
Later reprint.
Includes words, phrases, idioms, Indian terms,
Latin American etymologies, and the like.   Contains
a 46-page bibliography of great value for books and
articles dealing with regionalisms.

1121.   Santamaría, Francisco J.   Diccionario general de
americanismos.   México: Pedro Robredo, 1942-
43.   3 vols.
Includes common and scientific equivalents for
flora and fauna.   Useful tool for Mexicanisms.

Bilingual

1122.   Ayala, Francisco.   Diccionario Atlantic.   Bajo la di-

rección de Francisco Ayala. Con las pronuncia-
ciones del inglés británico e inglés americano indi-
cadas mediante el alfabeto de la Asociación Fonética
Internacional por Ivar Dahl. Buenos Aires: Editorial Sudamericana, 1977. 2 vols. in 1, 1,068 pp.
A good dictionary. It is current in scientific
terminology and has phonetic transcriptions of the
English entries using the International Phonetic Alphabet. Syllable length is indicated for the English.

1123. Cassell's Spanish Dictionary (Spanish-English, English-
       Spanish), revised by Anthony Gooch, et al. New
       York: Macmillan, 1978. xxv, 1,109 pp.
       Improvement over the original done by E. A.
       Peers, et al.

1124. Collins Spanish-English English-Spanish Dictionary.
       Compiled by Colin Smith, in collaboration with M.
       Bermejo Marcos and E. Chang-Rodríguez. London:
       Collins, 1971. xxxviii, 1,242 pp.
       A well-organized, up-to-date dictionary which
       embraces British and American English and penin-
       sular and South American Spanish. According to
       some lexicographers, this is the best dictionary of
       its type.

1125. Cuyás, Arturo; L. E. Brett; and H. S. Eaton. Ap-
       pleton's Revised English-Spanish and Spanish-English
       Dictionary. New York: Appleton-Century-Crofts,
       1961 (1903). xxxii, 697 pp.
       A good dictionary which has been used by sev-
       eral generations of students.

1126. Gerrard, A. Bryson, and José de Heras Heras. Cas-
       sell's Beyond the Dictionary in Spanish: A Hand-
       book of Everyday Usage. 2d ed., revised and en-
       larged. New York: Funk & Wagnalls, 1973 (1953).
       226 pp.
       Gives British and American translations. Usage
       of terms relating to household, office, automobile,
       food, and so forth. Attempts to bridge gap between
       Spanish acquired from grammar books and that spo-
       ken by natives.

1127. Gillhoff, Gerd A., and P. Morales. Crowell's Spanish-
       English and English-Spanish Dictionary. New York:
       Thomas Y. Crowell Co., 1963. xii, 1,261 pp.

Many Spanish American expressions. Special attention to commercial Spanish. Designed for student, businessman, and tourist. Not as complete as many other dictionaries.

1128. Gran diccionario general: Inglês-español español-inglês. Madrid: EDAF, 1966. 2 vols.
Contains archaic words useful for reading classical texts, neologisms for Spain and Spanish America, and many colloquial expressions.

1129. Peers, E. A., et al., eds. Cassell's Spanish Dictionary: Spanish-English English-Spanish. New York: Funk & Wagnalls, 1960 (1959). xvi, 1,477 pp.
A good dictionary that reflects British English.

1130. Raventós, Margaret. McKay's Modern Spanish-English English-Spanish Dictionary. New York: David McKay, 1962 (1953). xii, 1,230 pp.
Brief entries. This dictionary, suitable mainly for undergraduate students, is very careful in distinguishing different meanings. Oriented toward England and Spain.

1131. Simon and Schuster's International Dictionary: English/Spanish Spanish/English. New York: Simon & Schuster, 1973. xviii, 1,605 pp.
More than 200,000 entries, including Latin American, Iberian, American, and British variants; regionalisms; and technical and scientific terminology.

1132. Smith, C. C.; G. A. Davies; and H. B. Hall. Langenscheidt's Standard Dictionary of the English and Spanish Languages. New York: Barnes & Noble, 1966. 1,071 pp.
Words and expressions are British and Castilian. A good smaller dictionary.

1133. Velázquez de la Cadena, Mariano; E. Gray; and J. L. Iribas. A New Pronouncing Dictionary of the Spanish and English Languages. Chicago: Follett Publishing Co., 1980 (1852). 1,488 pp.
An old standby that has been somewhat modernized in recent editions.

1134. Williams, Edwin B. Spanish and English Dictionary/

Diccionario inglés y español. New York: Holt,
Rinehart & Winston, 1967 (1957). 1,226 pp. Expanded version published in 1963 (1,243 pp.)
Good, well-organized dictionary that marked an
advance over those of this type published previously.

Familiar Quotations, Proverbs, and Idioms

1135. Caballero, Ramón. Diccionario de modismos de la
lengua castellana. 2d Argentine ed. Buenos Aires:
Librería El Ateneo, 1947 (1905). 1,179 pp.
More than 60,000 idioms, with clear explanations
in Spanish.

1136. Correas, Gonzalo. Vocabulario de refranes y frases
proverbiales y otras fórmulas comunes de la lengua
castellana. Madrid: Real Academia Española,
1906 (based on a manuscript of 1627-30). 633 pp.
Rev. ed., Bordeaux: Institut d'Etudes Ibériques et
Ibero-Américaines de l'Université de Bordeaux,
1967.
Abundant collection of phrases current in Correa's time.

1137. Goicoechea Romano, Cesáreo. Diccionario de citas
verdades y semiverdades, axiomas y parodojas,
flores del genio y del ingenio de los grandes pensa-
dores, escritores y hombres célebres de todos los
tiempos, compilados en más de 12.500 frases y
ordenados según sus materias. 2d ed. Madrid:
Labor, 1962 (1952). 880 pp.
Indexed by abstract idea (ángeles, burlas, fan-
tasía, etc.) and also contains alphabetical indexes
of authors and phrases.

1138. Harbottle, Thomas B., and Martin Hume. Dictionary
of Quotations (Spanish). New York: Frederick Ungar, 1958. 462 pp.
Explanations of quotations; also translations into
English. Subject and author indexes.

1139. Iribarren, José María. El porqué de los dichos. 4th
ed. Madrid: Aguilar, 1974 (1955). 733 pp.
Covers meaning, origin, and use of sayings, idioms, and proverbs of Spain. The General Index

lists all phrases that are not arranged alphabetically.
Alphabetic index is found at back of book. Long
bibliography (pp. 675-701) of works consulted.

1140. Martínez Kleiser, Luis. Refranero general ideológico
español. Madrid: Real Academia Española, 1953.
xxx, 783 pp. Facsimile ed. Madrid: Hernando,
1978.
An extensive compilation of familiar sayings.

1141. Recio Flores, Sergio. Diccionario comparado de refranes y modismos: Spanish-English. México:
Libros de México, 1968. xv, 391 pp.
Many useful expressions in Spanish and English
listings. Contains bibliography of many types of
lexical works.

1142. Sbarbi, José María. El refranero general español.
Madrid: A. Gómez Fuentenebro, 1874-1878, 10
vols. New printing: Madrid: Atlas, 1980. 10
vols.
A standard reference.

1143. Sintes Pros, Jorge. Diccionario de aforismos, pro-
verbios y refranes: Con su interpretación para el
empleo adecuado y con equivalencias en cinco idio-
mas. 4th ed. Barcelona: Sintes, 1967 (1961).
894 pp.
Explained in French, Italian, English, German,
and Latin. Section on Latin proverbs, expressions,
and legal terminology.

1144. _____. Diccionario de máximas, pensamientos y
sentencias. 7th rev. ed. Barcelona: Sintes, 1970.
742 pp.
A useful, popular work.

1145. _____. Gran diccionario de frases célebres. Barcelona: Sintes, 1961. 3 vols.
Contains 40,000 Spanish and foreign quotes on
history, philosophy, and literature.

1146. Vega, Vicente. Diccionario ilustrado de frases célebres y citas literarias. 4th ed. Barcelona: Gustavo Gili, 1966 (1952). 939 pp.
Spanish and foreign quotations.

Synonyms and Antonyms

1147. Andrés, M. F. Diccionario español de sinónimos y
       equivalencias. 5th ed. Barcelona: Aedos, 1969.
       383 pp.

1148. Barcia, Roque. Diccionario de sinónimos castellanos.
       3d ed. Buenos Aires: Librería el Ateneo, 1944
       (1939). 735 pp.
       Also contains an extensive analytical index of the
       expressions and meanings cited or explained in the
       synonyms included in the work.

1149. Casares y Sánchez, Julio. Diccionario ideológico de
       la lengua española desde la idea a la palabra, desde
       la palabra a la idea. 2d ed. Barcelona: Gustavo
       Gili, 1981 (1942). 1,369 pp.
       Divided into three parts: synoptic, analogic, and
       the dictionary proper. The first two parts are set
       out like Roget's Thesaurus.

1150. Diccionario de sinónimos, antónimos e ideas afines.
       Buenos Aires: Editorial Andina, 1978. 213 pp.
       A handy list in three columns: palabras, sinóni-
       mos, antónimos.

1151. Diccionario de sinónimos e ideas afines y de la rima.
       2d ed. Paraninfo, Joaquim Horta Massanes (Bar-
       celona), 1978. 363 pp.
       An alphabetical listing like Roget's Thesaurus.

1152. Diccionario de sinónimos, ideas afines y contrarios.
       London: Harrap, 1967. 536 pp.

1153. Gili Gaya, S. Diccionario de sinónimos. 7th ed.
       Barcelona: Bibliograf, 1968. xvi, 352 pp.
       Interesting introduction and a well-organized and
       well-presented work.

1154. Sáinz de Robles, Federico C. Diccionario español de
       sinónimos y antónimos. 8th ed. Madrid: Aguilar,
       1978. 1,148 pp.
       Format like Roget's Thesaurus.

1155. Zainqui, José María. Diccionario razonado de sinóni-
       mos y contrarios. Barcelona: Editorial De Vecchi,
       1973. 1,073 pp.

Useful complement to bilingual and monolingual
dictionaries in the field of Castilian Spanish.

Linguistic Terminology

1156. Abraham, Werner. Diccionario de terminología lin-
       güística actual. Madrid: Gredos, 1981. 512 pp.
       Lists terms in Spanish or English, with defini-
       tions in Spanish. Includes an English index. Bib-
       liography.

1157. Ambrose-Grillet, Jeanne. Glossary of Transforma-
       tional Grammar. Rowley, Mass.: Newbury House
       Publishers, 1978. vii, 166 pp.
       Definitions of common terms and notions with
       examples from generative transformational grammar
       are contained in this reference work.

1158. Dubois, Jean, et al. Diccionario de lingüística. Ma-
       drid: Alianza, 1979. lxviii, 636 pp.
       A dictionary of linguistic terminology. Includes
       a lengthy bibliography of 25 pages.

1159. Lázaro Carreter, Fernando. Diccionario de términos
       filológicos. 4th ed. Madrid: Gredos, 1980 (1953).
       444 pp.
       Concise definitions with equivalents in foreign
       languages. At the end of the work there is a list
       of German, English, and French terms with Spanish
       equivalents.

1160. Pei, Mario A. Glossary of Linguistic Terminology.
       New York: Doubleday, 1966. 299 pp.
       Most common linguistic terminology. Where au-
       thorities differ in their uses of a term, Pei gives
       several definitions, attributing each to the particu-
       lar linguist.

1161. Steible, Daniel J. Concise Handbook of Linguistics:
       A Glossary of Terms. New York: Philosophical
       Library, 1967. 146 pp.
       Although intended for the student of English lin-
       guistics, this alphabetical listing can be useful for
       American students in other languages. Offers brief
       and simplified explanations.

Slang

1162. Bendezu Neyra, Guillermo E. Argot limeño o jerga
       criolla del Perú. Lima: Empresa Editora Lima,
       1977. 348 pp.
       Also contains essays on the theory of slang.
       Lists bibliographies consulted.

1163. Cela, Camilo José. Diccionario secreto. 2d ed.
       Madrid: Alfaguara, 1969 (vol. 1); Madrid: Alian-
       za, 1974 (vols. 2 and 3), (1st ed., 1968-71).
       A dictionary of Spanish taboo words. These
       words are illustrated in passages from different
       writers and their meanings are analyzed.

1164. León Núñez, Victor. Diccionario de argot español y
       lenguaje popular. Madrid: Alianza Editorial, 1980.
       157 pp.
       More than 2,500 entries taken from oral and
       written sources. Includes a bibliography and an
       18-page "Panorámica del argot español" written by
       Pilar Daniel.

1165. Martín Martín, Jaime. Diccionario de expresiones
       malsonantes del español. Madrid: Istmo, 1979.
       lxxx, 368 pp.
       A slang dictionary mostly of Madrid speech.

1166. Trejo, Arnulfo D. Diccionario etimológico latino-
       americano del léxico de la delincuencia. México:
       UTEHA, 1968. 226 pp.
       Mostly represents the jargon of the delinquents
       of Mexico City, but also includes the slang words
       spoken in Lima, Argentina, Brazil, Chile, Colom-
       bia, Panama, and southwestern United States.
       Trejo provides simple definitions and, wherever
       possible, the origins of the slang words. He has
       utilized the lexical studies of many Latin American
       and Spanish scholars and some Hispanic literary
       works for his definitions and etymologies. The
       largest sections cover thievery, fighting, and the
       authorities delinquents encounter, but also includes
       sections on penal institutions, parts of the body,
       dress, money, and the like. Extensive bibliogra-
       phy and index of words studied.

Rhyming

1167. Stahl, Fred A., and Gary E. A. Scavnicky. A Re-
       verse Dictionary of the Spanish Language. Urbana/
       Chicago and London: University of Illinois Press,
       1973. 181 pp.
           Basically a computer-programmed rhyming dic-
       tionary of 83,360 entries.

12. SCHOLARLY PERIODICALS

BIBLIOGRAPHIES AND GUIDES TO PERIODICALS

1168. Bleznick, Donald W. "A Guide to Journals in the Hispanic Field: A Selected Annotated List of Journals Central to the Study of Spanish and Spanish American Language and Literature." Hispania 49 (October 1966): 569-83 and 52 (October 1969): 723-37; rev. ed., 55 (March 1972): 207-21.
Fully annotated and indexed list of some 80 scholarly journals, both current and defunct. Provides information on types of articles, book reviews, and bibliographies. Other useful information.

1169. Carter, Boyd G. Historia de la literatura hispano-americana a través de sus revistas. México: Ediciones de Andrea, 1968. 271 pp.
Studies a large number of Spanish American literary publications from before Independence up to the 1960s. Extensive bibliography.

1170. _____. Las revistas literarias de Hispanoamérica: Breve historia y contenido. México: Ediciones de Andrea, 1959. 282 pp.
Information on important literary journals and on development of periodical literature and literary and philosophical currents.

1171. Catálogo de las publicaciones periódicas madrileñas existentes en la Hemeroteca Municipal de Madrid, 1661-1930. Madrid: Artes Gráficas Municipales, 1933- .
More than 3,000 titles for the years 1661-1930, listed chronologically and alphabetically. Information

on frequency of publication, size, number of pages, and dates.

1172. Charno, Steven M., comp. Latin American Newspapers in United States Libraries: A Union List. Austin: University of Texas Press, 1969. 619 pp. Detailed data on holdings of 70 libraries, with approximately 5,500 titles. Arrangement based on place of publication, first by country, then by city. Twenty Latin American republics and Puerto Rico represented.

1173. Directorio de publicaciones periódicas colombianas. Bogotá: Instituto Colombiano para el Fomento de la Educación Superior, 1975. 199 pp. Alphabetical listing of titles with information about publishing institution, place of publication, address and year when publication began.

1174. Forster, Merlin H. An Index to Mexican Literary Periodicals. New York: Scarecrow Press, 1966. iii, 276 pp. Index to 16 periodicals which began between 1920 and 1960.

1175. Gómez Rea, Javier. "Las revistas teatrales madrileñas (1790-1930)," Cuadernos bibliográficos, 31 (1974), 65-140. Data on 255 journals. Useful annotations.

1176. Guerrero, Fuensanta; Antonio Quilis; and Juan Manuel Rozas. La lengua y la literatura en el Consejo Superior de Investigaciones Científicas. Madrid: Consejo Superior de Investigaciones Científicas, 1965. 324 pp. Contains 3,000 titles on language and literature mainly taken from the books and journals of the Instituto Miguel de Cervantes of the CSIC. The years covered are chiefly 1940-64, but also included are issues of the Revista de filología española and its anejos for the years 1914-37. Also indexes the Boletín de filología española, Revista de literatura, Cuadernos de literatura, Cuadernos de literatura contemporánea, Anales cervantinos, Revista de bibliografía nacional, and Revista bibliográfica y documental.

1177. Hispanic American Periodicals Index 1978. Barbara
       G. Valk, ed. Los Angeles: UCLA Latin American
       Center, 1975- . Vol. 4 (1980), 749 pp.
       Lists annually (by subject and author) articles,
       reviews, documents, and original literary works
       appearing in nearly 250 journals throughout the
       world which deal with Latin America. Data base
       from 1970.

       Index to Latin American Periodical Literature, 1929-
       1960. See no. 151.

1178. "Indice general de publicaciones periódicas cubanas."
       Mimeographed. Humanidades y Ciencias Sociales.
       La Habana: Biblioteca Nacional José Martí, 1970- .
       A systematic attempt to compile an index to pe-
       riodical articles in Cuban journals in social sci-
       ences and humanities.

1179. Lafleur, Héctor René; Sergio D. Provenzano; and Fer-
       nando P. Alonso. Las revistas argentinas, 1893-
       1967. Rev. ed. Buenos Aires: Centro Editor de
       América Latina, 1969. 351 pp.
       A panorama of Argentine literary journals is
       given in chronological order with emphasis on lit-
       erary groups and movements. An index of journals
       concludes the study.

1180. Leavitt, Sturgis E., et al., eds. Revistas hispano-
       americanas: Indice bibliográfico, 1843-1935. San-
       tiago de Chile: Fondo Histórico y Bibliográfico José
       Toribio Medina, 1960. xxii, 589 pp.
       A listing and description of the most representa-
       tive magazines. Items are grouped according to
       subject.

1181. Levi, Nadia, et al., eds. Guía de publicaciones pe-
       riódicas de universidades latinoamericanas. Mé-
       xico: Universidad Nacional Autónoma de México,
       1967. 406 pp.
       Divided by country. Each national section con-
       tains alphabetical listing with bibliographic informa-
       tion.

1182. Madrid. Ministerio de Cultura. Dirección General
       del Libro y Biblioteca. Catálogo colectivo de pu-
       blicaciones periódicas en bibliotecas españolas. 5.

Humanidades. II. Lingüística y literatura. Instituto Bibliográfico Hispánico, 1979. Spanish equivalent to Union List of Serials. Covers 525 libraries in Spain. The Hemeroteca Municipal de Madrid could not be included. Pages 1 to 580 are devoted to periodicals arranged alphabetically by title. Holdings are indicated by years. An alphabetical index of institutions and their publications rounds out the volume.

1183.   MLA Directory of Periodicals: A Guide to Journals and Series in Languages and Literatures. Compiled by Eileen M. Mackesy, et al. New York: MLA, 1979, 1981. 541 pp.
        Furnishes basic information on all the journals and series on the Bibliography's Master List. Biennial updates are planned. Very useful.

        New Serial Titles. See no. 34.

1184.   Organization of American States. Index to Latin American Periodical Literature, 1966-1970. Columbus Memorial Library, Pan American Union. Boston: G. K. Hall, 1980. 2 vols.
        Periodicals indexed are generally of Latin American origin. Covers articles of cultural, economic, educational, historical, legal, political, and social content.

1185.   Rubio, Fanny. Revistas poéticas españolas, 1939-1975. Madrid: Turner, 1976. 550 pp.
        Useful bibliographical data on Spanish poetry magazines or on those that published poetry found throughout the book, but the reader is burdened in gleaning the data.

1186.   Shelby, Charmion, ed. Latin American Periodicals Currently Received in the Library of Congress and in the Library of the Department of Agriculture. Washington, D.C.: Library of Congress, 1944. vii, 249 pp.
        Basic information about serial literature except newspapers.

1187.   Tortajada, Armadeo, and C. de Amaniel. Materiales de investigación: Indice de artículos de revistas del Consejo Superior de Investigaciones Científicas, 1939-

1949. Madrid: Consejo Superior de Investigaciones
Científicas, 1952. 2 vols.
Author-subject index to 128 reviews of the CSIC
for the years indicated.

Ulrich's International Periodicals Directory. See no.
42.

1188. Union List of Periodicals in the Romance Languages
and Literatures in the British National, University,
and Special Libraries. London: University of London Library, 1964. vi, 150 pp.
Several hundred periodicals are listed.

1189. Valis, Noël. "Directory of Publication Sources in the
Fields of Hispanic Language and Literature." Hispania, 64 (1981), 226-57.
Essential data on 265 periodicals which will be
of special interest to those who wish to submit material to them for publication.

1190. Zimmerman, Irene. A Guide to Current Latin American Periodicals: Humanities and Social Sciences.
Gainesville, Fla.: Kallman, 1961. 357 pp.
Extensive coverage and very informative annotated
listing by country. Chapter 4 has a chronological
listing. Contains an annotated bibliography of reference sources.

1191. Zubatsky, David S. "A Bibliography of Cumulative In-
dexes to Hispanic American Language and Literary
Reviews of the Nineteenth and Twentieth Centuries."
Revista Interamericana de Bibliografía 20, no. 1
(January-March 1970): 28-57.
Annotated bibliography of some 180 journals pub-
lished in Latin America and the United States.

1192. _____. "A Bibliography of Cumulative Indexes to
Spanish Language and Literary Reviews of the Nineteenth and Twentieth Centuries." Hispania 51 (October 1968): 622-28.
Aims to include all periodicals dealing with the
Spanish and Catalan languages and literatures published in Spain during the periods covered.

1193. _____. "An International Bibliography of Cumulative

Indexes to Journals Publishing Articles on Hispanic
Languages and Literature. " Hispania, 58 (1975),
75-107.
Covers the 19th and 20th centuries. Lists reviews of general cultural interest, bulletins and
memoirs of major learned institutions and societies, when these include language and or literature
sections, and literary, critical, and philological
journals. Arrangement is by country and then alphabetical by journal title.

MAJOR JOURNALS IN THE HISPANIC FIELD

The following annotated list of journals central
to the study of Spanish and Spanish American
literatures and languages includes current and
defunct scholarly periodicals taken from the
original version of my "Guide to Journals in
the Hispanic Field" (Hispania 49 [1966]: 469-
83 and 52 [1969]: 723-37) and the revised edition (Hispania 55 [1972]: 207-21); also many
new journals are listed. The expanded list now
comprises 124 important 20th-century journals.
It should be emphasized that, as in previous
versions, this is a selected list of journals
which have a substantial frequency of articles,
bibliography, book reviews, and additional material related to the study of Hispanic language
and literature. The choice of journals, based
on my experience and the suggestions of colleagues, aims to provide a basic compilation
of periodical publications from throughout the
Hispanic world, the United States, and several
European countries.

The items included in each annotation, when
available and applicable, are found in the following order: title; subtitle; PMLA or other
standard abbreviation (if title is longer than
one word); original place of publication; date
the journal began, and if defunct, the date it
ceased publication; frequency; publishing organization and address; director or editor; in-
dex(es) of its contents; supplements it has published; language(s) of the text; nature of the articles and book reviews; and other pertinent in-

208 Scholarly Periodicals

formation. CSIC is the abbreviation for the
Consejo Superior de Investigaciones Científicas.

A number of the journals below are indexed
in Guerrero's and Tortajada's compilations (nos.
1176 and 1187 respectively, of this Sourcebook).

1194. Abside: Revista de cultura mejicana. México, 1937- .
Quarterly. Address: c/o Sergio Delmar Junco,
Apdo. Postal f-1335, San Luis Potosí, México.
Directed by Eduardo Enrique Ríos. Indexes: 1937-
56 in vol. 20 (1956); 1957-61 in vol. 25 (1961);
1962-66 in vol. 30 (1966).
Text in Spanish. Articles on Latin American
culture, literature, philosophy, and history.

1195. Al-Andalus: Revista de las Escuelas de Estudios
Arabes de Madrid y Granada (Andalus). Madrid,
1933- . Semiannual. Published by the Escuela
de Estudios Arabes, Hortaleza 104, Madrid 4,
Spain. Directed by Emilio García Gómez. Indice
de los veinte primeros volúmenes (Madrid: CSIC,
1962), 286 pp., indexed in Tortajada.
Text in French, Spanish, and English. Articles
and book reviews on Hispanic and Arabic studies in
linguistics, literature, history, art, and philosophy.
Includes lists of doctoral dissertations and necrol-
ogy.

1196. The American Hispanist (TAH). Clear Creek, Indiana,
1975- . 9 nos. per year. Address: P.O. Box
64, Clear Creek, IN 47426. Edited by John P. Dy-
son.
Text in English, Spanish, and Portuguese. Critical studies in Hispanic literature and news of the
profession. Book reviews, Newspaper format.

1197. The American Sephardi: Journal of the Sephardic
Studies Program of Yeshiva University. (Am. Seph).
New York, N.Y. 1966- . Semiannual. Address:
Sephardic Studies Program, Yeshiva University, Am-
sterdam Ave. and 186th Street, New York, N.Y.
10033. Edited by Herman Prins Salomon and Tomas
L. Ryan.
Scholarly and popular articles on all aspects of
Spanish, Portuguese, and Mediterranean Judaism,

including history, art, music, poetry, and folklore. Serialized pieces explaining Sephardic names, terminology and linguistic peculiarities. Book reviews.

1198. Anales cervantinos (A Cerv). Madrid, 1951- . Annual. Published by the CSIC, Instituto Miguel de Cervantes de Filología Hispánica, Duque de Medinaceli 4, Madrid 14, Spain. Directed by Alberto Sánchez. Annual index.

Text in Spanish. Articles on Cervantes, the Quijote, and themes applicable to Cervantes and other authors of his period. Includes a section entitled "Crónica cervantina," on people, books, studies, and other matter related to Cervantes. Contains reviews of books dealing with Cervantes or any of his works, and a "Bibliografía cervantina."

1199. Anales de la literatura española contemporánea (ALEC). Lincoln, Nebraska, Vol. 6, 1981- . Annual. Formerly Anales de la narrativa española contemporánea (1979-80), Vols. 4-5, and Anales de la novela de posguerra (1976-78), Vols. 1-3. Partially fills the gap left by the cessation of Journal of Spanish Studies: Twentieth Century (1973-80). Edited by Luis González-del-Valle at Dept. of Modern Languages and Literatures, University of Nebraska, Lincoln, NE 685888.

Text in English or Spanish. Scholarly articles on any aspect of 20th-century Spanish literature since the Generation of 1898 and modernismo. Current bibliography on fiction. Book reviews.

1200. Anales de la Universidad de Chile (AUC). Santiago, 1843- . Quarterly. Published by the Universidad de Chile, Alameda 1058, Casilla 10-D, Santiago, Chile. Directed by Alvaro Bunster. Indice general, 1843-1950 (Santiago: Editorial Universitaria, 1954), 285 pp.

Text in Spanish. Articles and book reviews on literature deal mostly with Spanish America. Publishes homenaje issues.

1201. Anales de literatura hispanoamericana. Madrid, 1976- . Annual. Published by the Cátedra de Literatura Hispanoamericana, Facultad de Filosofía y Letras, Instituto de Cultura Hispánica, CSIC, Madrid, Spain.

Text in Spanish. Articles, notes, and bibliographies on Latin American literature. Also has section on Rubén Darió. Book reviews.

1202. Anales galdosianos (An G). Pittsburgh, Pa., 1966- .
Annual. Published at University Professors Office,
Boston University, 745 Commonwealth Ave., Boston, MA 02215. Directed by Rodolfo Cardona.
Text in Spanish and English. Articles, texts,
and documents on Galdós's work and period and on
theoretical problems of the realistic novel. Bibliographies on Galdós.

1203. Annali Istituto Universitario Orientale, Napoli, Sezione
Romanza (AION-SR). Semiannual. Published by
Istituto Universitario Orientale, Largo San Giovanni
Maggiore 30, 80134 Napoli, Italy. Edited by Giuseppe Carlo Rossi.
Text in English, French, German, Italian, Portuguese, Spanish. Philological and literary studies
in Romance languages. Book reviews.

1204. Anuario de letras: Revista de la Facultad de Filosofía
y Letras. México, 1961- . Annual. Published
by the Centro de Lingüística Hispánica, 12 Piso,
Torre de Humanidades, México 20, D. F., México.
Edited by Juan M. Lope Blanch.
Text in Spanish. Articles, notes, and book reviews on Mexican and other Hispanic literatures and
languages.

1205. Anuario martiano. La Habana, 1969- . Annual.
Published by the Sala Martí, Biblioteca Nacional
de Cuba, La Habana, Cuba.
Text in Spanish. Articles devoted to all phases
of the life and work of José Martí. Includes book
review, notes, and an extensive bibliography.

1206. Arbor: Ciencia, pensamiento y cultura. Madrid,
1944- . Monthly. Published by the CSIC, Serrano 117, Madrid 6, Spain. Directed by Pedro
Rocamora Valls. Annual index and Indices de los
setenta y cinco primeros números (Madrid: CSIC,
1952), 1,600 pp., in Tortajada.
Articles and book reviews on culture and literature.

1207. Archivo de filología aragonesa (AFA). Zaragoza,
       1945- . Annual. Published by CSIC, Institución
       Fernando el Católico, Palacio de la Diputación Pro-
       vincial, Zaragoza, Spain. Directed by Manuel Al-
       var. Indexed in Tortajada.
           Text in Spanish and French. Articles and book
       reviews on linguistics of Spain and Portugal, and
       Spanish dialects, especially aragonés. Many lists
       of various lexicological distinctions found in certain
       areas of Spain.

1208. Archivum (Oviedo). Oviedo, 1951- . 3 issues per
       year. Published by the Facultad de Filosofía y
       Letras, Universidad de Oviedo, Spain. Directed
       by E. Alarcos Llorach and J. Ma. Martínez Ca-
       chero.
           Text in Spanish. Articles and book reviews on
       linguistics and some on Peninsular Spanish litera-
       ture.

1209. Archivum linguisticum: A Review of Comparative
       Philology and General Linguistics (ArL). Glasgow,
       1949- . Semiannual. Published by the University
       of Glasgow, Dept. of Linguistics and Phonetics,
       University of Leeds, Leeds L52, 9JT, England.
       Edited by I. M. Campbell and T. F. Mitchell.
           Text mainly in English and French but also in
       German, Italian, and Spanish. Articles frequently
       on Spanish topics. Book reviews and list of books
       received.

1210. Asomante: Revista literaria. San Juan, 1945-70;
       1972-76. Quarterly. Published by the Asociación
       de Graduadas de la Universidad de Puerto Rico.
       Directed by Venus Lidia Soto. Indices de "Aso-
       mante" (1945-1959) (San Juan: Instituto de Cultura
       Puertorriqueña, 1963), 82 pp.
           Text in Spanish. Articles and book reviews
       mainly on Hispanic literature. Also includes orig-
       inal poetry, short stories, and correspondence from
       Spain, Italy, and Paris on current literary affairs.

1211. Atenea: Revista de ciencia, arte y literatura. Con-
       cepción, 1924- . Title changed to Nueva atenea
       for nos. 423-24 (1970) and back to Atenea with no.
       425 (1972). Address: Casilla 1557, Concepción,

Chile. Directed by Tito Castillo. Indice general
for 1924-50, compiled by Arthur E. Gropp (Washington, D.C.: Pan American Union, 1955), 205 pp.
Text in Spanish. Articles on Hispanic literature
and long book reviews on Hispanic and general literature. Also concerned with culture and art.
Some numbers are homenajes.

1212. The Bilingual Review/La revista bilingüe (BR/RB),
Ypsilanti, Michigan. 3 nos. per year. Edited by
Gary D. Keller, Dept. of Foreign Languages and
Bilingual Studies, 106 Ford Hall, Eastern Michigan
University, Ypsilanti, MI 48197.
Text mainly in English and Spanish but also
French, Italian and Portuguese. Studies on lin-
guistics of bilingualism, bilingual education and
U.S. Hispanic language and literature. Book re-
views.

1213. Boletín cultural y bibliográfico (BCB). Bogotá, 1958-
73, 1979- . Monthly. Address: Banco de la República, Biblioteca Luis Angel Arango, Calle 11
No. 4, Bogotá, Colombia.
Text in Spanish. Articles and notes of Colombian writers, in the country and abroad, in the
areas of culture, literature and history.

1214. Boletín de dialectología española (BDE). Barcelona,
1941-68. Continued the Butlletí de dialectología
catalana (1913-36). Annual. Published by the Instituto Internacional de Cultura Románica ... de
Barcelona. Directed by A. Griera.
Text in Spanish, French, and Catalan. Articles
mostly on Spanish linguistics and dialectology.
Most of each issue is devoted to an extensive annotated bibliography.

1215. Boletín de filología (BFC). Santiago, 1934- . Title
was Anales for vols. 1-3. Annual. Published by
the Universidad de Chile, Facultad de Filosofía y
Letras, Depto. de Lingüística y Filología, Casilla
10136, Correo Central, Santiago, Chile. Index for
vols. 1-9 in vol. 10 (1958) and classified index of
articles previously published in vol. 20 (1969).
Text mostly in Spanish, some in German. Articles on Spanish language, especially phonology and
grammar. Also includes cultural matters and some

Hispanic literature.   Book reviews and list of books
received.

1216. Boletín de filología espanola (BFE).   Madrid, 1953- .
Quarterly.   Published by the CSIC, Instituto Miguel
de Cervantes de Filología Hispánica, Duque de Medinaceli 4, Madrid 14, Spain.   Directed by Manuel
Criado de Val.   Indexed in Guerrero.
Text in Spanish.   Articles mainly on linguistics
and some on literature.   Bibliographies of linguistics by subject and country.

1217. Boletín del Centro de Estudios del Siglo XVIII (Boces,
XVIII).   Oviedo, 1973- . Irregular.   Address:
Cátedra Feijoo, Facultad de Filosofía y Letras,
Universidad de Oviedo, Spain.   Edited by José
Miguel Caso González.
Text in Spanish.   Articles on the culture, liter-
ature and history of 18th-century Spain.   Extensive
bibliographies.   Also publishes anejos.

1218. Boletín de la Academia Argentina de Letras (BAAL).
Buenos Aires, 1933-51; 1956- . Semiannual.   Published by the Academia Argentina de Letras, Sánchez de Bustamante 2663, Buenos Aires 25a, Argentina.   Directed by Angel J. Batlistessa.   Index of
vols. 1-29 (1933-64) in vol. 30 (1965).
Text in Spanish.   Articles on Argentine and other
Hispanic literatures.   Bibliographies on specific literary figures.

1219. Boletín de la Academia Colombiana.   Bogotá, 1950- .
5 issues a year.   Published by the Academia Colombiana at Carrera 3-A, Número 17-34, Bogotá, Colombia.   Directed by Manuel José Forero.
Text in Spanish.   Articles, essays, and bibliographic notes on Colombian and other Spanish American (occasionally peninsular Spanish) literatures and
languages.   Includes some original poetry and news
of the Academy.

1220. Boletín de la Academia Norteamericana de la Lengua
Española (BANLE).   New York City, 1976- . An-
nual.   Edited by Eugenio Chang-Rodríguez, FDR
Post Office, P. O. Box 7, New York, NY 10022.
Text in Spanish.   Scholarly articles, usually on
linguistics, but also on history, literature, and edu-

cation of the Spanish-speaking people of North America. Also includes information on the activities of BANLE and major cultural institutions of the Hispanic world.

1221. Boletín de la Biblioteca de Menéndez Pelayo (BBMP). Santander, 1919-38; 1945- . Quarterly. Published by the Biblioteca de Menéndez y Pelayo, Santander, Spain. Directed by Ignacio Aguilera y Santiago. Index for 1919-59 in vol. 26 (1960). Text in Spanish. Articles and book reviews on language, literature, and ethnology of Spain. Menéndez Pelayo and classical Spanish writers are frequent subjects.

1222. Boletín de la Real Academia Española (BRAE). Madrid, 1914- . Publication suspended, 1936-44. 3 issues per year. Published by the Real Academia Española, Felipe IV, Madrid 4, Spain. Index for vols. 1-25 (1914-46) in vol. 25. Publishes anejos on linguistics and literature.
Text in Spanish. Scholarly articles on language, lexicology, grammar dialectology, phonology, and literature. Reviews journals and books and lists latest publications.

1223. Bulletin hispanique: Annales de la Faculté des Lettres de Bordeaux (BH). Bordeaux, 1898- . Quarterly. Published by the Institut d'Etudes Ibériques et Ibéroaméricaines, Univ. de Bordeaux III, Domaine Universitaire, 33405 Talence, France. Indexes for 1899-1928, 1929-48, 1949-58.
Text in French and Spanish. Articles on history, literature, history of ideas, and linguistics. Reviews of books and magazines, list of books received, and bibliography of Hispanic literature.

1224- Bulletin of Hispanic Studies (BHS). Liverpool, 1923- .
5.   Formerly called Bulletin of Spanish Studies. Quarterly. Published by the Liverpool University Press. Edited by A. L. Mackenzie and J-L. M. Marfany. P. O. Box 147, Liverpool L 69 3 BX, England. Indexes: vols. 1-30 in vol. 30; for years 1923-73 in vol. 50 (December 1973).
Text mostly in English, some in Spanish. Articles on whole range of Spanish, Portuguese, Catalan, and Latin American languages and literatures.

Many book reviews and six-monthly review of journals.

1226. Bulletin of the Comediantes (B Com). Madison, Wis.,
        1949- . Semiannual. Edited by James A. Parr,
        Dept. of Spanish and Portuguese, University of
        Southern California, Los Angeles, CA 90007.
        Text in English and Spanish. Articles are gen-
        erally short and deal with the Golden Age comedia
        and earlier drama. Lists current productions of
        comedias and other useful news. Includes current
        bibliography of foreign publications dealing with the
        comedia.

1227. The Canadian Modern Language Review/La Revue Ca-
        nadienne des langues vivantes (CMLR). Welland,
        Ontario, 1943- . Quarterly. Edited by Anthony
        S. Mollica, 4 Oakmont Rd., Welland, Ontario,
        Canada L3C4X8.
        Text preferably in English and French. Articles
        on literature, linguistics and pedagogy. Book re-
        views.

1228. Canadian Review of Comparative Literature/Revue Ca-
        nadienne de littérature canadienne (CRCL). Edmon-
        ton, Canada, 1974- . 3 nos. per year. Edited
        by Milan V. Dimic, Dept. of Comparative Litera-
        ture, The University of Alberta, Edmonton, Canada
        T6G2E6.
        Text preferably in English and French. Scholarly
        articles on literature from both an international and
        interdisciplinary view. Book reviews.

1229. Caravelle: Cahiers du monde hispanique et luso-
        brésilien. Toulouse, 1963- . Semiannual. Ad-
        dress: Univ. de Toulouse-le Mirail, 56 rue du
        Taur, 31000 Toulouse, France. Edited by Georges
        Baudot.
        Text in French, Spanish, Portuguese. Articles
        on the anthropology, history, sociology, geography,
        and literature of Latin America. Book reviews.

1230. Casa de las Américas (Casa-A). La Habana, 1960- .
        Bimonthly. Published by Casa de las Américas,
        G. y Tercera, Vedado 3, La Habana 4, Cuba. Di-
        rected by Roberto Fernández Retamar.
        Text in Spanish. Articles of broad scope on Latin

American social and political matters as well as
literature. Also contains excerpts from original
works and book reviews.

1231.   Celestinesca: Boletín informativo internacional, Athens, Georgia, 1977- . Semiannual. Edited by
Joseph T. Snow, Dept. of Romance Languages, University of Georgia, Athens, GA 30602.
Text in English and Spanish. Articles, news,
bibliography and notices of works in progress on
celestinesque literature. Book reviews.

1232.   Cervantes: Bulletin of the Cervantes Society of America. Gainesville, Fla., 1981- . Semiannual. Edited by John J. Allen, ASB 170, University of Florida, Gainesville, FL 32611.
Text in English and Spanish. Publishes scholarly
articles on Cervantes' life and works, plus reviews
and notes of interest to cervantistas.

1233.   Chasqui: Revista de literatura latino-americana.
1971- . 3 nos. per year. Edited by Ted Lyon,
142 F. O. B. , Brigham Young University, Provo,
UT 84602.
Text in English, Portuguese, and Spanish. Creative and critical work dealing with Latin American
literature. Book reviews and bibliographies.

1234.   Comparative Literature: Official Journal of the American Comparative Literature Association (CL). Eugene, Ore. , 1949- . Quarterly. Published by the
University of Oregon, Eugene, Oregon 97403, with
the cooperation of the Comparative Literature Section of MLA. Edited by Thomas R. Hart and Steven
F. Rendall, 223 Friendly Hall, Univ. of Oregon,
Eugene, OR 97403. Cumulative index for 1949-63.
Text mainly in English, occasionally in French,
German, Italian, and Spanish. Articles deal with
interrelations of literatures, theory of literature,
movements, genres, periods, authors, and problems of literary criticism. Book reviews.

1235.   Comparative Literature Studies (CLS), Urbana, Illinois, 1963- . Quarterly. Edited by A. Owen Al-
dridge, 2054 Foreign Language Bldg. , University of
Illinois, Urbana, IL 61801.
Text mainly in English, but other Romance lan-

guages and German accepted. Literary history and
the history of ideas from a comparatist perspective.
Book reviews.

1236. La corónica: Spanish Medieval Language and Litera-
ture Newsletter, 1972- . Semiannual. Edited by
John S. Miletich, Dept. of Languages, 1530SH,
University of Utah, Salt Lake City, UT 84112.

1237. Crítica hispánica (CH), Johnson City, Tenn., 1979- .
Semiannual. Address: P. O. Box 24302, East Tennessee State Univ., Johnson City, TN 37601. Edited by Laurentino Suárez.
Text in English and Spanish. Scholarly articles
and notes on Hispanic literature and linguistics.
Book reviews.

1238. Cuadernos americanos: La revista del Nuevo Mundo
(CA). Mexico, 1942- . Bimonthly. Published at
Avenida Coyoacán 1035, México 12, D. F., México.
Directed by Jesús Silva Herzog. Index for nos. 1-
100 (1942-58) published in 1959. Publishes anejos
on literature.
Text in Spanish. Articles on Spanish American
literature, philosophy, and history, with emphasis
on contemporary matters. Includes original works
and reviews of magazines and books.

1239. Cuadernos bibliográficos. Madrid, 1961- . Irregular. Edited by José Simón Díaz, CSIC, Vitruvio 8,
Apdo. 14-458, Madrid 6, Spain.
Text in Spanish. Monographic volumes and mis-
cellanies of bibliographies mainly on the literature
of Spain. The miscellaneous volumes contain articles, reviews, and notes relating to bibliography.

1240. Cuadernos de la Cátedra Miguel de Unamuno (CCU).
Salamanca, 1948- . Annual. Published by the
Servicio de Publicaciones de la Universidad de Salamanca, Patio de Escuelas Menores, Univ. de Salamanca, Spain. Directed by Fernando Lázaro Carreter.
Text in Spanish and French. Articles concern
the life, works, and philosophy of Unamuno. Bibliography on Unamuno in each issue.

1241. Cuadernos hispanoamericanos: Revista mensual de

cultura hispánica (CHA). Madrid, 1948- . Monthly. Published by the Centro Iberoamericano de Co-
operación, Avda. de los Reyes Católicos 4, Madrid
3, Spain. Directed by José Antonio Maravall. Author index for nos. 1-100 in no. 100 (1958).
Text in Spanish. Articles on Hispanic literature,
history, and philosophy, especially 20th-century.
Long book reviews, notes on literary events, and
special issues devoted to single authors.

1242. Cultura neolatina (CN). Modena, 1941- . 3 issues
per year. Published by S. T. E. M. Mucchi, Via
Tabboni 4, 41100, Modena, Italy. Directed by
Aurelio Roncaglia.
Text in Italian, Spanish, French, English, and
German. Articles on Romance languages and lit-
eratures with good representation of peninsular
Spanish. Book reviews and list of books received.

1243. Diacritics: A Review of Contemporary Criticism,
Ithaca, N. Y., 1970- . Quarterly. Edited by
Richard Klein, 278 Goldwin Smith, Cornell University, Ithaca, NY 14853.
Text in English. A review of contemporary criticism in literature, cinema, and the arts. Invites
critical responses to published opinion. Review articles and book reviews.

1244. Dieciocho: Hispanic Enlightenment, Aesthetics and
Literary Theory. 1978- . Semiannual. Edited
by Eva M. Kahiluoto Rudat, Dept. of Spanish and
Portuguese, Rutgers College, Rutgers University,
New Brunswick, NJ 08903.
Text in English, Spanish, and Portuguese. Stud-
ies of Hispanic Enlightenment (Peninsular and Latin
American), aesthetics and literary theory in gen-
eral. Book reviews.

1245. Dispositio: Revista hispánica de semiótica literaria.
1976- . 3 nos. per year. Edited by Walter Mi-
gnolo, et al., Dept. of Romance Languages, University of Michigan, Ann Arbor, MI 48109.
Text in English and Spanish, but also accepts
French. Articles and notes on Hispanic semiotics
in the field of literary studies.

1246. Los ensayistas: Boletín informativo, 1976- . Edited

by José Luis Gómez-Martínez, Dept. of Romance
Languages, University of Georgia, Athens, GA
30602.
  Text in Spanish, English, and Portuguese. Articles, notes, news, and bibliographies on the Hispanic essay. Book reviews.
  La estafeta literaria: Revista quincenal de libros,
artes y espectáculos. Madrid, 1944-78. See Nueva estafeta, no. 1271.

1247. Estudios filológicos. Valdivia, 1965- . Annual.
  Published by the Instituto de Filología, Facultad
  de Filosofía y Letras, Universidad Austral de Chile,
  Casilla 567, Valdivia, Chile. Directed by Guillermo
  Araya.
    Text in Spanish. Articles on Hispanic literature
  and philology.

1248. Explicación de textos literarios (ExTL), 1972- .
  Semiannual. Edited by Francisco E. Porrata, Dept.
  of Spanish and Portuguese, California State University, Sacramento, CA 95826.
    Text in Spanish. Scholarly studies dealing with
  literary works in Castilian. Book reviews.

1249. Filología. Buenos Aires, 1949- . Publication suspended, 1954-58. Annual. Published by the Ministerio de Educación, Facultad de Filosofía y Letras
  de la Universidad de Buenos Aires, 25 de Mayo 217,
  1002 Buenos Aires, Argentina. Directed by Angel
  J. Battistessa.
    Text in Spanish. Articles mainly on linguistics,
  but some on literature. Book reviews on general
  Hispanic works.

1250. Filología moderna (FMod). Madrid, 1960- . 3 nos.
  per year. Edited by Hans Juretschke, Facultad de
  Filosofía y Letras, A-38, Ciudad Universitaria, Madrid 3, Spain.
    Text in Spanish. Articles and notes on Hispanic
  and non-Hispanic literatures and languages. Book
  reviews.

1251. Germanisch-Romanische Monatsschrift (GRM). Heidelberg, 1909- . Publication suspended, 1943-October
  1950. Quarterly. Address: Am Hasenpfad 12, D

6300, Giessen, Germany.   Edited by Conrad Wiede-
mann.
Text in German.   Articles on literature and philology with adequate attention to Spanish.   Book reviews, notes, and list of books received.

1252. Hispamérica: Revista de literatura. 1972- . 3 nos.
per year. Edited by Saúl Sosnowski, 5 Pueblo
Court, Gaitherburg, MD 20760.
Text in Spanish.   Essays, interviews, fiction,
and reviews dealing exclusively with Spanish American literature.

1253. Hispania: A Journal Devoted to the Interests of the
Teaching of Spanish and Portuguese.   Cincinnati,
Ohio 45221, 1917- . Quarterly. Published by the
American Association of Teachers of Spanish and
Portuguese. Edited by Donald W. Bleznick, Department of Romance Languages and Literatures,
University of Cincinnati, Cincinnati, OH 45221.
Cumulative index every 10 years (most recently for
1968-77, published in 1980).
Text in English, Spanish, and Portuguese. Articles devoted to peninsular Spanish, Latin American,
and Portuguese literatures and languages. Also
contains pedagogical articles and news, general information on literary and cultural events, many
book reviews, list of books received, and an annual listing (May issue) of doctoral dissertations
completed and in progress.

1254. Hispanic Review: A Quarterly Journal Devoted to Research in the Hispanic Languages and Literatures
(HR). Philadelphia, 1933- . Quarterly. Published by the Department of Romance Languages,
University of Pennsylvania, Box 20, Philadelphia,
PA 19104. Edited by Russell P. Sebold. Index to
vols. 1-25 (1933-57) issued as supplement to vol.
25 (1958).
Text in English and Spanish. Mainly articles on
Hispanic and Portuguese literatures, and some on
linguistics. Many book reviews on literature and
linguistics, and list of books received.

1255. Hispanófila: Literatura, ensayos. Madrid, 1957- .
3 issues per year. Published at the University of
North Carolina, Chapel Hill, NC 27514. Edited by
A. V. Ebersole. Cumulative index every 3 years.

Text in Spanish and, occasionally, in English.
Articles on Spanish and Spanish American literatures of all genres and periods.   Book reviews.

1256. Iberoromania: Revista destinada a las lenguas y li-
teraturas de España, Portugal y Latinoamérica.
Munich, 1969- . Quarterly and now semiannual.
Published at Max Niemeyer Verlag, Pfrondorfer
Str. 4, 7400, Tübingen, W. Germany. Printed by
Ediciones Alcalá, Madrid. Directed by Dr. Hein-
rich Bihler, et al.
Text mainly in Spanish, Portuguese, and Catalan
but also in German, English, French, and Italian.
Articles on Iberian and Latin American linguistics
and literatures and information on congresses and
new and projected publications. Reviews.

1257. Ideologies and Literature, 1977- . Bi-monthly. Edited by Antonio Ramos-Gascón, et al., 9 Pleasant
St., S. E. 4 Folwell Hall, University of Minnesota,
Minneapolis, MN 55455.
Text in Spanish, English, and Portuguese. Socio-
historical approaches to Hispanic and Luso-Brazilian
literatures.

1258. Imagen: Quincenario de arte, literatura e información
cultural. Caracas, 1967- . Semimonthly. Published by the Instituto Nacional de Cultura y Bellas
Artes, Edificio Gran Avenida, Plaza Venezuela,
Apartado de Correos 12.497, Caracas, Venezuela.
Publishes articles, interviews, and reviews on
all phases of culture, with an emphasis on that of
Spanish America. Here, the term "culture" includes
literature, ballet, movies, music, art, art exhibits,
and the like. It is well illustrated. Often publishes
Spanish translations of both critical and creative material. Almost every number contains a supplement
devoted to the study of an individual or a topic.
Newspaper format.

1259. Indice. Madrid, 1945- . Monthly to 1968, now bimonthly. Published at Monte Esquinza 24, Madrid
4, Spain. Directed by J. Fernández Figueroa.
Text in Spanish. Articles on literature, art,
dance, theater, and the like. Most articles per-
tain to Spain, some to Spanish America and other
countries. Excerpts from literary texts and book
reviews. Newspaper format.

1260. Insula: Revista bibliográfica de ciencias y letras.
       Madrid, 1946- . Monthly. Published by Insula
       Librería, Benito Gutiérrez 26, Madrid 8, Spain.
       Directed by Enrique Canito. Index for 1946-56
       published by Insula (1958).
           Text in Spanish. Articles on literatures, poetry,
       theater, and movies of Spain, Spanish America, Eu-
       rope, and the United States. Many book reviews.
       Newspaper format.

1261. Journal of Hispanic Philology. 1976- . 3 nos. per
       year. Edited by Daniel Eisenberg, Dept. of Modern
       Languages, Florida State University, Tallahassee,
       FL 32306.
           Text in Spanish and English. Articles and re-
       views of the languages and literatures of the Iberian
       Peninsula from their origins through 1700. Pri-
       marily traditional in critical orientation.

1262. Kentucky Romance Quarterly (KRQ). Lexington, Ky.,
       1967- . Supersedes Kentucky Foreign Language
       Quarterly (1954-67). Quarterly. Published by the
       University of Kentucky, Lexington, KY 40506. Ed-
       ited by John E. Keller.
           Text mainly in English but also in French, Span-
       ish, and Portuguese. Articles on Hispanic, French,
       and other Romance literatures.

1263. Les langues néo-latines. Paris, 1906- . 4 nos.
       per year. Address: See latest issue. This is
       the official bulletin of the Société des Langues Néo-
       Latines.
           Text mainly in French but some in Spanish. Ar-
       ticles on Spanish, Spanish American, Portuguese,
       and Catalan literatures. Book reviews.

1264. Latin American Literary Review (LALR). Pittsburgh,
       Pa., 1972- . Semiannual. Published by the De-
       partment of Modern Languages, Carnegie-Mellon
       University, Pittsburgh, PA 15213. Edited by Yvette
       E. Miller.
           Text in English. Articles on the literatures of
       Latin America and Latin American minorities in the
       United States. Also includes creative writing and
       book reviews limited to the analysis of creative
       works.

1265. Latin American Theatre Review: A Journal Devoted
       to the Theatre and Drama of Spanish and Portuguese
       America (LATR). Lawrence, Kans., 1967- .
       Semiannual. Published by the Center of Latin
       American Studies. University of Kansas, Law-
       rence, KS 66044. Edited by George Woodyard.
       Text in English, Spanish, and Portuguese. Ar-
       ticles are historical, critical, or bibliographic in
       nature. Includes current theater activity, play syn-
       opses, works in progress, theater seasons, and fes-
       tivals. Book reviews.

1266. Letras de Deusto (LdD). Bilbao, 1971- . Semian-
       nual. Edited by Ignacio Elizalde Armendáriz, Fa-
       cultad de Filosofía y Letras, Universidad de Deusto,
       Bilbao, Spain.
           Text in Spanish, French, and English. Articles
       and reviews on linguistics, literature, philosophy
       and history.

1267. Les lettres romanes (LR). 1947- . Quarterly. Di-
       rected by Raymond Pouilliart, 146 Koning Albert-
       laan, 3040 Korbeek-Lo, Belgium.
           Text in French. Articles, critical reviews, book
       reviews, and bibliographic notes on Romance litera-
       ture. Addressed to the specialist.

1268. Lexis. Lima, Perú, 1977- . Semiannual. Address:
       Pontificia Univ. Católica, Depto. de Humanidades,
       Apdo. 12514, Lima 21, Perú. Edited by José Luis
       Rivarola.
           Text in Spanish. Articles on Hispanic linguistics
       and literary theory with special interest in Spanish
       America (particularly the Andean countries). Book
       reviews.

1269. MLN: Modern Language Notes (MLN). Baltimore,
       1886- . Changed title to MLN with vol. 77 (1962).
       6 issues per year. Published by Johns Hopkins
       Press, Baltimore, MD 21218. Edited by Paul Ol-
       son, et al. Indexes for vols. 1-50 (1935) and vols.
       51-60 (1946).
           Text in English, Spanish, and other modern lan-
       guages. One issue per year devoted to the Hispanic
       field, mainly literature. Book reviews dealing with
       Romance languages and German.

1270. Modern Language Review: A Quarterly Journal De-
       voted to the Study of Medieval and Modern Literature
       and Philology (MLR). Cambridge, 1905- . Quar-
       terly. Published by the Modern Humanities Re-
       search Association, St. Catharine's College, Cam-
       bridge, England. Edited by Colin Smith. Indexes
       for vols. 1-10 (1905-15), 11-20 (1916-25), and 21-
       30 (1926-38). Text in English. Articles and many book re-
       views on English, French, Italian, and Hispanic
       literature and language; several articles per year
       in the Hispanic field.

1271. Nueva estafeta, 1978- . Monthly. Supersedes La
       estafeta literaria (1958-77). Edited by Luis Ro-
       sales, Avenida José Antonio 62, Madrid 13, Spain.
       Text in Spanish. Articles and reviews of His-
       panic and world literatures, the arts, poetry, short
       stories.

1272. Nueva revista de filología hispánica (NRFH). México,
       1947- . Superseded Revista de filología hispánica
       (see no. 973). Semiannual. Published by El Cole-
       gio de México, Camino al Ajusco 20, México 20,
       D. F., México. Edited by Antonio Alatorre.
       Text in Spanish. Articles on Spanish and Spanish
       American literatures and languages, some Luso-
       Brazilian. Very extensive bibliography on all lit-
       erary genres and linguistics. Reviews of books and
       journals.

1273. Orbis: Bulletin international de documentation linguis-
       tique. Louvain, 1952- . Semiannual. Published
       by the Centre International de Dialectologie Générale,
       Blijde-Inkomstraat 21, Louvain, Belgium. Di-
       rected by Sever Pop (1952-60) and now A. J. Van
       Windekens.
       Text in French, Italian, Spanish, English, and
       occasionally other languages. Articles on language
       and linguistics, dialectology, grammar, and com-
       parative studies in these fields. Bibliographies and
       reviews of books.

1274. Papeles de Son Armadans (PSA). Palma de Mallorca,
       1956-79. Monthly. Directed by Camilo José Cela.
       Index for nos. 1-57 (1956-60) published in Palma de
       Mallorca, Spain (1961).

Text in Spanish. Articles and book reviews on
Spanish literature; original letters, poems, and
short stories.

1275. Plural: Crítica y literatura. México, 1971- .
Monthly. Published by the newspaper Excelsior,
Reforma No. 12/505, México 1, D.F., México.
Text in Spanish. Articles on Hispanic and world
literatures, culture, politics, society, art, and so
forth. Also includes original poetry and excerpts
from books and news of literary events. Newspaper
format.

1276. PMLA. Baltimore, 1884- . 6 issues per year.
Published by the Modern Language Association of
America, 60 Fifth Avenue, New York, NY 10011.
Edited by Joel Conarroe. Cumulative indexes for
vols. 1-50 (1935), 51-60 (1945), and 51-79 (1964).
MLA publishes annually an extensive international
bibliography (see no. 33).
Text in English and other modern languages.
Scholarly articles on modern literatures.

1277. Primer acto: Revista del teatro (PA). Madrid, 1957-
75; 2a época, 1980- . Published at Velázquez
138, Madrid 6, Spain. Directed by José Monleón.
Text in Spanish. Articles on Spanish and world
contemporary theater. Reviews other theater magazines. Articles by playwrights on various aspects
of the theater. Publishes original plays.

1278. Prohemio: Revista cuatrimestral de lingüística y crítica literaria. Madrid, 1970- . 3 issues per
year. Published by Cupsa Editorial, Cristóbal
Bordiu 35, of. 207, Madrid 3, Spain.
Text in Spanish. Mostly devoted to contemporary and past Hispanic linguistics and literature in
its articles and book reviews, but also covers world
linguistics and literatures.

1279. Quaderni ibero-americani: Attualità culturale nella
Penísola iberica e America latina (QIA). Torino,
1946- . Semiannual. Published by ARCSAL, Via
Po 19, 10126 Torino, Italy. Directed by G. M.
Bertini.
Text in Italian and Spanish. Articles on Hispanic
literature and comparative Italo-Spanish literature.

Includes news of intellectual life of Spain, Portugal,
and Latin America. Reviews of books and magazines.

1280. Razón y fe: Revista hispanoamericana de cultura
(RyF). Madrid. 1901- . Monthly. Published
by CESI (Casa de Escritores S. I.), Pablo Aranda
3, Madrid 6, Spain. Indexes for 1901-52 published
by Ediciones Fax (1954).
Text in Spanish. Articles on world literatures,
but most are on Spain and Latin America. Also
includes philosophy, especially Catholic, and its relation to literature, as well as concern with contemporary problems of tradition and progress. Bibliography of world philosophy, religion, and history;
and book reviews.

1281. Repertorio americano. San José de Costa Rica, 1919-
59; 1974- . Quarterly. Published by the Universidad de Estudios Latinoamericanos, Universidad
Nacional de Costa Rica, IDELA, Apdo. 86, Heredia,
Costa Rica. Index for years 1919-59 is being published; 5 vols. projected. Tomo I, letras A-B
(1981).
Text in Spanish. Articles devoted largely to the
literatures of Spanish America. One of the most
influential literary reviews of Latin America under
the direction of Joaquín García Monge in its first
period. Book reviews.

1282. Review. New York, 1968- . 3 issues per year
(since 1972). Published by the Center for Inter-
American Relations, Inc., 680 Park Avenue, New
York, New York 10021. Edited by Ronald Christ.
Text in English. Articles, reviews, interviews,
and news on Latin American literature. Has sections devoted to specific writers.

1283. Revista canadiense de estudios hispánicos (RCEH).
Toronto, 1976- . 3 nos. per year. Edited by
M. J. Valdés, 14045 Robarts Library, University
of Toronto, Ontario, Canada M5S 1A5.
Text in Spanish, English, French, Catalan and
Galician. Scholarly articles on Hispanic literature,
linguistics, history and philosophy. Book reviews.

1284. Revista chicano-riqueña (RD-R). 1970- . 3 nos.

per year.   Edited by Nicolás Kanellos, Dept. of
Spanish, University of Houston, TX 77004.
Text in English and Spanish.   Critical studies
of Chicano and Puerto Rican literature and art, as
well as original works.   Book reviews.

1284a.   Revista de archivos, bibliotecas y museos (RABM).
Madrid, 1871-78, 1883, 1897-1931, 1947-52, 1953- .
Semiannual.   Published by the Ministerio de Cultura,
Biblioteca Nacional, Paseo Calvo Sotelo 20, Madrid
1, Spain.   Index for 1871-1957 (1958) published in
Madrid in 1959.
Text in Spanish.   Articles on Spanish libraries,
archaeology, history, music, literature, and lan-
guage.   Book reviews.

1285.   Revista de dialectología y tradiciones populares (RDTP).
Madrid, 1945- .   Quarterly.   Published by CSIC,
Instituto Miguel de Cervantes, Departamento de Dialectología y Tradiciones Populares, Duque de Medinaceli 4, Madrid 14, Spain.   Indexed in Tortajada.
Text in Spanish.   Articles on all regions of Spain
and their dialects, geography, history, culture, literature, music, religion, folklore, and ethnology.
Book reviews.

1286.   Revista de estudios hispánicos (REHisp).   Río Piedras,
1928-30; 1971- .   Semiannual.   Published by the
Seminario de Estudios Hispánicos "Federico de
Onís," Facultad de Humanidades, Universidad de
Puerto Rico, Río Piedras, Puerto Rico 00931.   Di-
rected by Daisy Carballo Abreu.
Text in Spanish.   Articles on Hispanic literature,
linguistics, culture, folklore, and bibliographies.
Book reviews and list of books received.

1287.   Revista de estudios hispánicos (REH).   University,
Ala., 1967- .   3 issues per year.   Published by
the University of Alabama, Department of Romance
Languages, University, AL 35486.   Edited by En-
rique Ruiz-Fornells.
Text mainly in Spanish and English.   Articles on
Hispanic literature.   Also reviews journals and
books.

1288.   Revista de filología española (RFE).   Madrid, 1914- .
Suspended, 1938-40.   Quarterly.   Published by CSIC,

Instituto Miguel de Cervantes, Duque de Medinaceli
4, Madrid 14, Spain. Directed by Dámaso Alonso.
Indexes: vols. 1-46 (1963) in vol. 47 (1964); Alice
M. Pollin and Raquel Kersten, Guía para la consulta de la "RFE," 1914-1960 (New York: New
York University Press, 1964); in Guerrero. Publishes anejos on Spanish language and literature.
Text in Spanish. Articles on early Spanish literature and language, grammar, and dialects. Reviews of articles in related journals. Annual bibliography of Spanish linguistics, philology, literature,
history, poetry, and theater (all early Spanish).
Also contains a word index and many book reviews.

1289. Revista de filología hispaánica (RFH). Buenos Aires
       and New York, 1939-46. Superseded by Nueva re-
       vista de filología hispánica (see no. 1272). Quar-
       terly. Directed by Amado Alonso.
          Articles on Spanish, Latin American, and Portu-
       guese literatures and philology of early times. Ex-
       tensive bibliographies of peninsular Spanish litera-
       ture and language. Reviews of books and journals.

1290. Revista de ideas estéticas (RIE). Madrid, 1943- .
       Quarterly. Published by the CSIC, Instituto Diego
       Velázquez (Sección de Estética), Duque de Medina-
       celi 4, Madrid 14, Spain. Directed by José Camón
       Aznar. Indexed in Tortajada.
          Text in Spanish, occasionally in English and
       French. Articles and book reviews on aesthetics
       of art, music, and literature.

1291. Revista de literatura (RL). Madrid, 1952-70; 1978- .
       Semiannual. Published by the CSIC, Instituto de
       Miguel de Cervantes de Filología Hispánica, Duque
       de Medinaceli 4, Madrid 14, Spain. Directed by
       Joaquín de Entrambasaguas. Indexed in Guerrero.
          Text in Spanish. Articles and book reviews
       mostly on Spanish literature. Extensive bibliogra-
       phies that list latest books and articles on Spanish
       authors and Darío.

1292. Revista de occidente (RO). Madrid, 1923-36; 1963-77;
       1980- . 4 nos. per year. Published at Génova
       23, Madrid 4, Spain. Directed by José Ortega y
       Gasset in its first period. Edited by Soledad Or-
       tega. Index for 1923-36 published by CSIC in 1952.

Text in Spanish. Articles and book reviews on
literature, philosophy, art, history, religion, sociology, and political science. One of the most influential Spanish journals of this century in its first
period.

1293. Revista española de lingüística: Organo de la Sociedad
       Española de Lingüística (REL). Madrid, 1971- .
       Semiannual. Published by Sociedad Española de
       Lingüística, Duque de Medinacelli 4, Madrid 14,
       Spain. Edited by Francisco R. Adrados.
       Text in Spanish, English, French, German, Cata-
       lan. Articles mainly on linguistics relating to Span-
       ish and other languages. Also includes news of lin-
       guistic symposia and the latest research in struc-
       tural linguistics. Many reviews of books published
       in England, France, the United States, and other
       countries.

1294. Revista hispánica moderna (RHM). New York, 1935- .
       Quarterly. Published by the Hispanic Studies Pro-
       gram, Columbia University, 612 West 116th Street,
       New York, NY 10027. Edited by Karl-Ludwig Selig.
       Text in English, Spanish, Portuguese, French,
       German. Articles and book reviews on the modern
       literature of Spain, Portugal, and Latin America.
       Extensive quarterly bibliographies on Latin Ameri-
       can literature and language ended with volume 34
       (1968).

1295. Revista iberoamericana (RI). Mexico, 1939- . Semi-
       annual. Published by the Instituto Internacional de
       Literatura Iberoamericana, CL 1312, University of
       Pittsburgh, Pittsburgh, PA 15260. Edited by Al-
       fredo A. Roggiano. Index for vols. 1-15 (1939-50)
       published in 1954 by the Unión Panamericana.
       Text mainly in Spanish. Articles on Latin Amer-
       ican literature, notes and documents, bibliographies.
       Reviews of books and journals.

1296. Revista interamericana de bibliografía/Inter-American
       Review of Bibliography (RIB). Washington, D.C.,
       1951- . Quarterly. Published by the Department
       of Cultural Affairs, General Secretariat of the OAS,
       Washington, DC 20006. Edited by Elena Castedo-
       Ellerman. Cumulative index of vols. 1-15 (1951-65)
       in vol. 15 (1965).

Text in Spanish, English, French, and Portuguese. Articles mainly on Latin American literature and literary figures. Also includes recent information on new publications, authors, and libraries of Latin America. Bibliographies of books, pamphlets, and articles recently acquired by the Pan American Library and other select libraries. Many book reviews and lists of books received.

1297. Revista nacional de cultura (RNC). Caracas, 1938- .
Quarterly. Published by the Instituto Nacional de la Cultura, Apartado de Correos 50995, Caracas, Venezuela. Directed by Vicente Gerbasi. Index for nos. 1-150 by author, subject, and title.
Text in Spanish. Articles on Venezuelan, other Spanish American, and some Spanish literatures. Also includes comparative studies, culture, short stories, and poetry. Bibliographies of Venezuelan works and reviews of books in all fields, written in other languages as well as Spanish.

1298. Revue de linguistique romane (RLiR). Strasbourg, 1925- . Published by the Institut Pierre Gardette, 23 rue du Plat, 69288 Lyon Cedex 1, France. Edited by M. G. Tuaillon.
Text mainly in French, some English, German, Italian and Spanish. Articles and book reviews on Romance linguistics, grammar, lexicology, and phonology. Bibliographies of Romance linguistics, dictionaries, and glossaries.

1299. Revue de littérature comparée (RLC). Paris, 1921- .
Publication suspended, July 1940-September 1946. Bimonthly. Published by Univ. François Rabelais, 3 rue des Tanneurs, 37000 Tours, France. Edited by Jacques Voisine. Index cumulative every 10 years; 1921-50 in 2 vols.
Text mainly in French but some in English, German, Italian, and Spanish. Articles on comparative literature with Spanish frequent. Bibliographies and book reviews.

1300. Revue hispanique (RH). New York, 1894-1933. Edited by Raymond Foulché-Delbosc (to 1929). Index by tome of vols. 1-80 (1894-1930) in The Hispanic Society of America's Catalogue of Publications, by Clara L. Penney (New York, 1943), pp. 31-43.

Text in Spanish, French, English, German, and
Italian. Articles and book reviews on Spanish and
Portuguese history, literatures, and languages.
Also general cultural topics. Bibliographies on
language, history, the arts, folklore, and litera-
ture.

1301. Romance Notes (RomN). Chapel Hill, N.C., 1959- .
3 nos. per year. Published by the Department of
Romance Languages, University of North Carolina,
Dey Hall 014-A, Chapel Hill, NC 27514. Edited
by Edouard Morot Sir.
Text in English, some French, and Spanish.
Short articles, frequently by young scholars, on
Romance literatures and languages; many on Spain
and Latin America.

1302. Romance Philology (RPh). Berkeley, Calif., 1947- .
Quarterly. Published by the University of California
Press, Berkeley, CA 94720. Edited by Yakov Malkiel.
Text in English, French, Italian, Spanish, Portuguese, and German. Articles and book reviews on
Romance linguistics, dialectology, phonology, lexicology, and medieval literary theory. Spanish literature and linguistics appear frequently.

1303. Romania. Paris, 1872- . Quarterly. Published at
19 rue de la Sorbonne, 75005 Paris, France. Edited by Jacques Monfrin. Cumulative indexes for
1872-1901 and 1901-34.
Text mainly in French, but some in English,
German, Spanish, and Italian. Articles on Romance linguistics and literatures with good representation for Spanish. Bibliographies of journal
articles and book reviews.

1304. Romanic Review (RR). New York, 1910- . Quarterly. Published by the Department of Romance
Languages, Columbia University through the Columbia University Press, New York, NY 10025. Edited by Michael Riffaterre.
Text mainly in English; some French, Spanish,
and Italian. Articles and book reviews on Romance
literatures with occasional articles on Hispanic literature, mostly peninsular.

1305. Romanische Forschungen: Vierteljahrschrift für ro-
       manische Sprachen und Literaturen (RF). Frank-
       furt, 1883- . Publication suspended, 1943-50.
       Quarterly. Published at Köln am Rhein, Univ.
       Romanisches Seminar, Albertus Magnus Platz,
       Germany. Edited by Fritz Schalk.
       Text in French, Spanish, English, German, and
       Italian. Articles and book reviews on Romance
       philology and literatures. Yearly analytical sur-
       vey of philological studies.

1306. Romanistisches Jahrbuch (RJ). Hamburg, 1947- .
       Annual. Published by the Romanisches Seminar
       and Ibero-Amerikanisches Forschunginstitut of Ham-
       burg University, Von Melle Park 6, VI, D-2000,
       Hamburg 13, West Germany.
       Text in German, Spanish, French, Italian, and
       English. Articles and book reviews on Romance
       philology and literatures with good representation
       of Hispanic literature and language.

1307. Sefarad: Revista del Instituto Arias Montano de Es-
       tudios Hebraicos y Oriente Próximo. Madrid,
       1940- . Published by the Instituto Arias Mon-
       tano, Duque de Medinaceli 4, Madrid 14, Spain.
       Edited by Francisco Cantera Burgos. Cumulative
       index every 15 years.
       Text in Spanish, also English, French, German,
       Italian, and Hebrew. Articles on Judeo-Spanish
       life, literature, culture, and history. Bibliography
       on problems of Jewish culture. Reviews of maga-
       zines and books.

1308. Segismundo: Revista hispánica de teatro. Madrid,
       1965- . Semiannual. Published by the CSIC, In-
       stituto Miguel de Cervantes, Duque de Medinaceli
       4, Madrid 14, Spain.
       Text in Romance languages, English, and Ger-
       man. Scholarly articles on the Hispanic theater.

1309. Sin nombre: Revista trimestral literaria. San Juan,
       1970- . Quarterly. Published at Calle Cordero
       No. 55, Santurce, PR00911; Apartado 4391, San
       Juan, PR 00905. Directed by Nilita Vientós Gas-
       tón.
       Text in Spanish. Articles and book reviews on
       Puerto Rican and other Hispanic literatures and
       news of the literary world.

1310.   Sur.   Buenos Aires, 1931- . Semiannual.   Index
        for nos. 1-302 (1931-66) in nos. 303-5 (November
        1966-April 1967).   Directed by Victoria Ocampo
        until her death in 1979.
        Text in Spanish.   Articles and book reviews on
        literary studies, mostly Spanish American.   Much
        original work of contemporary Hispanic authors and
        others (in translation).   Bibliographies on contem-
        porary literature.

1311.   Symposium: A Quarterly Journal in Modern Litera-
        tures.   Syracuse, N.Y., 1946- .   Quarterly.   Pub-
        lished by the Department of Romance Languages of
        Syracuse University with the Centro de Estudios
        Hispánicos, through the Syracuse University Press,
        Syracuse, NY 13210.   Edited by J. H. Mathews.
        Text mainly in English, some French, German,
        and Spanish.   Articles and book reviews on many
        modern literatures with good representation in the
        Hispanic field.

1312.   Texto crítico.   Xalapa, Veracruz, México, 1975- .
        3 nos. per year.   Address: Centro de Investigacio-
        nes Lingüístico-Literarias, Universidad Veracru-
        zana, Apdo. 369, Xalapa, Veracruz, México.   Ed-
        ited by Jorge Ruffinelli.
        Text in Spanish but articles may be written in
        French, English, Italian, German, or Portuguese.
        Literary criticism and theory on any genre of Latin
        American literature.

1313.   Thesaurus: Boletín del Instituto Caro y Cuervo.   Bo-
        gotá, 1945- .   3 issues per year.   Published by
        the Instituto Caro y Cuervo, Apartado Aéreo 51502,
        Bogotá, Colombia.   Edited by Ismael Enrique Del-
        gado Tíllez.   Indices de los tomos I-XXV (1945-
        1970) by Elena Alvar, published by the Instituto
        Caro y Cuervo (1974).   518 pp.
        Text in Spanish.   Articles on Spanish American,
        Spanish, and Colombian literatures, linguistics,
        grammar, dialectology, phonology, lexicology, and
        folklore.   Reviews of books and leading philological
        magazines.

1314.   La torre: Revista general de la Universidad (Torre).
        Río Piedras, 1953-73.   Quarterly.   Published by
        Editorial Universitaria, Río Piedras, PR.   Directed
        by Jaime Benítez.   Index for years 1953-60.

Text in Spanish. Articles on Puerto Rican and
other Hispanic literatures, philosophy, history, and
politics. Bibliography on Puerto Rico, Argentina,
Mexico, and Spain. Book reviews on world literatures.

1315. Universidad de la Habana (UH). La Habana, 1934- .
Bimonthly. Published by the Departamento de Inter-
cambio Universitario, La Habana, Cuba. Directed by
Elías Entralgo y Vallina. Index for nos. 1-124/129
(1934-56) in 1959.
Articles and book reviews on Cuban and other
Hispanic literatures, comparative literature, history, philosophy, politics, and culture. More po-
litically oriented since 1958.

1316. World Literature Today (continues Books Abroad),
Norman, Okla., 1927- . Quarterly. Edited by
Ivar Ivask, 630 Parrington Oval, Room 110, Nor-
man, OK 73019.
Text in English. Short articles on contemporary
writers and literary movements in foreign countries.
Many book reviews.

1317. Zeitschrift für romanische Philologie (ZRP). Tübingen, 1877- . Suspended, 1914-23 and 1945-48.
6 issues per year. Published at Höhenstrasse 24,
D-6900 Heidelberg Ziegelhausen, West Germany.
Edited by Kurt Baldinger. Cumulative indexes for
vols. 1-30 and 31-50.
Monographs on linguistics. Text in German,
French, Spanish, English, and other Romance languages. Articles and book reviews on Hispanic and
other Romance languages and literatures. Bibliographic supplements of literature and linguistics
have extremely wide coverage, especially since the
publication of the volume for the years 1940-50.
With the four-volume bibliography for the years
1961-62, ZRP has been publishing its valuable bibliography under the title Romanische Bibliographie/
Bibliographie romane/Romance Bibliography.

GUIDES

1318. Barberena B., Elsa. Directorio de bibliotecas de la
Ciudad de México. 2d ed. México: Universidad
de las Américas, 1967.
Describes services and holdings of 244 libraries.

1319. Boston Public Library. Catalogue of the Spanish Library and of the Portuguese Books Bequeathed by
George Ticknor to the Boston Public Library. Boston: Boston Public Library, 1879. Rpt., Boston:
G. K. Hall & Co., 1970, 550 pp.
An extensive listing arranged by author. Some
3,200 books and pamphlets in the Luso-Hispanic
field are among the nearly 10,000 works. Also
includes analytical references to works in larger
collections and in serial publications.

1320. Columbus Memorial Library of the Pan American
Union. Guía de bibliotecas de la América latina:
Edición provisional. 2d ed. Washington, D.C.:
Pan American Union, 1962 (1942). viii, 166 pp.
Alphabetical arrangement within each country by
name of institution. Data given for each: address,
name of head librarian, number of volumes in library, date of founding, type of library, and indication whether exchange service provided. Includes
general libraries with more than 2,000 volumes and
scholarly libraries with more than 1,000.

Downs. American Library Resources. See no. 28.

1321. Esdaile, Arundell. National Libraries of the World.
2d ed., revised by F. J. Hill. London: Library
Association, 1957 (1934). 413 pp.

History, important collections, building description, catalogs, place in national system, staff, and finances are data supplied for each library.

1322. Gropp, Arthur E. Guide to Libraries and Archives in Central America and the West Indies, Panama, Bermuda, and British Guiana, Supplemented with Information on Private Libraries, Bookbinding, Bookselling, and Printing. New Orleans, La.: Tulane University Press, 1941. 721 pp.
Libraries, archives, book industry, trade librarians, government appropriations, and historical background are data included.

1323. Guía de las bibliotecas de Madrid. Madrid: Servicio de Publicaciones del Ministerio de Educación Nacional, 1953. 556 pp.
Public and private libraries, with addresses, numbers of volumes, and descriptions of manuscripts and special collections.

1324. Hill, Roscoe R. The National Archives of Latin America. Cambridge, Mass.: Harvard University Press, 1945. xx, 169 pp.
History, organization, contents, and publications of the 19 existing national archives. Illustrations.

1325. International Library Directory. London: A. P. Wales Organization, 1963- .
Thorough listing by country. Description and address of each library.

1326. Martijevic, Nicolás. Guía de las bibliotecas universitarias argentinas. Bahía Blanca: Casa Pardo, 1976. 171 pp.
Basic information about the holdings of Argentine university libraries.

1327. Peraza Sarausa, Fermín. Directorio de bibliotecas de Cuba, 1968. Gainesville, Fla.: Biblioteca de Bibliotecario, 1968.
The last of six editions (from 1942). Useful information, including scope and holdings, of Cuban libraries.

1328. The World of Learning, 1981-82. 32d ed. London: Europa Publications Limited, 1982. 2 vols.

Lists alphabetically by nation the universities and
libraries with their mailing addresses and names of
many university administrative officials and professors. Also lists learned societies and research in-
stitutes.

CATALOGS

1329. Aguilar Piñal, Francisco. Impresos castellanos del
siglo XVI en el British Museum. Madrid: Consejo
Superior de Investigaciones Científicas, 1970. 137
pp.
Annotated listing of 442 books which complements
Thomas's Short-Title Catalogue (see no. 120).

1330. Bancroft Library. Catalog of Printed Cards. Berkeley and Los Angeles: University of California
Press; Boston: G. K. Hall & Co., 1964. 22 vols.
A photocopy of author and title cards of an important Hispanic collection.

1331. Biblioteca Nacional de Madrid. Inventario general de
manuscritos de la Biblioteca Nacional. Madrid:
Ministerio de Educación Nacional, 1953-70. 9 vols.
Annotated bibliographic descriptions of 3,026 manuscripts, dealing mostly with literature and history.

1332. Bibliotheek der Rejksuniversitiet te Utrecht. España
e Hispanoamérica: Catálogo de libros españoles y
publicaciones extranjeras sobre España e Hispanoamérica. Utrecht: Rejksuniversitiet te Utrecht,
1948-60. 1 vol., 10 vols. of Supplements. Utrecht:
1949-68.
Includes linguistics, literature, periodicals, dictionaries, grammars, histories of literature, anthologies, and translations. Foreign entries in languages of sources but annotations in Spanish.

1333. Castañeda, Carlos E., and Jack A. Dabbs. Guide to
the Latin American Manuscripts in the University
of Texas Library. Cambridge, Mass.: Harvard
University Press, 1939. x, 217 pp.
Complete listing of manuscripts on the history
and culture of Latin America and of former Spanish
colonies now part of the United States.

1334. Florida University Libraries. Catalog of the Latin
       American Library. Boston: G. K. Hall & Co.,
       1973. 13 vols.; First Supplement, 1980, 7 vols.
       Lists approximately 120,000 volumes, pamphlets,
       periodicals, and government documents in their
       original forms. Greatest strength in Cuban, Hai-
       tian, and Dominican Republic materials, but also
       good in other Latin American materials. Includes,
       in order of strength, history, social and political
       sciences, literature, and the other humanities.

1335. Harvard University Library. Latin American Litera-
       ture: Classification Schedule; Classified Listing by
       Call Number; Author and Title Listing; Chronologi-
       cal Listing. Cambridge, Mass.: Harvard Univer-
       sity Press, 1969. 489 pp.

1336. Hispanic and Luso-Brazilian Councils, Canning House
       Library, London. Author and Subject Catalogues.
       Boston: G. K. Hall & Co., 1967. Hispanic Coun-
       cil, 4 vols.; First Supplement, 1973, 288 pp.
       This library contains 30,000 Latin American,
       Portuguese, and Spanish books, mostly of the 19th
       and 20th centuries. Philosophy, religion, education,
       history, economics, the arts, and language and lit-
       erature are among the broad range of cultural areas
       covered. The library also houses important cul-
       tural and economic serials.

1337. Hispanic Society of America. Catalogue of the Li-
       brary of the Hispanic Society of America. Boston:
       G. K. Hall & Co., 1962. 10 vols.; First Supple-
       ment, 1970, 4 vols.
       Photocopies of cards for every book printed since
       1700. Manuscripts, most periodicals, and pre-1700
       books are not included. Emphasis is on the art,
       history, and literature of Spain, Portugal, and co-
       lonial Hispanic America. More than 100,000 titles.

1338. Ibero-Amerikanisches Institut. Berlin. Schlagwortka-
       talog des Ibero-Amerikanischen Instituts, Preussis-
       cher Kulturbesitz in Berlin (Subject Catalog of the
       Ibero-American Institute, Prussian Cultural Heritage
       Foundation in Berlin). Boston: G. K. Hall, 1977.
       30 vols.
       Catalog of one of leading libraries in Latin Amer-
       ican studies. Subject Catalog. Contains about

300,000 volumes, including books and periodical articles. Imprint dates go back to 1945. Subject indexes in English and in Spanish.

1339. Jones, Harold G. Hispanic Manuscripts and Printed Books in the Barberini Collection. Vatican City: Biblioteca Apostolica Vaticana, 1978. 2 vols. A rich collection, especially on the Spanish Golden Age.

1340. Latin American Serials Vol. 3: Literature with Language, Art and Music. London: Committee on Latin America, 1977. 253 pp. Catalogue of holdings of over 150 British libraries and collections of reviews concerning Latin American artistic matters in general.

1341. McKnight, William, and Mabel Barrett Jones. A Catalogue of "comedias sueltas" in the Library of the University of North Carolina. Chapel Hill: University of North Carolina Press, 1965. vii, 240 pp. Author index follows list of plays. Title listing also includes opening and final lines. More than 1,900 items, covering Catalonian and Spanish plays of the Golden Age and the 18th century.

1342. Molinaro, J. A.; J. H. Parker; and Evelyn Rugg. A Bibliography of "comedias sueltas" in the University of Toronto Library. Toronto: University of Toronto Press, 1959. vii, 149 pp. Covers 17th- and 18th-century drama. First entry dated 1703 and last 1825. Lists original title with shortened version of publication's name, first and last printed lines, publisher, date, and number of pages.

1343. National Library, Peru. Author Catalog of the Peruvian Collection of the National Library of Peru. Boston: G. K. Hall, 1979. 6 vols. Contains about 94,000 items of works by Peruvians and about Peru published between 1583 and 1977. Lists approximately 10,000 periodicals.

Penney. Printed Books, 1468-1700. See no. 109.

1344. Regueiro, José M. Spanish Drama of the Golden Age:

A Catalogue of the "comedia" Collection in the University of Pennsylvania Libraries. New Haven, Conn.: Research Publications, 1971. 106 pp.

1345. Rodríguez-Moñino, Antonio, and María Brey Mariño. Catálogo de los manuscritos poéticos castellanos existentes en la biblioteca de The Hispanic Society of America (siglos XV, XVI y XVII). New York: Hispanic Society of America, 1965-66. 3 vols. Catalog of 248 manuscripts of lyric poetry, divided into three major sections: collections, authors, and anonymous works.

1346. Rogers, Paul P. The Spanish Drama Collections in the Oberlin College Library: A Descriptive Catalogue. Oberlin, Ohio: Oberlin College Press, 1940. ix, 468 pp. Supplement, under same title, published in 1946, 157 pp. Lists 7,400 dramatic works dating from 1678 to 1924. Annotated as to condition of manuscript, notes, cross-references, imprint, pagination, size, and series.

Thomas. Short-Title Catalogue. See no. 120.

1347. Tudela de la Orden, José. Los manuscritos de América en las bibliotecas de España. Madrid: Cultura Hispánica, 1954. 586 pp. Catalog divided into two parts: Madrid, and the provinces. A bibliographic essay is included.

1348. Tulane University. New Orleans. Catalog of the Latin American Library of the Tulane University Library. Boston: G. K. Hall, 1970. 9 vols. First Supplement, 1973. 2 vols.; Second Supplement, 1975. 2 vols.; Third Supplement, 1978. 2 vols. Includes material from all of Latin America, most of which deals with the social sciences and humanities. Specializes in Mexico and Central America. Arranged in dictionary form.

1349. University of Buenos Aires. Argentine Bibliography: A Union Catalogue of Argentinian Holdings in the Libraries of the University of Buenos Aires. Boston: G. K. Hall, 1980. 7 vols. More than 105,000 cards of the 53 libraries of

the University of Buenos Aires. Lists all works
written by Argentine authors and works about Argentina published anywhere in the world through
1977.

1350. University of Miami. Coral Gables, Fla. Catalog
of the Cuban and Caribbean Library of the University of Miami. Boston: G. K. Hall, 1977. 6
vols.
Also contains material on Mexico and Colombia
as well as on the entire Caribbean area. Strong
in 20th-century Cuban history and literature.

1351. University of Texas at Austin. Catalogue of the Latin
American Collection of the University of Texas Library. Boston: G. K. Hall, 1969. 31 vols.
First Supplement, 1971. 5 vols.; Second Supplement, 1973. 3 vols.; Third Supplement, 1975. 3
vols.; Fourth Supplement, 1977. 3 vols.; Bibliographic Guide to Latin American Studies: 1978,
1979. 3 vols.; Bibliographic Guide to Latin American Studies: 1979, 1980. 3 vols.; Bibliographic
Guide to Latin American Studies: 1980, 1981. 3
vols.
In the library's 160,000 volumes dating from the
15th century to the present can be found information
on virtually any subject relating to Latin America.

1352. Chatham, James R., and Enrique Ruiz-Fornells. Dissertations in Hispanic Languages and Literatures: An Index of Dissertations Completed in the United States and Canada, 1876-1966. Lexington: University Press of Kentucky, 1970. xiv, 120 pp. Vol. 2: 1967-77. Compiled by James R. Chatham with Carmen C. McClendon. Lexington: University Press of Kentucky, 1981. xi, 162 pp.

Includes literatures and linguistics of Spain, Spanish America, Brazil, and Portugal. The general index gives a topical analysis of the entries under each of the categories together with names of authors of dissertations and the literary figures to whom dissertations have been devoted.

Vol. 2 contains data on more than 3,500 dissertations written in the United States and Canada and also includes dissertations on the teaching and learning of Catalan, Portuguese, and Spanish and on bilingualism.

1353. _____, and Sara Matthews Scales. "Western European Dissertations in the Hispanic and Luso-Brazilian Languages and Literatures: A Retrospective Index." Draft (1982) in two volumes: "Author List" and "Index."

Retrospective list of 6,050 dissertations accepted in Western European universities starting before the middle of the 19th century. The detailed index is very useful.

1354. Dissertation Abstracts International. Sec. A, "Humanities." Ann Arbor, Mich.: University Microfilms, 1935- . Vols. 1-11 (1935-51) issued as Microfilm Abstracts; vols. 12-29 (1952-June 1969) issued as

Dissertation Abstracts. The present title began with
vol. 30 (July 1969). Monthly compilation.
Contains abstracts of dissertations accepted by
most American and Canadian universities and, since
1969, European universities (in Section C).

1355.   Fichier Central des Thèses, l'Université de Paris X
(Nanterre). Directed by Madame Falaise. Estab-
lished under the auspices of the Ministère des Uni-
versités in 1970.
Contains over 70,000 dissertation titles, approximately 50,000 in preparation and 20,000 completed
(in 1982), in the fields of humanities, theology, law,
economics, political science, and business. Con-
tact Mme Falaise, Directrice, Fichier Central des
Thèses, 200 Avenue de la République, Univ. de
Paris X, Nanterre, France.

1356.   Hispania. "Dissertations in the Hispanic Languages
and Literatures." Vol. 18, 1935- . Published
annually in the May issue.
List of completed and in-progress Ph.D. dissertations. Through 1949, M.A. theses were also
listed.

1357.   Jones, C. A. "Theses in Hispanic Studies Approved
for Higher Degrees by British Universities to 1971."
Bulletin of Hispanic Studies 49 (October 1972): 325-
54. Updated by F. W. Hodcroft for 1972-74 (52,
1975, 325-44) and by D. Mackenzie for 1975-78 (56,
1979, 283-304).
Begins with 1913. The largest number of theses
is devoted to literature and history, but such fields
as language, Spanish-Arabic studies, education, religion, politics, and economics are also represented.
Index of authors.

1358.   Modern Language Journal. "American Doctoral De-
grees Granted in the Field of Modern Languages."
Vol. 7, 1922- . Published annually.
Lists currently include dissertations granted in
Romance languages and literatures, comparative ed-
ucation, foreign-language education, and linguistics.

1358a. Tesis doctorales aprobadas en las universidades españolas durante el curso 1976/77. Madrid: Ministerio de Educación y Ciencia, Centro de Proceso de

Datos, 1978. The 1978/79 volume appeared in 1979
and the 1978/79 volume in 1981.

This Fichero Mecanizado de Tesis Doctorales includes an annual collection of brief abstracts of dissertations accepted in all disciplines in public and
private universities. Useful indexes of authors,
subjects, etc.

1359. Zubatsky, David S. "An International Guide of Completed Theses and Dissertations in the Hispanic
Languages and Literatures." Hispania 55 (May
1972): 293-302.

A very useful annotated list arranged by country
or by geographical region, then by type of published
list. This list should be the starting point for any-
one seeking to find what theses and dissertations
have been written in the United States and abroad.

15. OTHER USEFUL REFERENCES IN THE HISPANIC FIELD

BIOGRAPHICAL DICTIONARIES

1360. Arze, José Roberto. Ensayo de una bibliografía biográfica boliviana. La Paz: Amigos del libro,
1981. 71 pp.
Includes 367 unannotated items on biographies
published mainly in books and pamphlets. Index
of writers included in the listing.

1361. Asenjo, Conrado, ed. Quién es quién en Puerto Rico:
Diccionario biográfico de record personal. 4th ed.
San Juan: Imprenta Venezuela, 1948-49. 216 pp.

1362. Canals, S. Olives, and Stephen S. Taylor, eds. Who's
Who in Spain: A Biographical Dictionary Containing
About 6,000 Biographies of Prominent People in and
of Spain and 1,400 Organizations. Montreal: Inter-
continental Book and Publishing Co., 1963. 998 pp.
Data include present occupation, date and place
of birth, education, career, address, ancestors'
awards, memberships, recreation, and family.

1363. Coll y Toste, Cayetano. Puertorriqueños ilustres.
2d ed. Río Piedras, 1971 (1967). xxx, 372 pp.
Rpt. in 1976.
Contains biographical sketches of a good number
of Puerto Ricans in both editions.

1364. Diccionario biográfico de Chile. 13th ed. Santiago:
Empresa Periodística Chile, 1967 (1936). liv, 1,732
pp. 14th ed., 1970.
One of the most complete biographical dictionaries
in Latin America.

1365. Diccionario biográfico de México. Monterrey: Revesa,
       1968. 643 pp.
       Provides basic biographical information on prom-
       inent Mexican academics and social figures.

1366. Diccionario biográfico de Venezuela. Madrid: Blass,
       1953. li, 1,558 pp.
       Divided by region or state.

1367. Esperabé Arteaga, Enrique. Diccionario enciclopédico
       ilustrado y crítico de los hombres de España. 2d
       ed. Madrid: Artes Gráficas Ibarra, 1957. 530
       pp.
       Around 3,000 entries.

1368. Hilton, Robert, ed. Who's Who in Latin America:
       A Biographical Dictionary of Notable Living Men
       and Women of Latin America. 3d ed., revised
       and enlarged. Stanford, Calif.: Stanford Univer-
       sity Press, 1946-51 (1935). 7 vols. Rpt., De-
       troit: Blaine Ethridge Books, 1971, 2 vols.
       About 8,000 entries.

1369. Inguíniz, Juan Bautista. Bibliografía biográfica mexi-
       cana. México: Porrúa and Universidad Nacional
       Autónoma de México, 1969. 431 pp.
       Annotated listing of 1,314 references to books,
       pamphlets, and periodical and newspaper articles
       containing biographical data on Mexicans. Includes
       a name index.

1370. Instituto Nacional del Libro Español. Quién es quién
       en las letras españolas. 3d ed., revised and en-
       larged. Madrid, 1980 (1969). 495 pp.
       Brief biographies of living Spanish authors.

1371. National Directory of Latin Americanists: Biobibli-
       ographies of 1884 Specialists in the Social Sciences
       and Humanities. 2d ed. Washington, D.C.: Li-
       brary of Congress, Hispanic Foundation, 1971 (1966).
       684 pp. New edition is being prepared (1982).
       Biographies of 2,695 specialists in the social sci-
       ences and humanities.

1372. Peraza Sarausa, Fermín, ed. Diccionario biográfico
       cubano. La Habana: Anuario Bibliográfico Cubano,
       1951-60 (vols. 1-11); and Gainesville, Fla., 1966-
       68 (vols. 12-14).

Alphabetical biographical dictionary of deceased persons who were born in Cuba or had some connection with Cuba. Volumes 12-14 present new biographies.

1373. _____. Personalidades cubanas. La Habana: Anuario Bibliografíco Cubano, 1957-65. 8 vols. Vol. 8, Cuba en el exilio.
Biographies of living Cubans and those who have had some importance in Cuban life.

1374. Peruanos notables de hoy. Lima: Manuel Beltroy, 1958. 202 pp.
Alphabetical biographical dictionary containing complete data on living Peruvians. Index with classification by profession.

1375. Quién es quién en Colombia: Biografías contemporáneas. Bogotá: Editorial Temis Librería, 1978. 400 pp.

1376. Quién es quién en el Uruguay. Ed. by Central de Publicaciones SRL. Montivideo: Gráfica "33," 1980. 688 pp.

1377. Quién es quién en la Argentina: Biografías contemporáneas. 9th ed. Buenos Aires: Kraft, 1968 (1939). 1,083 pp.
Biographical information for some 8,000 Argentines.

1378. Quién es quién en Venezuela, Panamá, Ecuador, Colombia. Bogotá: O. Perry, 1952- .
Very complete biographical dictionary of living people.

1379. Rosa-Nieves, Cesáreo, and Esther M. Melón. Biografías puertorriqueñas: Perfil histórico de un pueblo. Sharon, Conn.: Troutman Press, 1970. 487 pp.
Alphabetical listing of more than 300 biographical sketches of outstanding Puerto Ricans. Contains bibliography.

1380. Slocum, Robert B., ed. Biographical Dictionaries and Related Works: A Bibliography. Detroit: Gale Research Co., 1967. 1,056 pp. Supplement (1972), 852 pp. 2d Supplement (1978), 912 pp.

Latin American countries and Spain included
among the 4,829 references in the basic volume
and the approximately 3,500 additional items in the
Supplements. Each entry has full bibliographic information and a descriptive annotation. Contains
such material as collective biographies, biobibliographies, epitaphs, genealogical works, dictionaries
of antonyms and pseudonyms, historical and specialized dictionaries. Indexes of authors, titles, and
subjects.

ENCYCLOPEDIAS

1381. Enciclopedia Barsa de consulta fácil.   México: Ency-
       clopaedia Britannica, 1980 (1957).   16 vols.
       Prepared with the advice of the editorial board
       of Encyclopaedia Britannica.   Volume 15 includes
       atlas; volume 16, guides to further reading.

1382. Enciclopedia de México.   México: Instituto de la En-
       ciclopedia de México, 1966-78.   12 vols.
       Prepared along the lines of the Britannica.   In-
       cludes all that pertains to Mexico in such fields as
       anthropology, bibliography, biography, science, his-
       tory, literature, and semantics.

1383. Enciclopedia dello spettacolo.   Rome: Unione Editori-
       ale, 1975 (1954-62).   10 vols.
       Embraces dramatic and musical theater, movies,
       and television from their artistic, social, juridical,
       and economic points of view.   Covers the "specta-
       cle" from ancient times to present.

1384. Enciclopedia el Ateneo.   2d ed.   Buenos Aires: Ate-
       neo, 1965-66.   12 vols.
       Each volume covers a broad theme: the uni-
       verse; man, his history and beliefs; thought and the
       world of letters; art, music, and spectacles; the
       world of science; man the builder.

1385. Enciclopedia universal ilustrada europeo-americana.
       Barcelona and Madrid: Espasa-Calpe, 1907?- .
       103 vols.   Supplement for 1977/78, published in
       1982.   1,036 pp.
       One of the most valuable encyclopedias in any
       language.

1386. Gran enciclopedia argentina: Todo lo argentino orde-
       nado alfabéticamente; geografía e historia, topo-
       nomías, biografías, ciencias, artes, letras, de-
       recho, economía, industria y comercio institucio-
       nes, flora y fauna, folklore, léxico regional. Ed-
       ited by Diego A. de Santillán. Buenos Aires:
       Ediar, 1956-64. 9 vols.
           A national, not a general, encyclopedia. Bio-
       graphical entries for Argentines are numerous.

1387. Gran enciclopedia Rialp. (GER). 2d revised printing.
       Madrid: Ediciones Rialp, 1981-82 (1971-77). 24
       vols.
           One of the important recent European encyclo-
       pedias. Signed articles by more than 3,000 scien-
       tists and specialists from all over the world.

                         HANDBOOKS

1388. Handbook of Latin American Studies (HLAS). Cam-
       bridge, Mass.: Harvard University Press, 1935-
       47 (vols. 1-13); Gainesville: University of Florida
       Press, 1961-78 (vol. 14-); University of Texas
       Press, 1979- (vol. 41-). Since 1964, the hu-
       manities and social studies have been rotated yearly.
           Sections on anthropology, including linguistics,
       art, education, geography, government, history, in-
       ternational relations since 1830, Latin American
       language, law, literature, music, philosophy, soci-
       ology, travel, and description. Special articles on
       bibliography collections, archives, and the like.
       The Author Index to Handbook of Latin American
       Studies, compiled by Francisco José Cardona and
       María Elena Cardona (Gainesville: University of
       Florida Press, 1968, 421 pp.) covers volumes 1-
       28 (1936-66). A subject index is in preparation.

1389. Hilton, Ronald, ed. Handbook of Hispanic Source Ma-
       terials in the United States. 2d ed. Stanford,
       Calif.: Stanford University Press, 1956 (1942).
       xiv, 448 pp. Spanish ed., Los estudios hispánicos
       en los Estados Unidos (Madrid: Ediciones Cultura
       Hispánica, 1957). xiii, 493 pp.
           Embraces Spain, Portugal, and Latin America in
       pre- and post-Columbian times and Florida, Texas,
       Southwest United States, and California until their

respective annexations. Describes archives, libraries, museums, scientific societies, works of finished
investigations, philanthropic entities or cooperatives
interested in progress of Hispanic studies, all up to
January 1, 1956.

1390. Sable, Martin H., ed. Guide to Latin American Stud-
       ies. Los Angeles: UCLA Latin American Center,
       1967. 2 vols.
       Annotated bibliography of text and reference
       books, government documents, pamphlets, and news-
       paper articles, mostly in Spanish and English but
       also in French, German, and Portuguese on all cul-
       tural aspects.

1391. _____. Latin American Jewry: A Research Guide.
       Cincinnati, Ohio: Hebrew Union College, 1978. 633
       pp.
       Covers almost all aspects of the impact of Jewry
       in and on Latin America and its individual nations,
       regions, and places from 1492 to 1974.

1392. _____. Master Directory of Latin America: Contain-
       ing Ten Directories Covering Organizations, Associa-
       tions, and Institutions, Communications, Education-
       Research, Government, International Cooperation,
       Labor Cooperations, Publishing, Religion, and So-
       cial and Social Services Organizations and Associa-
       tions. Los Angeles: UCLA Latin American Cen-
       ter, 1965. xiv, 438 pp.
       Supplies names and addresses of associations,
       organizations, and institutions with relevance and
       interest in the 20 countries and Puerto Rico and
       British, Dutch, and French Caribbean and South
       Atlantic islands belonging to Spanish American
       countries.

1393. Véliz, Claudio, ed. Latin America and the Caribbean:
       A Handbook. New York: Frederick A. Praeger;
       London: A. Blond, 1968. 840 pp.
       Collection of brief interpretative essays by some
       80 well-known British, United States, and Latin
       American scholars. Deals with history, politics,
       economics, and social and cultural backgrounds.
       Basic bibliographies but no subject index.

MISCELLANEOUS

History

1394. Altamira, Rafael. Manual de historia de España,
       desde los orígenes hasta nuestros días. 2d ed.
       Buenos Aires: Sudamericana, 1946 (1933). 601
       pp. English translation by Muna Lee, A History
       of Spain (Princeton, N. J.: D. Van Nostrand Co.,
       1949). 748 pp.
       A basic general history.

1395. Bleiberg, Germán, director. Diccionario de historia
       de España. Rev. ed. Madrid: Revista de Occi-
       dente, 1979 (1952). 3 vols.
       Handy reference work. Contains a chronology
       of Spanish history from the year 850 B. C. E., bib-
       liography and maps.

1396. Castro, Américo. La realidad histórica de España.
       6th ed. México: Porrúa, 1975 (1948). 479 pp.
       Revised version of his earlier España en su his-
       toria (cristianos, moros y judíos). English transla-
       tions. The Structure of Spanish History (Princeton,
       N. J.: Princeton University Press, 1954, 689 pp.);
       and The Spaniards: An Introduction to Their His-
       tory (Berkeley and Los Angeles: University of Cal-
       ifornia Press, 1971).
       Important work on the development of the Spanish
       nation whose character was formed by the symbiotic
       relationships of Christians, Moors, and Jews in the
       Middle Ages.

1397. Crow, John A. The Epic of Latin America. 3d ed.
       Garden City, N. Y.: Doubleday & Co., 1980 (1946).
       xxvi, 729 pp.
       From Indian civilizations to the 20th century,
       dealing with cultural, economic, literary, and po-
       litical history of Latin America.

1398. _____. Spain: The Root and the Flower. Rev.
       ed. New York: Harper & Row, 1975 (1963). 475
       pp.
       Well-written overview of Spanish history.

1399. Diccionario de historia de España desde sus orígenes.

Rev. ed. Madrid: Revista de Occidente, 1979
(1952). 3 vols.
Handy reference work. Useful for world history, also. Chronological index, bibliography, and
maps.

1400. Diccionario Porrúa de historia, biografía y geografía
de México. 4th ed., revised and enlarged. México: Porrúa, 1980 (1964). 2 vols. 2,746 pp.
Biographical material on Mexicans or those whose
activities have linked them to Mexico.

1401. Griffin, Charles C., and J. Benedict Warren, eds.
Latin America: A Guide to the Historical Literature. Published for the Conference on Latin American History. Austin: University of Texas Press,
1971. 700 pp.
Selective, scholarly bibliography with 7,087 critical annotations covering Latin American history.
Divided into the following sections: reference, general, background, colonial Latin America, Independence, Latin America since Independence, and international relations since 1830.

1402. Historia general de España y América. Madrid: Ediciones Rialp, 1981- . 19 vols. planned.
From the origins of Spain through the Franco
period. Vol. 18 will cover the American nations
in the 20th century and 19 will consist of Indexes.
Prepared with the collaboration of over 20 specialists.

1403. Indice histórico español, 1953-57. Quarterly. Published by the Centro de Estudios Históricos de la
Universidad de Barcelona through Editorial Teide.
Founded by Jaime Vicens Vives.
Contains information on studies relating to the
history of Spain from prehistoric times to the 20th
century as well as of Spanish America from the
discovery to Independence. Published annual author and subject indexes.

1404. Sánchez-Albornoz, Claudio. España: Un enigma histórico. 6th ed. Barcelona: Edhasa, 1971 (1956).
2 vols.
A refutation of Américo Castro's La realidad histórica de España. Besides criticizing Castro's

scholarship, it traces the formation of the Spanish
character to the early inhabitants of Spain.

1405. Sánchez Alonso, Benito. Fuentes de la historia española e hispanoamericana. 3d rev. ed. Madrid:
Consejo Superior de Investigaciones Científicas,
1952 (1919). 3 vols.
A fundamental source for Hispanic historical bibliography.

1406. Studemund, Michael. Bibliographie zum Judenspani-
schen. Hamburg: Helmut Buske Verlag, 1975. 148
pp.
Excellent bibliography of 1,368 entries on Judeo-
Spanish culture, history, and civilization.

1407. Werlich, David P. Research Tools for Latin American Historians: A Selected, Annotated Bibliography.
New York and London: Garland, 1980. 269 pp.
A classified annotated bibliography of almost
1,400 reference works, compendiums of source
materials, and periodicals. Part I includes general reference works and II covers individual nations.

Philosophy

1408. Abellán José Luis. Historia crítica del pensamiento
español. Madrid: Espasa-Calpe, 1979-81. 3 vols.
Vol. 4 in press.
Deals with Spanish philosophy, history, and intellectual life of Spain. Vol. 1 contains methodology
and historical introduction; Vol. 2 covers the Spanish Golden Age; and Vol. 3 the 17th and 18th centuries. Includes bibliographies and indexes.

1409. Ferrater Mora, José. Diccionario de filosofía. 6th
ed. Madrid: Alianza, 1980 (1941). 2 vols., xix,
3,589 pp.
A remarkable work by an internationally recognized scholar. Alphabetically arranged, it includes
all aspects of world philosophy from classical antiquity to the present. Besides biobibliographic
studies and analyses of the works of many philoso-
phers--Hispanic philosophers are extremely well
represented--there are entries on philosophical

terms, concepts, schools, and movements. Substantial bibliographies accompany most entries.

1410.   Repertoire bibliographique de la philosophie. Supple-
        ment to the Revue philosophique de Louvain. Lou-
        vain, 1949-70.
        Includes philosophical literature published in Ger-
        man, English, Spanish, Catalan, French, Italian,
        and Portuguese.   Contains general studies as well
        as studies on individual philosophers organized by
        historical periods and by countries.   Covers books
        and articles and book reviews in periodicals.

16. SELECTED PUBLISHERS AND BOOK DEALERS

PUBLISHERS

United States and Canada

Barnes and Noble Books. 81 Adams Dr., Totowa, NJ 07512.

R. R. Bowker Company. 1180 Avenue of the Americas, New York, NY 10036.

Burt Franklin Reprints. 235 East 44th Street, New York, NY 10017.

Cambridge University Press. 32 East 57th Street, New York, NY 10022.

Catholic University of America Press. 620 Michigan Avenue, NE, Washington, DC 20064.

Columbia University Press. 562 W. 113th St., New York, NY 10025.

Cornell University Press. 124 Roberts Place, Ithaca, NY 10025.

Dover Publications. 180 Varick Street, New York, NY 10014.

Duke University Press. Box 6697 College Station, Durham, NC 27708.

G. K. Hall and Co. 70 Lincoln St., Boston, MA 02111.

Garland Publishing Inc. 136 Madison Ave., New York, NY 10016.

Greenwood Press. 88 Post Rd., Greenwood, CT 06881.

Hafner Press. 866 3rd Ave., New York, NY 10022.

Harvard University Press. 79 Garden Street, Cambridge,
MA 02138.

The Hispanic Society of America. Broadway between 155th
and 156th Streets, New York, NY 10032.

Indiana University Press. 10th and Morton Streets, Bloomington, IN 47401.

Irvington Publishers, Inc. 551 5th Ave., New York, NY
10176.

Johns Hopkins University Press. Baltimore, MD 21218.

Johnson Reprint Corp. 111 Fifth Ave., New York, NY 10013.

Juan de la Cuesta. 270 Indian Road, Newark, DE 19711.

Kraus Reprint Company. Route 100, Millwood, NY 10546.

Louisiana State University Press. Baton Rouge, LA 70803.

New York University Press. Washington Square, New York,
NY 10003.

Northwestern University Press. 1735 Benson Avenue, Evanston, IL 60201.

Ohio State University Press. 2070 Neil Avenue, Columbus,
OH 43210.

Penguin Books. 625 Madison Ave., New York, NY 10022.

Pennsylvania State University Press. 215 Wagner Bldg.,
University Park, PA 16802.

Princeton University Press. 41 William St., Princeton, NJ
08540.

Regents Press of Kansas. 303 Carruth-O'Leary, Lawrence,
KS 66045.

Scarecrow Press, Inc. P.O. Box 656, Metuchen, NJ 08840.

Southern Illinois University Press. P. O. Box 3697, Carbondale, IL 62901.

Stanford University Press. Stanford, CA 94305.

University Microfilms International. 300 North Zeeb Road, Ann Arbor, MI 48106.

University of Alabama Press. Box 2877, University, AL 35486.

University of California Press. 2223 Fulton St., Berkeley, CA 94720.

University of Chicago Press. 5801 Ellis Avenue, Chicago, IL 60637.

University of Georgia Press. Terrell Hall, Athens, GA 30602.

University of Illinois Press. P. O. Box 5081, Station, Champaign, IL 61820.

University of Miami Press. P. O. Box 4836, Hampden Sta., Baltimore, MD 21211.

University of Michigan Press. P. O. Box 1104, Ann Arbor, MI 48106.

University of Minnesota Press. 2037 University Avenue Southeast, Minneapolis, MN 55455.

University of Missouri Press. 200 Lewis, Columbia, MO 65211.

University of Nebraska Press. 901 N. 17th St., Lincoln, NE 68588.

University of New Mexico Press. Albuquerque, NM 87131.

University of North Carolina Press. Box 2288, Chapel Hill, NC 27514.

University of Oklahoma Press. 1005 Asp Ave., Norman, OK 73019.

University of Pennsylvania Press. 3933 Walnut Street, Philadelphia, PA 19104.

University of Tennessee Press. 293 Communications Bldg.,
  Knoxville, TN 37996-0325.

University of Texas Press. P. O. Box 7819, Austin, TX
  78712.

University of Toronto Press. Toronto, Ont., Canada M5S
  1A6.

University of Washington Press. Seattle, WA 98105.

University of Wisconsin Press. 114 N. Murray St., Madison,
  WI 53715.

University Press of Kentucky. Lexington, KY 40506.

University Presses of Florida. 15 Northwest 15th St.,
  Gainesville, FL 32603.

Vanderbilt University Press. 2505 (Rear) West End Ave.,
  Nashville, TN 37203.

Yale University Press. 92 A, Yale Sta., New Haven, CT
  06520.

Spain

Aguilar, S. A. de Ediciones. Juan Bravo 38, Madrid 6.

Alianza Editorial. Milán 38, Madrid 38.

Consejo Superior de Investigaciones Científicas. Vitrubio 8,
  Madrid 6.

EDHASA. Diagonal 519-521, Barcelona 29.

Ediciones Cátedra, Grupo Editorial. Don Ramón de la Cruz
  67, Madrid 1.

Ediciones Destino. Consejo de Ciento 425, Barcelona 9.

Ediciones Guadarrama. Calabria 235-239, Barcelona 29.

Ediciones Rialp. Preciados 34, Madrid 13.

Editorial Castalia. Zurbano 39, Madrid 10.

Editorial Ebro. Avenida Goya 71, Zaragoza 5.

Editorial Gredos. Sánchez Pacheco 83, Apartado 2076, Madrid 2.

Editorial Gustavo Gili. Rosellón 87-89, Barcelona 29.

Editorial Juventud. Provenza 101, Barcelona 29.

Editorial Planeta. Córcega 273-277, Barcelona.

Editorial Seix Barral. Tambor del Buch S. N. , San Juan Despi, Barcelona.

Espasa- Calpe. Carrera de Irún, Madrid 34.

Insula. Benito Gutiérrez 26, Madrid 8.

Porrúa Turanzas. Cea Bermúdez 10, Madrid 3.

Taurus Ediciones. General Mola 86, Madrid 6.

Spanish America

Casa de la Cultura Ecuatoriana. Avenida Seis de Diciembre 332, Apdo. 67, Quito, Ecuador.

Casa de las Américas. G. y Tercera, Vedado 3, La Habana, Cuba.

El Colegio de México. Camino al Ajusco 20. México 20, D. F.

Costa Amic, Mesones 14, Apdo 29-188, México 1, D. F.

Ediciones Macchi. Alsina 1535. P. B. 1088, Buenos Aires, Argentina.

Editorial Joaquín Mortiz. Tabasco 106, Apartado 7-832, México 7, D. F.

Editorial Losada. Alsina 1131, 1088 Buenos Aires, Argentina.

Editorial Porrúa. Argentina 15. México 1, D. F.

Editorial Sopena Argentina. Echeverría 5037-39, Buenos
Aires, Argentina.

Editorial Sudamericana. Humberto lo. 545, 1103 Buenos
Aires, Argentina.

Editorial Universitaria. San Francisco 454, Casilla 10220,
Santiago, Chile.

EDUCA (Editorial Universitaria Centroamericana). Apartado
37, Ciudad Universitaria "Rodrigo Facio," San José, Costa
Rica. (See book dealers).

Emecé Editores. Carlos Pellegrini 1069, 1009 Buenos Aires,
Argentina.

EUDEBA (Editorial Universitaria de Buenos Aires). Rivadavia
1571-73, 1033 Buenos Aires, Argentina.

Fernando García Cambeiro. Cochabamba 244, 1150 Buenos
Aires, Argentina.

Fondo de Cultura Económica. Avenida Universidad 975, Apdo.
44975, México 12, D. F. (See book dealers).

Instituto Caro y Cuervo. Apartado Aéreo 51502, Bogotá,
Colombia.

Librería Andina. Jr. Calao 309, Of. 2, Lima 1, Perú.

Monte Avila Editores. Apartado 70712, (Zona 1070), Caracas, Venezuela.

Siglo Veintiuno Editores. Cerro del Agua 248, Apdo. 20626,
México 20, D. F.

Siglo Veintiuno Editores de Colombia. Apdo. aéreo 19434,
Bogotá, Colombia.

Universidad Central del Ecuador. Editorial Universitaria,
Quito, Ecuador.

Universidad de Costa Rica. Departmento de Publicaciones,
Ciudad Universidad de "Rodrigo Facio," San José, Costa
Rica.

Universidad de San Carlos de Guatemala. Imprenta y Librería
Universitarias 10a, Calle 9-59, Zona 1, Guatemala.

Universidad Nacional Autónoma de Honduras. Centro Universitario de Estudios Generales, Tegucigalpa, D. C., Honduras.

Universidad Nacional Autónoma de México. Departamento de Distribución de Libros Universitarios, Porto Alegre 216, México 13, D. F.

Universidad Nacional de Colombia. Dirección de Divulgación Cultural, Publicaciones, Bogotá, Colombia.

Universidad Nacional de Zulia. Editorial Universitaria, Maracaibo, Venezuela.

Universidad Nacional Mayor de San Marcos. Departamento de Publicaciones, Avenida República de Chile 295, Apdo. 508, Lima, Perú.

University of Puerto Rico Press. Apdo X, Estación UPR, Río Piedras, PR 00931.

BOOK DEALERS

United States and Canada

Adler's Foreign Books, Inc. 162 Fifth Ave., New York, NY 10010.

Continental Book Company, Inc. 11-03 46th Ave., Long Island City, NY 11101.

Editorial Excelsior. 15 North Market St., San José, CA 95113.

Four Continent Book Corp. 156 Fifth Ave., New York, NY 10010.

French and European Publications, Inc. 610 Fifth Ave., New York, NY 10020.

Girol Spanish and Portuguese Books. P. O. Box 5473, Sta. F, Ottawa, ON K23 3M1, Canada.

Imported Books. P. O. Box 4414, Dallas, TX 75208.

Johnson Reprint. 111 Fifth Ave., New York, NY 10003.

Kraus Periodicals and Reprints. Route 100, Millwood, NY 10546.

L. A. Publishing Company. 37A Union Sq. W., New York, NY 10003.

Larousse and Company. 572 Fifth Ave., New York, NY 10036.

Lectorum Publications, Inc. 137 W. 14th St., New York, NY 10011.

Libros Españoles, S. A. 1898 SW. 8th St., Miami, FL 33135.

Ling's International Books. P. O. Box 82684, San Diego, CA 92138.

Mexican Book Service. St. Peters, PA 19470.

Midwest European Publications. 915 Foster St., Evanston, IL 60201.

Albert J. Phiebig, Inc. P. O. Box 352, White Plains, NY 10602.

Rizzoli International Bookstore. Spanish Department. 712 Fifth Ave., New York, NY 10019.

Spanish Book Corporation. 610 Fifth Ave., New York, NY 10020.

Eliseo Torres. P. O. Box 2, Eastchester, NY 10709.

Spain

Aguilar, S. A. de Ediciones. Juan Bravo 38, Madrid.

Julián Barbazán. Calle de los Libreros 4, Madrid 13.

Delsa. Serrano 80, Madrid 6.

Insula Librería. Benito Gutiérrez 26, Madrid 8.

Librería Passim. Bailén 134, Barcelona 9.

Librería Puvill. Boters y Paja 29, Barcelona 2.

Librería Rubiños. Alcalá 98, Madrid 9.

Miessner Libreros. José Ortega y Gasset 14, Madrid 6.

Porter-Libros. Avenida Puerta del Angel 9, Barcelona 2.

León Sánchez Cuesta. Serrano 29, Madrid 1.

Spanish Book Center. Milanesado 21-23, Barcelona 17.

Spanish America

Los Amigos del Libro. Casilla 450 (Calle Perú, esquina
España), Cochabamba, Bolivia.

Herta Berenguer. Avenida Pocura 2738, Santiago, Chile.

Juan A. Bove Trabal. Casilla de Correo 610, Montevideo,
Uruguay.

Distribuidora "Artigas." Dr. José Pugnalini 1844, Montevideo, Uruguay.

Editora Cosmos, Ltda. Calle 18 No. 6-47, Ofna 702, Apdo.
aéreo 37035, Bogotá, Colombia.

EDUCA (Editorial Universitaria Centroamericana). Apartado
37, Ciudad Universitaria "Rodrigo Facio," San José, Costa
Rica. (Distributes for the Editorial Universitaria of El
Salvador, Guatemala, and Nicaragua and for the Universidad Nacional Autónoma de Honduras.)

Fondo de Cultura Económica. Avenida Universidad 975, Apdo.
44975, México 12, D. F.

Fernando García Cambeiro. Cochabamba 244, 1150 Buenos
Aires, Argentina.

José María Herrera, Libros de Colombia y Latino-América.
Apartado aereo 12053, Bogotá, Colombia.

E. Iturriaga y Compañía. Jirón Ica 441, Oficina 202, Casilla
de Correos 4640, Lima, Perú.

Librería Cultural Panameña. Apdo. 2018, Panamá.

Librería Cultural Salvadoreña. Apdo. 2296, Calle Arce 423, San Salvador, El Salvador.

Librería del Plata. Sarmiento 1674, 1042 Buenos Aires, Argentina.

Librería Delta Editorial. Avenida Italia 2817, Montevideo, Uruguay.

Librería Hispanoamericana. Apdo. 20830, Avenida Ponce de León 1013, Río Piedras, PR 00928.

Librería Lehmann. Apdo. 10011, San José, Costa Rica.

Librería y Editorial Nascimento. San Antonio 390, Casilla 2298, Santiago, Chile.

Librería y Editorial Universitaria. María Luisa Santander 0447, Casilla 10220, Santiago, Chile.

Librerías de Cristal. Av. Alvaro Obregón 85, México, D. F.

Llartantse, S. R. Ltda. Jirón Chimú 286, Lima 21, Perú.

MACH (Materiales Académicos de Consulta Hispanoamericanos). Apartado Postal 7-854, México 7, D. F.

Adolfo Montero Linardi. 1 Carlos Gómez 1418, Montevideo, Uruguay.

Organización Difusora del Libro Americano. Apdo. 557, Montevideo, Uruguay.

Porrúa Hermanos y Cía., S. A. Apartado Postal 7990, México 1, D. F.

Soberbia. Edificio Dillon, Local 4, Este 2, No. 139, Puente Yanes a Tracabordo 1010, Caracas, Venezuela.

Others

B. H. Blackwell, Ltd. 48-51 Broad Street, Oxford OX1 3BQ, England.

E. J. Brill. Oude Rijn 33a-35, Leiden, Netherlands.

Dolphin Book Co. (Treduor) Ltd.   Llangrannoy, Llandsysul,
Dyfed SA 44 68A, Great Britain.

Grant and Cutler, Ltd.   Buckingham St., Strand, London,
WC2N 6DQ 01-839-3136, England.

Hachette International.   254 Blvd. St. Germain, F-75340,
Paris cedex 07, France.

Otto Harrassowitz.   Taunustrasse 5, Postfach 2929, 6200
Wiesbaden, West Germany.

Kraus Reprint Company.   FL 9491 Nendeln, Liechtenstein.

Mouton Publishers.   Postfach 110240, D-1000 Berlin 11,
West Germany.

Martinus Nijhoff.   Postbus 566, 2501CN, Lange Voorhout 9-
11, The Hague, Netherlands.